MW00760479

Prayers & GUIDELINES

for Young Catholics

Pflaum Publishing Group
Dayton, OH 45439
Milwaukee, WI 53051

Edited by Jean Larkin
Designed by Larissa Thompson

Nihil obstat: † Reverend Monsignor John F. Murphy, *Censor Librorum*, November 22, 2002.

Imprimatur: Most Reverend Timothy M. Dolan, Archbishop of Milwaukee, December 6, 2002.

Pflaum Publishing Group
2621 Dryden Road, Suite 300
Dayton, OH 45439
www.pflaum.com

ISBN 0-89837-231-3

Table of Contents

The Liturgical Year

Season	Time	Liturgical Color
Advent	Four weeks preceding Christmas	Violet Rose–3rd Advent
Christmas	Christmas Eve through the feast of Jesus' baptism (Sunday after Epiphany)	White
Ordinary Time	Monday after the feast of Jesus' baptism until Ash Wednesday	Green
Lent	Ash Wednesday to the Mass of the Lord's Supper on Holy Thursday	Violet Rose–4th Lent Red–Palm Sunday
Triduum	Last three days of Holy Week, beginning with the Mass of the Lord's Supper	Violet
Easter	Easter Vigil through Pentecost	White
Ordinary Time	Monday after Pentecost to the first Sunday of Advent	Green

Prayers

for Young Catholics

The Sign of the Cross

In the name of the Father,
and of the Son,
and of the Holy Spirit. Amen.

Lord's Prayer

Our Father, who art in heaven,
hallowed be thy name;
thy kingdom come; thy will be done
on earth as it is in heaven.

Give us this day our daily bread;
and forgive us our trespasses
as we forgive those
who trespass against us;
and lead us not into temptation,
but deliver us from evil. Amen.

Hail Mary

Hail Mary, full of grace!
The Lord is with you!
Blessed are you among women,
and blessed is the fruit of your
womb, Jesus.

Holy Mary, Mother of God,
pray for us sinners,
now and at the hour of our death.
Amen.

Prayer of Praise

Glory be to the Father,
and to the Son,
and to the Holy Spirit.

As it was in the beginning,
is now, and ever shall be,
world without end. Amen.

Morning Prayer

O Jesus, through the Immaculate Heart of Mary, I offer you my prayers, works, joys, and sufferings of this day in union with the Holy Sacrifice of the Mass throughout the world.

I offer them for the intentions of our bishops and for all our associates, and in particular for those recommended by our Holy Father this month. Amen.

Prayer to Guardian Angel

Angel of God, my guardian dear, to whom God's love commits me here, ever this day [night] be at my side, to light and guard, to rule and guide. Amen.

Apostles' Creed

I believe in God, the Father almighty, creator of heaven and earth.

I believe in Jesus Christ, his only Son, our Lord. He was conceived by the power of the Holy Spirit and born of the Virgin Mary.

He suffered under Pontius Pilate, was crucified, died, and was buried. He descended to the dead. On the third day he rose again.

He ascended into heaven and is seated at the right hand of the Father. He will come again to judge the living and the dead.

I believe in the Holy Spirit, the holy catholic Church, the communion of saints, the forgiveness of sins, the resurrection of the body, and the life everlasting. Amen.

Act of Faith

O my God, I believe that you are one God in three divine persons, Father, Son, and Holy Spirit. I believe that Jesus became man, died for us, and will come to judge us. I believe all the truths of the holy, catholic Church, because they reveal your word. Amen.

Act of Hope

O my God, because your goodness never ends, I hope to receive pardon for my sins and spend life everlasting in your loving presence. Amen.

Act of Love

O my God, I love you with my whole heart and soul, because you are all good and worthy of all my love. I love my neighbor as myself, and I forgive all who have injured me. I ask pardon of all whom I have injured. Amen.

Act of Contrition

My God, I am sorry for my sins with all my heart. In choosing to do wrong and failing to do good, I have sinned against you, whom I should love above all things. I firmly intend, with your help, to do penance, to sin no more, and to avoid whatever leads me to sin.

Our Savior Jesus Christ suffered and died for us. In his name, my God, have mercy. Amen.

Blessing Before Meals

Bless us, O Lord, and these your gifts, which we are about to receive from your goodness, through Christ, our Lord. Amen.

Grace After Meals

We give you thanks, O Lord, for these your gifts, which we have received from your goodness, through Christ our Lord. Amen.

Memorare

Remember, most loving Virgin Mary, never was it heard that anyone who turned to you for help was left unaided.

Inspired by this confidence, though burdened by my sins, I run to your protection for you are my mother.

Mother of the word of God, do not despise my words of pleading but be merciful and hear my prayer. Amen.

Our Lady of Guadalupe

Remember, O most gracious Virgin of Guadalupe, that in your apparitions on Mount Tepeyac you promised to show pity and compassion to all who, loving and trusting you, seek your help and protection.

Accordingly, listen now to our supplications and grant us consolation and relief. We are full of hope that, relying on your help, nothing can trouble or affect us.

As you have remained with us through your admirable image, so now obtain for us the graces we need. Amen.

Mysteries of the Rosary

Joyful Mysteries (Mon. and Sat.)
Jesus' Infancy and Childhood

1. Mary is told she will be the mother of Jesus.
2. Mary visits her cousin Elizabeth.
3. Mary gives birth to Jesus.
4. Jesus is presented in the Temple.
5. Jesus is found in the Temple.

Luminous Mysteries
(Thurs.)
Jesus' Public Ministry

1. Jesus is baptized in the Jordan River.
2. Jesus performs his first miracle at the wedding of Cana.
3. Jesus proclaims the Kingdom of God and calls us to conversion.
4. Jesus is transfigured before Peter, John, and James on Mount Tabor.
5. Jesus institutes the Eucharist at the Last Supper.

Sorrowful Mysteries

(Tues. and Fri.)
Jesus' Passion and Death

1. Jesus suffers his agony in the Garden.
2. Jesus is scourged at the pillar.
3. Jesus is crowned with thorns.
4. Jesus carries his cross to Calvary.
5. Jesus dies on the cross.

Glorious Mysteries

(Sun. and Wed.)
The Glory of Jesus and Mary

1. Jesus rises from the dead.
2. Jesus ascends into heaven.
3. Jesus sends the Holy Spirit.
4. Mary ascends into heaven.
5. Mary is crowned queen of heaven.

Prayer to Holy Spirit

Come, Holy Spirit, fill the hearts of your faithful, and kindle in them the fire of your love.

Send forth your Spirit, O Lord, and our hearts shall be created. And you shall renew the face of the earth.

Let us pray.
O God, who taught the hearts of the faithful by the light of the Holy Spirit, grant us by the same Spirit to delight in what is right and always to rejoice in his consolation. Through Jesus Christ our Lord. Amen.

Prayer of St. Francis of Assisi

Lord, make me an instrument
of your peace.

Where there is hatred,
let me sow love;
where there is injury, pardon;
where there is doubt, faith;
where there is despair, hope;
where there is darkness, light;
where there is sadness, joy.

O divine Master, grant that I may not
seek so much to be consoled as to
console, to be understood as to understand, to be loved as to love.

For it is in giving that we receive, it is
in pardoning that we are pardoned,
and it is in dying that we are born to
eternal life. Amen

Stations of the Cross

Pause between each station for a brief reflection.

1. Jesus is condemned to death.

2. Jesus carries his cross.

3. Jesus falls the first time.

4. Jesus meets his mother.

5. Simon of Cyrene helps Jesus carry his cross.

6. Veronica wipes the face of Jesus.

7. Jesus falls the second time.

8. Jesus speaks to the women of Jerusalem.

9. Jesus falls the third time.

10. Jesus is stripped of his garments.

11. Jesus is nailed to the cross.

12. Jesus dies on the cross.

13. Jesus is taken down from the cross.

14. Jesus is placed in the tomb.

Guidelines

for Young Catholics

Ten Commandments

(Catechism of the Catholic Church, Part 3, Section 2)

1. I am the Lord your God: you shall not have strange Gods before me.
2. You shall not take the name of the Lord your God in vain.
3. Remember to keep holy the Lord's day.
4. Honor your father and your mother.
5. You shall not kill.
6. You shall not commit adultery.
7. You shall not steal.
8. You shall not bear false witness against your neighbor.
9. You shall not covet your neighbor's wife.
10. You shall not covet your neighbor's goods.

Two Great Commandments

(Catechism of the Catholic Church, No. 2196)

You shall love the Lord your God with all your heart, and with all your soul, and with all your mind, and with all your strength.

You shall love your neighbor as yourself.

Seven Sacraments

Baptism
Confirmation
Eucharist
Penance (Reconciliation)
Anointing of the Sick
Holy Orders
Matrimony

Precepts of the Catholic Church

(The Catechism of the Catholic Church *lists five precepts. See Nos. 2042-43.)*

1. You shall attend Mass on Sundays and on holy days of obligation and rest from servile labor.
2. You shall confess your sins at least once a year.
3. You shall receive the sacrament of the Eucharist at least during the Easter season.
4. You shall observe the days of fasting and abstinence established by the Church.
5. You shall help to provide for the needs of the Church.

(The traditional precepts included two more.)

1. Study Catholic teaching.
2. Observe the marriage laws of the Church and provide religious training for one's children.

Beatitudes

(Matthew 5:3-10)

Blessed are the poor in spirit, for theirs is the kingdom of heaven.

Blessed are they who mourn, for they will be comforted.

Blessed are the meek, for they will inherit the land.

Blessed are they who hunger and thirst for righteousness, for they will be satisfied.

Blessed are the merciful, for they will be shown mercy.

Blessed are the clean of heart, for they will see God.

Blessed are the peacemakers, for they will be called children of God.

Blessed are they who are persecuted for the sake of righteousness, for theirs is the kingdom of heaven.

Corporal Works of Mercy

Feed the hungry.
Give drink to the thirsty.
Clothe the naked.
Visit the imprisoned.
Shelter the homeless.
Visit the sick.
Bury the dead.

Spiritual Works of Mercy

Convert the sinner.
Instruct the ignorant.
Counsel the doubtful.
Comfort the sorrowful.
Bear wrongs patiently.
Forgive all injuries.
Pray for the living and the dead.

Gifts of the Spirit

(Catechism of the Catholic Church, No. 1831)

Wisdom
Understanding
Counsel (right judgment)
Fortitude (courage)
Knowledge
Piety (reverence)
Fear of the Lord (respect for God)

Fruits of the Spirit

(Catechism of the Catholic Church, No. 1832)

Charity	Generosity
Joy	Gentleness
Peace	Faithfulness
Patience	Modesty
Kindness	Self-control
Goodness	Chastity

Holy Days of Obligation

In the United States

Mary, Mother of God	January 1
Ascension of Jesus	40 days after Easter or 7th Sunday of Easter
Assumption of Mary	August 15
All Saints' Day	November 1
Immaculate Conception	December 8
Christmas	December 25

In Canada

Mary, Mother of God	January 1
Christmas	December 25

GIN AND DAGGERS

GIN AND DAGGERS

A MURDER, SHE WROTE MYSTERY

Jessica Fletcher
AND Donald Bain

McGRAW-HILL PUBLISHING COMPANY
New York   St. Louis   San Francisco   Hamburg
London   Mexico   Sydney   Toronto

Based on the Universal television series created by Peter S. Fischer, Richard Levinson & William Link.

1 2 3 4 5 6 7 8 9 DOC DOC 8 9 2 1 0 9

ISBN 0-07-003239-4

Library of Congress Cataloging-in-Publication Data

Fletcher, Jessica.
  Gin and daggers.
    I. Bain, Donald.   II. Title.
III. Title: Murder, she wrote.
PS3556.L516G56 1989   813'.54   89-8088
ISBN 0-07-003239-4

Book design by Eve Kirch

29704

To my dear friends in Cabot Cove, to the millions of readers of my books who graciously allow me a red herring or two, and to my friend Donald Bain, with whom writing this book has been an absolute delight.

Jessica Fletcher
Cabot Cove, Maine

To my daughters, Laurie and Pamela, who, on rare occasions, are delightful mysteries to me. And to my friend and colleague Jessica Fletcher, who has taught me so much about the craft of writing a murder mystery.

Donald Bain
New York City

And to our staunchly loyal and creative editor, Anne Sweeney, who saw the wisdom of our literary marriage from the beginning.

Jessica and Donald

Chapter

1

"Care to take a closer look, Mrs. Fletcher?"

"Well, I suppose so," I said.

"Hold on, then, here we go."

My heart, which had been nestled securely in its usual place, now moved up to my throat and lodged there, beating as though a crazed bass drum player were doing a paradiddle on it. I reached over and touched him on the arm. "Please, maybe we shouldn't . . ."

He banked the Cessna 310 into a tight turn, forcing me back against my seat. "There it is, Mrs. Fletcher, right down there in that clump o' trees."

My eyes were closed. I forced them open and looked in the direction his finger was pointed until I spotted my home in Cabot Cove.

"There's the firehouse," he said, guiding the small aircraft down closer to the trees. His name was Jed Richardson, and he operated Jed's Flying Service out of our small airport.

"Yes, I see. But maybe we should land now, Jed. I have an appointment."

"Right you are, Mrs. Fletcher," he said, laughing and bringing the aircraft back to a straight-and-level attitude.

1

Jed had flown me to Bangor, where I'd been interviewed on a local television station about the publication of my latest novel. I'd offered to drive, but the station had insisted upon flying me in.

Seth Hazlitt, my good friend from Cabot Cove, was waiting for me at the airport.

"You all right, Jess?" he asked as we walked away from the plane.

"Yes, I think so."

"You look a little green."

"It must be the light." He didn't know how rubbery my legs were.

"Mort's at the house waitin' for you. He says he's come up with some new clues."

"Really? I hope they make more sense than the last batch. Do we really have to get into it now?"

"Won't take long, Jess. He's pretty eager to wrap it up."

"How did you identify the murderer so fast, Jessica?" Mort asked as we sat in Seth's living room.

"Elementary, my dear Metzger. The initial clues pointed clearly—too clearly, I think—to the Oriental woman who owned the shop, but then I learned—and it really was made too easy for me—that the letter opener used to kill Marc Silbert was missing from the ornate holder in which it usually sat. The art collector certainly had a motive, too, but it had to be the brother, and that's the problem with the whole case."

Seth patted our sheriff and friend, Morton Metzger, on the back. "It just needs some more refinement, Mort, that's all."

"I've been refinin' it forever." Mort looked at me. "Maybe you're not the best one to make a judgment about it, Jess. You write murder mysteries, and solve 'em, too. You're a professional. This here game is for people who don't know anything about murder mysteries."

I smiled at him; he looked dejected. "Maybe you're right, Mort, maybe I'm being too picky. I think you've invented an absolutely wonderful murder mystery board game. You just need to iron out a few wrinkles."

"Maybe if I figure a way to use dice," he said. "People like to roll dice in games."

"Yes, that might be a good idea," I said. "I have to run home now. See you both tonight at the church supper?"

"We'll be there," Seth said.

I returned to my house and sat at my kitchen table. It was a little past noon; crisp, cool air sent my white curtains fluttering and heralded the coming of fall to Maine in all its peacock splendor. I looked through the open window to a clump of white pine trees that had always given me particular pleasure. They stood majestically, and every time I looked at them I felt, at once, gratitude for their beauty and sadness at knowing the state's powerful lumber interests were methodically seeing to it that there would be fewer of them in coming years.

I forced myself out of my reverie and went to work on a speech I was to give in London to the International Society of Mystery Writers. I was making good progress when Josh, the mailman, approached the house. I knew when he was coming because he whistled, always the same tune—"Tea for Two" —and always off-key. I jumped from my desk and met him at the door.

"Mornin', Mrs. Fletcher."

"Good morning, Josh. Lovely day. Like fall."

"Seems that way."

"I love the fall," I said. "October is my favorite month."

"Not mine, Mrs. Fletcher. October means December and January are comin', and that means snow."

I nodded. "Yes, I suppose the seasons mean different things to different people, depending upon how you make a living. How's your wife?"

"Feelin' better. The new medicine Doc Hazlitt put her on

seems to be working, although sometimes I think the gout got to her brain."

"Really?" Could gout go to the brain?

"Seems like she gets more testy every day, but I suppose that's what naturally happens with women."

I was tempted to argue, but I had learned long ago that arguing with anyone so committed to a preconceived notion of male and female behavior was an exercise in futility. I smiled and accepted the letters and magazines he handed me.

"Got one all the way from London, England," he said.

"Really? How wonderful. I'm going there next week."

"Yes, Mrs. Fletcher, I know that. Everybody's talkin' about it."

"They are? Oh well, of course they are." In a town the size of Cabot Cove, there was very little that remained private, including what over-the-counter drugs you bought at the local pharmacy.

Josh resumed whistling as he went down the walk, same song, same out-of-tune rendition of it. I returned to my desk and immediately opened the letter from England; the bills and junk mail could wait. Just seeing the return address on the envelope filled me with excitement. The letter was from Marjorie Ainsworth, the world's most famous and successful writer of murder mysteries. We'd become friends years ago when I was introduced to her in London by P. D. James, and we'd kept in touch by letter ever since. Not that we communicated with great frequency; I wrote her only two or three times a year, but the number of letters didn't matter. Just being in touch with someone as talented as Marjorie Ainsworth was sufficient for me.

Marjorie Ainsworth's books sold in the millions and were translated into virtually every language on earth. She *defined* the genre, and all murder mysteries written by others were judged against hers.

The letter was typewritten, which had been the case for

the last three or four. I knew the typing had been done by Marjorie's faithful niece, Jane Portelaine, the daughter of Marjorie's older brother, now deceased. Earlier letters had been handwritten, but Marjorie was in failing health and had taken to dictating her correspondence.

My dear Jessica,

You mentioned in one of your recent letters that you had a friend in Cabot Cove, a Dr. Seth Hazlitt. By coincidence, I recently found myself reading something by another Hazlitt, William Hazlitt, no relation, I'm sure, but perhaps I'm wrong.

At any rate, I've been reading Hazlitt's "On Living to One's Self," and something struck me as being relevent to my present level of existence. He wrote, "What I mean by living to one's self is living in the world, as in it, not of it . . . It is to be a silent spectator of the mighty scene of things; . . . to take a thoughtful, anxious interest or curiosity in what is passing in the world, but not to feel the slightest inclination to make or meddle with it."

I have always taken perverse pleasure in meddling in the world through my books, but would never dream to do it in real lives. Alas, my current frail condition invites meddling by those around me, and I abhor it (as I speak this to dear, devoted Jane, I see the sourness in her face because, of course, she is one of the prime intruders in my life). Please, do not misunderstand. If I have said it once, I have said it countless times that were it not for Jane over the years, my life would be in considerably worse shambles than it presently is. I adore her but I cannot help protesting my plight, and what it has spawned. Still, this headstrong lady (the head is strong, the body less so) manages to prevail at times.

The weekend we've planned here at the house is still on, and I look forward with great anticipation to your arrival and the chance to spend time with my American colleague. What I am hoping, Jessica, is that you can come a day earlier than the others. This will give us time to leisurely explore our lives of the moment, and to thoroughly trash all those who will be arriving later.

I warn you: I am not the woman you last saw. I always recall a line from the play *Twigs*, a line that rings with great truth: "Men get better looking as they get older, and women get to look more like men." You will see for yourself the wisdom of that dialogue when you arrive.

Safe journey, Jessica, and bring your woollens. The winds are brisk this time of year at Ainsworth Manor, and I would be devastated should the keynote speaker at this year's confab of mystery writers come down with a cold that would render her words gratingly nasal.

Affectionately,
Marjorie

P.S. An autographed copy of *Gin and Daggers* awaits you.

I placed the letter on the desk, sat back, and shook my head, a smile upon my face. What a remarkable woman. No wonder the world adores her.

I went to the bedroom and took from a shelf in a cedar closet the sweaters I would bring to protect against the brisk winds of Ainsworth Manor. As I stood kneading the wool, a jet aircraft passed overhead, and I realized I'd be on such a plane in two days—destination, London.

I couldn't wait to return to England, to spend time with Marjorie Ainsworth, and to join my colleagues at the annual meeting of the International Society of Mystery Writers, or ISMW, as it was commonly referred to. As much as I adopted a toe-in-the-sand response to people in town when they congratulated me on being chosen to be the speaker this year, inside—deep inside—I was proud as could be.

Chapter

2

"Enjoy your stay," the passport inspector at London's Heathrow Airport said as he handed me back my passport.

"Thank you. I certainly hope to."

I went to the baggage area, where my luggage had already arrived on the carousel. I loaded it onto one of hundreds of available trolleys, the existence of which always confirmed for me London's heroic attempt to remain civilized. Because I had nothing to declare, I went through the Customs area marked in green, and immediately spotted Lucas Darling, who was with a crowd of people behind portable barriers.

Lucas was the unpaid secretary of ISMW; a sizable family inheritance allowed him to indulge himself. He was a cherubic little man of fifty, with pink cheeks and gossamer blond-gray hair that he allowed to grow just oh-so-long, giving him what he considered to be a literary look. He was fond of bow ties, and wore a large, floppy red one with white polka dots this day, along with a double-breasted blue blazer with large brass buttons, and gray slacks. A long, slender black umbrella dangled from his wrist. He was virtually hopping up and down as he called, "Jessica, Jessica, over here!"

"Hello, Lucas," I said.

"Oh, Jessica, how good to see you again," he said, shaking my hand.

"It's good to see you, too, Lucas, and wonderful to be back in London."

"You brought a brolly, I hope. It's been raining here for days." Before I could say anything, he added, "No matter, I brought one for you." He handed me the umbrella he was carrying.

Lucas took over wheeling the baggage trolley and led us to a taxi stand, where a young man graciously loaded my luggage into the space next to him in the front, held open the door for us, and, once we were settled in the spacious rear compartment (more blessed civilization, those London cabs), headed for the city.

"Everything shaping up for the conference?" I asked.

Lucas's face soured. "I wish that were the case, Jessica, but I'm afraid it's not."

I raised my eyebrows.

"So many last minute details. I can't trust them to anyone else anymore. The members keep promising to do things and then don't, which means I have to do them myself—although, Lord knows, I don't mind. Sometimes I think I'm the only one who takes these yearly conferences seriously."

I laughed and patted his arm. "That isn't true at all, Lucas. *I* take them seriously."

"You're a pleasant exception, Jessica Fletcher. By the way, have you read Marjorie's new book, *Gin and Daggers*?"

"No, I haven't, but there's a good reason for it. You do know I'll be spending the weekend with her before the conference starts."

He pouted. "Yes, and I was terribly disappointed that you wouldn't be in London over the weekend. I had some splendid social outings planned for us."

"I'm sure there'll be lots of time during the conference for socializing, Lucas. The point I was making was that Marjorie told me in a recent letter that she had a copy of *Gin and Daggers* waiting for me at the manor, and wanted personally to give it to me. You can imagine the willpower it took for me not to buy a copy back in the States. From everything I hear, it's her finest work, a masterpiece."

Lucas shifted on the seat so that he was facing me. He said earnestly, "There's no debate about that, Jessica. The only question has to do with the book's authorship."

My laugh this time was one of dismissal.

"You may laugh, Jessica, but the rumors are getting serious."

"That's preposterous," I said. "If there is one person in this world who does not need a ghostwriter, it's Marjorie Ainsworth." As I said it, I realized my protest was probably overblown. Reports of Marjorie's ill health were consistent and compelling. The letter to me just before I left Cabot Cove gave credence to the fact that she was obviously not well, although the condition of a writer's body, unless in chronic pain, needn't influence the quality of writing. Her letter to me was lucid enough. Her mind was sharp. If she had to dictate, that didn't mean less direct involvement in the book. I said this to Lucas.

"I hope you're right," he said. "As you know, ISMW is still carrying the fight to break through that pretentious barrier between genre fiction and what they love to term 'serious literary works.' If any book is destined to do that, it's *Gin and Daggers*."

"The more you talk, the harder I have to fight the urge to have the driver stop at the nearest bookstore so I can get a copy. It's that good, Lucas?"

"Even better than that, Jessica, it's a tour de force, but it doesn't read consistently like Marjorie Ainsworth. Don't get me wrong, I'm not implying that the rumors might be right. It's just that . . ."

"Not like her at *all*?"

He smiled sheepishly. "There I go again, my penchant for overstating things. Of course it's filled with classic Ainsworth plotting, insight into the human dilemma, things like that, but there's a philosophical depth that isn't evident in her previous books. Do you know what I mean?"

I shrugged. "I don't know; I always found quite a bit of depth to Marjorie's writing."

He sighed and looked out though raindrops on his window. We'd entered central London now; sprawling industrial complexes and blue-collar housing had given way to the more genteel architecture of the West End. He turned to me. "Ignore everything I've said, Jessica, until you've had a chance to read *Gin and Daggers*. Then we'll sit down over a long, leisurely dinner and discuss it, like two matrons at a literary luncheon."

"You have a deal, Lucas. I look forward to it."

The driver turned off the Strand and into a broad courtyard, at the end of which was the main entrance to the Savoy Hotel. Until the driver made that turn, I'd managed to avoid thinking about previous arrivals at the Savoy with my late husband, Frank. Now, as the splendidly uniformed doorman stood waiting to assist us, those feelings threatened to overflow. I turned away from Lucas in case my eyes had misted.

"Here we are, Jessica," Lucas said brightly. "I would have opted for a more intimate setting for the conference, but the site selection committee, God bless them, insisted upon the Savoy." When I didn't turn to acknowledge his comment, he said, "Jessica, are you all right?"

I drew a breath and smiled at him. "Yes, of course. I'm just overwhelmed at being back in this wonderful city."

We were graciously whisked through the elegant Thames Foyer, where tea would be served in the afternoon—and where theatergoers would snack before curtain time—and went·to the reception desk. I was warmly greeted by name.

Then, in the tow of a handsome, gregarious porter dressed in pinstripes, we were led to my room.

Room? It was a magnificent suite, spacious and airy, a fireplace on one wall, fine paintings on another establishing the Victorian panache for which the Savoy was famous.

I went to a window and looked out over the leafy embankment of the river Thames.

"Is everything to your satisfaction, Mrs. Fletcher?" the porter asked.

I turned. "Yes, it's splendid. I didn't expect to be in a suite, especially one with such opulence."

Lucas Darling laughed. "Nothing but the best for the famous Jessica Fletcher. Do you realize, Jessica, that . . . ?"

I cocked my head. "Realize what, Lucas?"

"Well, I hate to sound maudlin, but when Marjorie Ainsworth passes away, Jessica Fletcher will become, without doubt, the world's most revered writer of the murder mystery."

I couldn't help the guffaw that came from me. "Don't be silly, Lucas. I am firmly entrenched in a wonderful and large group of good writers. Then there are the Marjorie Ainsworths of this world. But thank you. You've always had an ability to flatter."

After the porter left, tipped handsomely by Lucas, he asked if I would join him for a drink downstairs.

"Oh, thank you, Lucas, but I really need some time to straighten out my circadian rhythms. The flight was long."

"Aha, the plot for the next Jessica Fletcher murder mystery is already developing. Circadian rhythms out of whack, claims of a suspect to have feasted on smoked salmon, caviar, and London broil on her flight when, in fact, our detective hero knows that particular flight served capon, country pâté, and vanilla mousse topped with raspberries."

We laughed. "Get out of here, Lucas, and let me pull myself together. Marjorie's chauffeur will be here tomorrow at noon to take me to Ainsworth Manor. I want to be rested, don't want to miss a moment of my time with her."

"Of course, I understand. Is there anything I can do for you?"

"No, but I would like to see the public room where I'll be making my speech, get a feel for it, that sort of thing."

"Whenever you say."

"Give me three hours of solitude. I'll meet you in the foyer."

"I'll be there. Three hours will give me time to run some errands. There are always so many errands to run in preparation for the conference, and no one seems willing to run them except me."

Poor suffering Lucas, I thought. Instead, I said, "Yes, but don't think your dedication isn't appreciated. I hear all the time from members about how the society would be nothing without Lucas Darling."

He kissed me on the cheek. "Bless you, Jessica Fletcher, you give Americans a good name." He went to the door, turned, and added, "A word of caution. London is not what it used to be. The crime rate is dreadful here, and getting worse every day. Rumor has it that the bobbies are carrying concealed weapons, quite a change from their nightsticks-only days. Packs of vile young men are roaming the streets and preying on visitors, particularly . . ."

I finished his sentence for him: "Particularly older women."

"I didn't say that, nor would I ever. Anyway, keep your handbag close to you and, no matter how tempted you might be to taste the less elegant areas of jolly old London, control your temptation. See you at three downstairs." He bounced jauntily out of the room.

"Thank God," I said aloud, but not *too* loud. I quickly unpacked and got out of the clothes I'd been living in since leaving Cabot Cove for Boston's Logan Airport and my connecting flight to London. A quick shower in the beautifully appointed bathroom revived my spirits while, at the same time, relaxing me enough to slide in for a nap between fresh sheets on the queen-sized bed.

Damn the mind. I wanted sleep to rescue me from those sad thoughts I'd had in the taxi, but I lost the race. I could hear the music, the happy sounds of men and women enjoying themselves, the delicious and comforting feel of being led around the dance floor downstairs in the River Room Restaurant:

> Savoy, the home of sweet romance,
> Savoy, it grabs you at a glance,
> Savoy, gives happy feet a chance
> To dance. . . .

It seemed like only yesterday, but I knew it wasn't; another mean trick played by the mind.

Now my topsy-turvy circadian rhythms, more commonly known as jet lag, came rushing over the hill to my rescue. The last thing I remember before falling asleep was changing songs from "Stompin' at the Savoy" to "Tea for Two," and smiling at the realization that I whistled more in tune than my mailman.

Chapter

3

Marjorie Ainsworth's chauffeur, Wilfred, was a proper gentleman in his sixties who stood forever straight, and who looked as though he could stand that way for hours, perhaps even days, waiting for a passenger. He never smiled, although not from a lack of pleasantness. It was more a matter of not having a smile born into him, which probably accounted for the lack of lines on his face. "It's a pleasure to see you once more, Mrs. Fletcher," he said, opening the door of the vintage maroon Morgan.

We pulled away from the hotel, smoothly negotiated London's clotted lunchtime traffic, and were soon on our way to the little town of Crumpsworth, an hour's drive. Ainsworth Manor, as I recalled, was a few minutes outside Crumpsworth, which, like all small, quaint British towns—it was in fact not much more than a large village—was founded at some astoundingly ancient date—1270 seemed to ring a bell with me, a hundred years give or take.

It took a few minutes for me to become comfortable riding on the "wrong" side of the road. I remembered . . . I tried not to remember how I balked at driving a car here, and how Frank had eagerly gotten behind the wheel, considering it a challenge, and, within minutes, drove as though he'd lived here his entire life.

I watched the countryside slide by, gently rolling hills, idyllic herds of cows grazing on rich grass, fancy sports cars passing us at grand prix speed, tiny villages with women sweeping their sidewalks. How I loved this place, and once again questioned why I'd never followed my instincts to move here. I knew why, of course. Cabot Cove, my home in Maine, was too precious to me to pull up stakes. I also knew that there were few places I'd ever visited that hadn't spurred in me a desire to live in them. The grass always seems greener; most times, of course, it isn't.

As we entered Crumpsworth, I recognized a few shops, even saw a person standing on a corner who looked familiar. I wondered how the residents of Crumpsworth felt about being home to Marjorie Ainsworth, the world's most famous mystery writer. They probably didn't think much about it, considering the British psyche and inherent tendency to downplay such things. Still, Ainsworth Manor and its illustrious occupant must be grist for dinner table conversation. Did any of the residents of Crumpsworth read Marjorie's books? A few, probably, but not enough to put her on the bestseller lists. The rest of the world saw to that.

We navigated a roundabout and proceeded down a narrow, pockmarked macadam road that eventually gave way to dirt. Wilfred drove with caution along the rutted road until we were abreast of Ainsworth Manor. It stood high on the slope of a hill, gothic in aura, although its architecture was not precisely that. I remembered the last time I approached it and thinking there should be streaks of lightning on a dark scrim behind it. Moviemakers would undoubtedly agree.

We turned onto an access road that was lined with poplar trees and drove for a couple of minutes until coming to a gate that had not been designed to keep out anyone who really wanted to get in. Wilfred got out of the Morgan, opened the gate, returned to the car, drove through, got out again, shut the gate, and drove on.

A minute later we were in front of Ainsworth Manor.

"Mrs. Fletcher, how nice to see you again," Jane Portelaine, Marjorie Ainsworth's niece, said to me as I stepped through massive oak doors into a stone-floored foyer.

"It's good to be back," I said, meaning it, although I thought to myself that Jane's presence did not necessarily add to my pleasure. She was obviously a good person, as evidenced by the devotion she'd demonstrated to Marjorie for so many years. The problem with Jane Portelaine was that her severe appearance, coupled with an enigmatic personality, tended to be off-putting, at best. She was tall and slender, skinny actually, an angular woman with sharp, chiseled features, except for her mouth, which was full and earthy and out of proportion to the rest of her. She always wore her brown hair pulled back tight, and her choice in clothing ran to drab suits and overly long and simple dresses, shoes sensible beyond even British standards. This day she wore a slate-gray dress buttoned to the neck and a black cardigan sweater, her long, bony hands shoved deep into its pockets.

The reason I use the term "enigmatic" to describe Jane is that behind her austere façade there seemed to be a parallel unstated sensuality, undoubtedly suppressed but, like rage, threatening to spring forth at any moment.

In contrast with her generally spartan approach to life, Jane was, simultaneously, enamored of perfumes and colognes. She used them to excess; the scent of Victorian posy hung heavy in the foyer as I entered Ainsworth Manor. Marjorie once told me that perfume was Jane's abiding passion, and that the account she maintained at Penhaligon's, on Wellington Street, was, in her estimation, "obscenely high." Then again, she went on to tell me, her real objection was not the amount of money her niece spent on such things, but the fact that she liberally doused herself with them, which made Ainsworth Manor smell like "a French whorehouse."

"Was your trip pleasant?" Jane asked me.

"Yes, tiring, but a good night's sleep took care of that."

The foyer was exactly as I remembered it, large and chilly, with two full and tarnished suits of armor flanking the archway leading to the living room, embroidered tapestries hanging on facing walls, a few oversized pieces of dark furniture, and a single light fixture on the high ceiling that cast tentative illumination.

What had changed was the member of the household staff who stood silently at the foot of a long, curving staircase until Jane said to him, "Marshall, please take Mrs. Fletcher's luggage and show her to her room." To me: "My aunt hasn't been feeling well, I'm afraid, and naps more than before. She's napping now."

"Oh, I wouldn't think of disturbing her. I just hope we have some time to chat a little later."

"I'm sure you will, Mrs. Fletcher. Might I suggest you spend a few minutes freshening up before joining me in the library. You know where that is."

"Yes, I do."

"Tea, or would you prefer sherry?"

"Tea would be fine, thank you."

I'd been assigned a room at the rear of the house which, I knew, was next to Marjorie Ainsworth's bedroom. Marshall, who violated the clichéd stereotype of the butler—too young, too of-his-generation—pulled back heavy drapes, allowing gray light to spill into the room. I went to the window and looked down at the magnificent English gardens that had always been Marjorie's pride and joy. "It's so beautiful, even in this gray weather," I said.

"They forecast sunshine tomorrow, Mrs. Fletcher," said Marshall as he busied himself with my luggage.

"Oh, don't bother, I'll take care of that."

"No bother, ma'am. I've heard much about you from Miss Ainsworth."

"All good, I hope."

"Oh yes, always positive comments about Jessica Fletcher. You're one of . . . the few."

It was an inappropriate comment for someone in his position to make, but I didn't challenge him.

After he left, I stood at the window and looked more closely at the gardens below. Two men were working in a far corner. It was hard to tell for certain, but they appeared to be of Mediterranean origin. They were digging up a small tree and I watched with interest, just the way I always watch construction going on in big cities. I then remembered that Jane Portelaine would be waiting for me downstairs. I stepped into the hallway—eight feet wide, very long, and lined with bookcases—and looked down over a railing upon the formal dining room. Beyond it was a drawing room; a fire crackled in the fireplace there, its flickering orange fingers playing on a large and well-worn oriental rug. Everything in the manor was oversized, but not in relationship to its mistress. Marjorie Ainsworth's image in the world was larger than life, and it was only fitting that her domicile would be, too.

I turned and looked at the door to her bedroom. Was she sleeping, dozing in a half-awake state, perhaps fully awake and looking out the window on her treasured gardens? The temptation to knock was strong; I walked away before it overruled good judgment.

Jane was seated in a large wing chair in the library. Her legs were crossed and she held a cup and saucer. A fireplace in the library also housed a healthy fire, spreading a pleasant warmth through the dank room.

"Tea, Mrs. Fletcher? Please help yourself."

"Thank you." I poured the tea into a cup through a small silver strainer from a brown teapot that was cradled in blue-

and-white quilted chintz. A tiny sponge attached to the lip caught inadvertent drips. I returned to my chair and tasted. "Wonderful," I said. "Different."

"Lapsang Souchong," Jane said. "It's an oolong."

"Yes," I said, taking another sip so that I wouldn't trigger a long and detailed explanation of the proper tea one should use, and how to brew it. Jane Portelaine was an expert on tea.

I let a moment pass, then said, "You say your aunt hasn't been well. Her most recent letter to me indicated the same thing. How serious?"

Jane's reply was to take another sip of tea and to stare at me over her cup.

"I don't mean to pry and, please understand, I don't wish to meddle in her life or . . ." Marjorie's letter about meddling came to mind. "I got quite a kick out of the letter in which she talked about meddling, especially her tongue-in-cheek asides about you as you took her dictation."

"Asides?" What could pass for a smile crossed her mouth. "That's kind."

I dropped the subject of Marjorie's health, content to sip my tea, the room's silence broken only by the crackle of the burning hardwood logs. After a few minutes I asked, "Who else will be coming this weekend?"

"The usual people who flock around my aunt."

"The usual people?" I laughed. "I suppose we all have 'usual people' in our lives, but your aunt's entourage must be bigger and more diverse than most."

Jane started to get up. "I can provide you with a list if you'd like."

"Gracious, no, nothing that formal. I was just . . ." I wanted to say I was just making conversation. Instead, I said, "I was just mildly curious about whom I would be meeting this weekend."

She looked up at the rococo ceiling and said, "Well, there will be my other aunt, Ona Ainsworth-Zara, and her husband;

my aunt's New York agent, Bruce Herbert; her American publisher, Mr. Perry, and her British publisher, Archibald Semple,
and . . . yes, I think William Strayhorn will be here."

"The book critic?"

"Yes, and Sir James Ferguson, the producer of *Who Killed
Darby and Joan?*"

"I loved it," I said. "I saw it the last time I was in London.
How long has it been running now?"

Jane shrugged. "Six, seven years, I suppose."

Who Killed Darby and Joan? was the name of one of Marjorie
Ainsworth's previous novels that had been adapted for the
London stage and that had been a hit from the day it opened.
The term "Darby and Joan," I knew, was slang for the arche-
typical elderly, happily married British couple. There were
Darby-and-Joan clubs in cities and towns all over Great Britain.

"Quite an impressive list of visitors," I said. "I've never
met Marjorie's younger sister."

"Well, you certainly will, won't you?"

There was that tone of voice again. It was to be hoped that
when the others arrived, I would have to spend only minimal
time with Jane Portelaine.

We spent another awkward half hour before she got up
and said, "I'll check on her now. If she's awake, I'll see if
she's well enough to come down."

"Please, don't put any pressure on her. I'll be content to
see her whenever it's comfortable for her. Perhaps she'd prefer
I come to the bedroom."

"I think not." Jane's long, lanky frame disappeared
through a doorway.

A few minutes later she reappeared and said, "She's coming down. Marshall will wheel her."

"Wheel . . . ? I didn't realize she was in a wheelchair."

"Only recently, and not always. It depends on the day.
We've had an elevator installed in the rear of the house."

"That sounds like a good idea," I said, a flush of excitement

coming over me as I awaited Marjorie's arrival. Then anticipation became reality as the young butler wheeled his mistress
through the door and to the center of the study.

"Jessica, I am so sorry to have kept you waiting. Welcome."

Those warm and sincere words buoyed me after the
strained conversation with Jane.

I got up and took the hand she offered in both of mine.
"How wonderful to see you again, Marjorie. I must say you
look a lot better than your last letter indicated you would."

"Bull! I look like the wrath of God, probably because I am
closer to him than I have ever been before. But, my dear
poppet, thank you for being the kind friend you have always
been. Jane has seen to it that you've had tea?"

"Yes, she's been very gracious."

Marjorie looked at me through squinted eyes. "That's bull,
too. One thing my niece is not is gracious." I was relieved
there were just the two of us in the room.

I took my chair again and closely observed Marjorie Ainsworth. She had grown old and feeble. Her hand, when I took
it, seemed nothing but bone and vein covered loosely by leathery skin. Her hair was completely white and appeared not to
have been washed and brushed in too long a time. She wore
a Black Watch plaid dress that was stained on the bosom. An
old, handmade shawl covered her legs. Most telling of her
advanced age, however, were her eyes. I don't think I'd ever
met anyone in my life whose eyes sparkled with such mischief.
Now that sparkle was evident only in fleeting bursts, replaced
by dark eyes that had sunk into the bony structure of her face,
like fresh soil sinking after a heavy rain; dark circles around
them gave her skin a puttied appearance. This close scrutiny
by me was, at first, upsetting, but then I reminded myself that
she was indeed an old woman growing older, and had every
right to look it.

The thing that stayed in my mind after the first few minutes
was her unkempt condition, and I wondered at the compe-

tence and interest of whatever household staff served her these days.

"Jane!" Marjorie shouted in a surprisingly strong and vibrant voice. A moment later Jane Portelaine stood in the doorway. "I'd like a gin," said Marjorie, "and fetch the book for Jessica."

When Jane returned, she carried a glass filled with gin and a copy of *Gin and Daggers*. She handed the drink to Marjorie, the book to me.

"Thank you, I've been looking forward to this ever since it was published." I eagerly opened to the first page and saw that it had been inscribed to me in Marjorie's own handwriting:

For Jessica,

Whose forays into the matter of murder, both on the printed page and in real life, delight everyone, particularly this old woman who has always been content to confine her snooping to the typewriter. Your reputation in the world as an author is well deserved. More important to me, Jessica Fletcher, I count you as a friend, which puts you in a small group indeed.

Affectionately,
Marjorie

I was sincerely touched. "You're much too kind with your praise, Marjorie."

"Not in the least. Would you like to join me in a gin, or whiskey if you prefer, before dear Jane departs us again?"

"Thank you, no." At those words, Jane was gone.

We chatted about *Gin and Daggers*, and I must admit I suffered conflicting thoughts. On the one hand, I wanted to sit with Marjorie forever. On the other hand, I couldn't wait to begin reading. There'd be plenty of time for that later, I knew, and my instincts told me the book would see to a relatively sleepless night for me.

We talked about many things, including the subject of death, which Marjorie seemed to dwell upon. Understandable: older people think about their mortality most of the time, I'm told. What was upsetting was that after ten minutes her conversation, lucid and insightful at times, would slip into vague comments that had nothing to do with what we'd been discussing. Let me give you an example.

She was saying, ". . . and so I talked to my solicitor and changed provisions in my will, knowing full well that the end could come at any moment. He's a fuddy-duddy, but, as we all know, the last thing anyone needs is a gregarious and creative solicitor. Mine fusses for days over a clause which is in my best interest but . . ." At that point she literally shuddered in the wheelchair and closed her eyes against something only she could identify—pain, a sudden and unexpected thought?–and then completed her sentence with, ". . . the flowers turned dry and brittle. I watched them die . . . how sad, how sad. . . ."

I said, "Yes, I'm sure that's true, Marjorie. You were saying that your solicitor . . ."

Her eyes opened wide and she looked at me as though I had intruded upon a precious moment. "I . . . my solicitor? Yes, of course, he's an old fusspot but, I suppose, that is in my best interests." She sipped her gin, closed her eyes, and drew a series of deep breaths. When she opened her eyes she smiled. "Jessica Fletcher. You and I have so much to talk about, but you'll forgive me if my physical stamina does not always match my mental intentions. If I fall asleep in this chair, just ignore me, leave the room, and busy yourself with something else."

I forced a laugh. "Oh, don't worry about me, I certainly will take care of myself. If you should nod off on me, Marjorie, I will not consider it a comment on my conversation. I will take it as a good opportunity to begin reading *Gin and Daggers*."

She said slowly, deliberately, and with a modicum of anger, *"Gin and Daggers.* I trust you'll find it interesting, Jessica."

"Of course I will. I find all your books—"

She interrupted with, "Interesting in a different sense, Jessica. Are you certain you don't want something stronger than Jane's tea? Gin is good for you, my doctor says, which, despite the fact that he is an inept physician, endears him to my heart. I would never think of giving him the heave-ho as long as his prescription pad continues to have 'gin' printed on it."

I laughed heartily and we shifted into a conversation about the guests who would be arriving the next day—Friday—for the weekend at Ainsworth Manor.

A minute later she did as she'd predicted: dozed off in the chair, the light from the fireplace casting a flattering orange glow across her old, tired face. She seemed very much at peace, which pleased me. I opened *Gin and Daggers* to the dedication page:

> *To my faithful niece, Jane,*
> *without whom this modest effort*
> *would never have been possible*

I turned to page one:

> He stepped out of the shadows and she knew immediately he was not a man to be trusted, not with that downturn at the corners of his mouth which, to the untrained eye, indicated amusement at what went on around him but, for this trained eye, represented pure evil.

I quickly finished the very short first chapter, quietly closed the book, stood, looked down at the woman in whose brain the words I'd just read had been formulated, and tiptoed from the room. On my way up to my bedroom, I passed the butler, Marshall, who stood at the foot of the stairs with a heavyset woman who I remembered was Mrs. Horton, and who ran Ainsworth Manor's kitchen.

"Hello, Mrs. Horton," I said.

My sudden appearance seemed to have interrupted a serious conversation. Mrs. Horton flashed a quick smile at me and said she was pleased to have me as a guest once more— "Do you have a preference for dinner, Mrs. Fletcher?" I told her anything would be fine as long as it was prepared with her skilled hands. It was a silly platitude, I know, but I couldn't think of anything else to say. I passed between them and went to my room, where, after reading the next two chapters of what was, without doubt, a remarkable piece of writing, I dozed off myself.

Chapter

4

"But that's one of Dorothy's enduring traits, Clayton," William Strayhorn, London's most respected book critic, said to Marjorie Ainsworth's American publisher, Clayton Perry. "Read a Dorothy Sayers mystery and you'll always learn something."

"Yes, readers love to learn something while being entertained," Archibald Semple, Marjorie's British publisher, chimed in. "But that doesn't make her better than a writer who doesn't give a tinker's damn about educating readers."

It was Friday night, and we'd been at the dinner table for two hours. The chief topic of discussion throughout the meal—throughout the entire day for that matter—had been the relative merits of mystery writers, past and present. The quality of the debates ranged from intently interesting to snide and gossipy. No matter what level they took, however, the presence of the invited guests and their conversation seemed to buoy Marjorie Ainsworth's spirits. She'd spent most of the day with us and, aside from an occasional lapse of concentration and a few brief naps in her wheelchair, had been an active participant.

I'd been more of an observer than an involved member of

these spirited discussions. I've always preferred to listen; you learn so much more that way than being compelled to verbalize what you already know. I'd drifted from group to group, enjoying some more than others, laughing at myriad witty lines that erupted from time to time, and generally enjoying the ambiance of Ainsworth Manor and its weekend visitors.

Mrs. Horton and two very young girls in starched uniforms cleared the remnants of the main course and prepared to deliver dessert. Marjorie sat at the head of the table. The long day had taken its toll on her; she looked exhausted and was obviously fighting to remain with the group until the last possible minute.

There had been a spirited, somewhat comic debate earlier in the day between Marjorie and her niece, Jane, about the seating arrangements at dinner. Jane had insisted that couples be split up in the time-honored tradition of a formal dinner, but Marjorie insisted couples sit together. "As far as I'm concerned," Marjorie had said, "they deserve each other, and I see no reason for me to provide a respite from those with whom they've chosen to spend their lives." That settled it; guests sat at the dinner table where Marjorie wanted them to sit.

I had been placed to Marjorie's immediate left. Across from me was William Strayhorn, the critic, whose face had the bloated, flushed look of a heavy drinker; watery blue eyes further confirmed my impression. He was pleasant enough, but too full of himself for my personal taste, although I've been accused in the past of being too quick in making that judgment about people. To my left sat Clayton Perry, the American publisher of Marjorie Ainsworth's novels, and his wife. Neither of them drank or smoked, and both had the lightly tanned, sinewy bodies of people devoted to health and exercise.

Directly across from the Perrys sat Mr. and Mrs. Archibald Semple. It was obvious to me from the beginning that Mr.

Semple was not especially fond of Mr. Perry, and that the feeling was mutual. They were certainly physical opposites; while Perry was dressed immaculately in a three-piece gray suit, pale blue shirt, and perfectly knotted red paisley tie, Semple was the picture of slovenliness. He was obese, one of those people who sweat no matter what the temperature. He consumed his food with the zeal of a stray mongrel who's been on the run for days, some of it ending up on his wrinkled, stained green-and-brown-striped tie. Because he was heavy, his suit, although probably the correct size, looked as though it belonged to someone else. His fingernails were highly lacquered, and the broad expanse of bare skin on top of his head was sparsely covered with long, wet strands of hair that he brought up from just above his left ear. Mrs. Semple, too, was overweight. She'd started the day staunchly Victorian but, by the time dinner was served, had consumed enough alcohol to turn her into a giggling libertine. She wore a black taffeta dress that was cut very low, exposing the upper reaches of a large bosom. Talcum powder was caked in her cleavage.

To continue down my side of the table, Jane Portelaine sat next to the Perrys, and next to her was Bruce Herbert, Marjorie's New York agent. They made an interesting couple. Herbert was as outgoing as Jane was taciturn. He was a handsome man in his early forties who seemed always to say the right thing at the right time, a distinct advantage at such gatherings, but invariably making me wonder what he was really thinking. It was he who'd proposed the toast at the beginning of dinner:

"To the world's finest crime novelist, Marjorie Ainsworth, who has given millions of people supreme joy through her books, who has set the standard for all writers of the genre, today and for future generations. I suspect, Marjorie, that you would be hailed as the best by Dame Agatha Christie were she around to make such a proclamation. I suppose I should also add that you have provided a splendid living for all of us . . . well, for most of us at this table. To you, Marjorie, may *Gin and Daggers* be only the latest of your wonderful writings."

"Hear, hear," Archibald Semple said, his words slurred.

"I have a toast," Marjorie said.

We all looked at her as she raised her glass and said:

> A thumbprint on the teacup,
> the telltale rigid chin;
> a murder's been committed here,
> beware the next of kin.

"Bravo," Bruce Herbert said.

"Did you write that?" I asked her.

"Heavens, no, and I have no idea who did. I heard it once and . . ."

Count Antonio Zara, Marjorie's brother-in-law, suddenly stood, cleared his throat, and said in a heavy accent, "As we all know, Italians are not noted for writing murder mysteries. Instead, we have devoted our creative energies to wine, fine food, and an appreciation of beautiful women. That I have married into this illustrious family, and sit at this table tonight, gives me distinct pleasure. I salute my British and American friends, and insist the next time this distinguished group gathers, it be at my villa on Capri."

There was polite applause. He'd mentioned his villa on Capri many times that day, prompting Bruce Herbert to whisper to me, "*His* villa. Everything he has is the result of marrying Marjorie's sister. He's as phony as his title. 'Count'? He's a handsome, oily gigolo who scored."

Ona Ainsworth-Zara, the count's wife and Marjorie's sister, was, I judged, twelve to fifteen years younger than Marjorie. She was an attractive woman, regal in bearing, beautifully dressed, and adorned with an array of expensive jewelry. She'd kept to herself most of the day, probably because getting too close to her older and famous sister triggered razor-sharp barbs. I wondered at one point why Marjorie had bothered to invite her, and had my question answered when Bruce Herbert muttered, "The count and his lady have managed to infiltrate another party. Why Marjorie puts up with it is beyond me."

I'd never met Ona before, and Marjorie had had little to say about her during our brief previous encounters. Although she'd never said anything overtly negative about Ona, there was always an edge to her voice when she brought her up, and I gathered that if there was not an outright estrangement, they certainly weren't loving siblings. Strange, I thought as I sat at the table, that Marjorie had never married. I knew of no romantic interest in her long life, although one had to assume there were some flirtations along the way. Few people, even those committed to avoiding intimacy, successfully avoid it over a lifetime.

Marshall supervised the serving of dessert.

"Can we trust this?" Bruce Herbert asked. Marjorie, who'd been dozing, jerked awake and said in a strong voice, "Trust it? What in heaven's name do you mean by that?"

Herbert laughed and said, "I've read at least a thousand murder mysteries, Marjorie, in which victims are poisoned by dishes that look like this."

There was laughter at the table. Strayhorn, the critic, said, "I'd debate you on that, Mr. Herbert. I'd say the whiskey decanter has done more people in than syllabub."

"Syllabub?" I said. "What's that?"

Mrs. Semple said with a giggle, "Our answer to zabaglione."

Her husband chimed in, "It goes back to Elizabethan times."

"What's in it?" I asked.

Mrs. Horton, who stood at the door to the kitchen, said, "Whipped cream, sherry, and lemon juice. They used to make it with warm cow's milk."

I looked at my hostess and said lightly, "You haven't decided to poison us all with your syllabub, have you, Marjorie?"

She raised her head and moved her nose, as though a disagreeable odor had reached it. A tiny smile came to her lips as she said, "My dear Jessica, I must be slipping not to have thought of that. What a wonderful way to clear my decks before leaving."

Laughter quickly dissipated as her final words sunk in.

"Whatever do you mean by saying 'leaving'?" asked Archibald Semple.

"You know only too well what I mean, Archie. I don't expect this dicky body to support me much longer."

Clayton Perry laughed. "You'll probably outlive us all," he said.

"I doubt that," remarked Jane Portelaine, sounding as though she meant it. No one challenged her. By now we were all too used to her depressing comments.

Bruce Herbert broke the tension by suggesting to Marjorie that it was time she did a cookbook. "Everyone else has," he said. "There's the Lord Peter Wimsey cookbook, and one of the best cookbooks I've ever seen—I use it all the time—is the Nero Wolfe cookbook."

"Food is of no interest to me," Marjorie said.

"It was to Agatha," Strayhorn said. "Remember *Funerals Are Fatal?*"

That led into a new topic of discussion: food and the use of it as a vehicle to deliver lethal poisons. As the argument heated up, I looked down the table at the other guests. Looking every bit the contented land baron, was the producer of *Who Killed Darby and Joan?*," Sir James Ferguson. He was stocky, but not portly, and wore a beautiful tan tweed jacket, a maroon V-neck sweater, and a loosely woven brown tie. He was one of those people who seem to enjoy whatever they're doing with a minimum of effort. He didn't laugh much, but he was never without an amused smile on his handsome, ruddy face. As we all know, there are people in this world whom you immediately like, and Sir James Ferguson was one of them. I intended to find time for more conversation with him before the weekend was over.

The young man across from him was not one of those who instantly produce a positive reaction. His name was Jason Harris, and he defined "brooding young man."

He'd arrived late Thursday night. I was in my room reading *Gin and Daggers*, and had come downstairs at about eleven o'clock to pour a small glass of port as a stomach-settling nightcap. Harris had just arrived and was in the library with Jane Portelaine. They were startled by my sudden appearance (it seems that everywhere I went in the manor I startled someone), but they quickly recovered. He was introduced to me by Jane as a writer whom Marjorie Ainsworth had taken under her wing.

"How wonderful," I said, offering my hand, which, after some hesitation, he accepted. "My nephew, Grady Fletcher, is an aspiring writer, too." The moment I said it I knew I should have left out the word 'aspiring.' He glowered at me. He was too old to be viewed as aspiring to anything, just as one reaches a certain age when one can no longer refer to a companion of the opposite sex as "girlfriend" or "boyfriend." He was handsome enough, a head of brown curls falling gently over his forehead and ears, a nicely sculptured face, square jaw, aquiline nose, and sensual, doelike brown eyes —bedroom eyes they were called in my youth. What was missing was a smile or, more correctly, the ability to smile. It went with being the struggling artist.

Oh well, I told myself as I asked a couple of questions of him and received answers that were little more than mono-syllabic grunts.

My final question was "Are you currently working on a novel, Mr. Harris?"

Harris and Portelaine looked at each other. He said to me, "I have a work in progress."

"Well," I said, "I think I'll take this splendid port upstairs with me and read one more chapter of *Gin and Daggers*. It's remarkably good, don't you think?" No answer. "Good night. It was a pleasure meeting you, Mr. Harris. I'm sure we'll have time to talk tomorrow."

As much as I tried to dismiss Jason Harris—to perceive him as simply amusing, as all such brooding young men are—I couldn't, and I made a mental note to ask Marjorie about him. I read another chapter, then sat on a window seat and looked out over the gardens. There was a full moon; it was as though someone had turned on a floodlight to illuminate the beautiful plantings. One of my final thoughts before retiring was that besides being a weekend guest at Marjorie's country home, I was a character in a murder mystery being written by her. The idea amused me, and I fell into a blissful sleep.

That thought came back to me as I sat at the dinner table and ate my syllabub, which, by the way, was absolutely delicious, although I have to admit that what had been said in jest about it had planted the idea of a foreign substance, arsenic perhaps, having been added to the ingredients. I laughed aloud as I thought it, which caused some of my table companions to look at me. I shook my head. "Just imagining what it would be like to be poisoned," I said.

"I assure you, Jessica, that had I the notion to do away with you, I would never spoil a dinner party," said Marjorie. "As you know, I've always believed in treating my victims to a splendid final meal, then doing away with them somewhere removed from the table to avoid offending the sensitive digestive tracts of other guests."

"A considerate murderer," Clayton Perry said.

"Let's hear it for blood, the sort brought about by daggers and revolvers, not poison. I hate death by poisoning," Archie Semple said. "It's bloody dull, but I suppose I've picked up my love for violence from reading too many of your American books and watching too many of your American productions on the telly." He looked across the table at Perry, who gave him a condescending smile and pushed his barely touched cup of syllabub away. His wife had done the same moments earlier. Fattening; no poisoning them with desserts. It would have to be a main course, soup, or from the classic decanter.

I looked down the table at Jason Harris; his usual scowl was on his face. He wore a forest-green corduroy jacket over a black turtleneck. He established eye contact with Jane Portelaine and raised one eyebrow—something I've never been able to do—which said to me that he found the dinner boring and would be happy when it ended.

It ended a half hour later. We retired to the library. Marshall, the butler, stood behind a rolling cart and portioned out after-dinner drinks. I'd just been handed a Cognac when Clayton Perry's wife came up to me. Her name was Renée. "I've been admiring that pendant all evening, Mrs. Fletcher."

I lifted the gold pendant to which she was referring, and smiled. "It's my favorite piece of jewelry, Mrs. Perry. My husband gave it to me."

"It's lovely."

"Yes, it's very special. In fact, he bought it for me when we were in London together a number of years ago. You can imagine that coming back here always has special meaning for me."

"Of course. By the way, I'm a big fan of your novels."

"Thank you."

"Clayton would give his eyeteeth to have you as an author at Perry House."

"That's very flattering, but I've been with my present publishers for years now, wouldn't think of changing unless they committed outright theft of my royalties, or insisted upon multiple four-letter words and interminable car chases and mass murders."

We both laughed. "I assure you, Mrs. Fletcher, Clayton would see that nothing like that ever happened to you."

"I'm sure he would. He has a fine reputation. . . ." (I seemed to recall some gossip about Perry House's being in serious financial trouble but, of course, didn't mention that.) "By the way, please call me Jessica for the rest of the weekend."

"Yes, and it's Renée."

We all turned in the direction of Marjorie Ainsworth's voice, which announced she was going to bed. I was amazed at her stamina. She'd been gracious and witty all day and evening. Again, there were those mental lapses that were disquieting, but everyone seemed to accept them as nothing more than periods of fatigue in a brain that had been working at top creative effort for so many years.

Marjorie's departure broke up the gathering. Most of us said good night and retired to our respective rooms, leaving Bruce Herbert, Jason Harris, Jane Portelaine, and "Count" Antonio Zara to accept another drink from Marshall, and to settle down on large couches in front of the fireplace, which had recently been stoked by the butler. I walked upstairs with Ona Ainsworth-Zara.

"It's been so good to meet you after all these years," I said.

"My sister speaks often and well of you, Mrs. Fletcher."

"That's always nice to hear, especially from someone like her. By the way, your husband is a charming man."

"He has to be. He has little else."

I didn't know what to say, so I said nothing. She bade me a curt good night and walked down the hall. I watched her go into her room, then entered mine, closed the door behind me, and prepared for bed. I was tired; I looked at the copy of *Gin and Daggers* that sat on my night table and wondered whether I would be able to stay awake long enough to read more. I knew I would; it was that compelling, that rich, that much of a page-turner.

I got into bed, opened the book to where I'd left off, and before starting to read, thought back to my conversation in London with Lucas Darling. He was right; it was like no other Marjorie Ainsworth novel I'd ever read. He was also right when he'd said that there were numerous examples of the classic Ainsworth style and touch, but that they were isolated, cropping up at intervals rather than being the basis for the narrative. I wondered at it, could do nothing else. Dare I ask Marjorie whether she'd been *helped*? I answered my own question with a resounding no. That would be a terrible offense. Undoubtedly, though, others would be asking her as the rumor swelled and those who read her book arrived at the same conclusion as Lucas Darling.

What if Marjorie hadn't written *Gin and Daggers*? Would that be taking unfair advantage of the reading public? I didn't know the answer to that question and decided not to grapple with it at that point. I finished a chapter, laid the book down beside me, got into my robe and slippers, and went to an adjacent bathroom that was assigned to me, which could be reached only from the hallway. I returned ten minutes later, pausing at the railing and listening to muffled conversations from the library. Mrs. Horton stepped into the dining room and looked up at me. "Good night, Mrs. Horton," I said. She mumbled something and left the room. A few minutes later I was in my bed, asleep.

I sat bolt upright. I didn't know what time it was. Had I been asleep ten minutes, an hour, four hours?

It was a sound that had awakened me, and it seemed to come from Marjorie's room. How to describe it? A cry for help? Not really. Sounds from someone engaged in a struggle?

More like it, but hardly accurate. Whatever it was, it had been loud enough to awaken me and sinister enough to cause me to get out of bed, slip into my robe and slippers, and open my door. I looked up and down the hallway, which was dimly lighted by low-wattage sconces along the wall. I listened, heard nothing. I immediately tried to calculate how much time had elapsed between when I had first heard the noise and had looked into the hallway. Five minutes perhaps, considering the time it had taken me to process what I'd heard, to decide to investigate it, to find my slippers, one of which I'd inadvertently kicked under the bed, to get into my robe, and to cross the darkened room to the door. Five minutes.

I entered the hallway, stepping gingerly as the ancient floorboards creaked beneath my feet, a sound I hadn't heard since awakening.

I stood outside Marjorie's bedroom door. It was ajar, not enough so that you could see through the opening, but certainly not closed tight. I put my ear to it and listened, heard nothing but silence. The steeple bell at a nearby country church suddenly went into action: one, two, three chimes. It was three o'clock in the morning, unless the clock controlling the bell hadn't been set correctly.

I placed my fingertips against the door and pushed. It was heavy and did not swing open, had to be pushed more. I did that and peered into the room. Marjorie's bed was king-sized and covered with a canopy. The room was dark except for a sharp shaft of moonlight that poured through an opening in the drapes. It was perfectly aimed, as though a theater lighting technician had highlighted a section of a stage where major action would occur.

I stepped over the threshold and walked to the side of the bed, like a moth drawn to a summer candle. A whole arsenal of grotesque sounds rose up inside me but stopped at my throat, sounds of protest, of outrage, of shock and horror. Yet not a sound came from me as I looked down at the body of

Marjorie Ainsworth, the grande dame of murder mystery fiction, sprawled on her back, arms and legs flung out, a long dagger protruding from her chest like a graveyard marker.

All I managed to say—and it was in a whisper—was "Oh my God." As I turned to leave, my slippered foot hit a metal object and propelled it under the bed. I didn't stop to see what it was. I returned to the hallway and stood at the railing, my hands gripping it as I drew a deep breath to fill my lungs. I shouted, "Help! Please come quickly! There's been a murder!"

Chapter

5

We huddled together in the study like survivors of a shipwreck or plane accident, each having experienced a tragedy that bound us to one another.

As expected, everyone reacted to the shocking event in his or her own way. There was the hysterical camp, which included Archibald Semple, Marjorie's British publisher; Bruce Herbert, her New York agent; Sir James Ferguson, the producer of *Who Killed Darby and Joan?* (his lack of control surprised me, based upon my observation of him at the dinner table); and, even more surprising, Renée Perry, the wife of Marjorie's American publisher, Clayton Perry. My surprise wasn't based upon any dramatic change in her demeanor, although it certainly had changed. Murder tends to cause that. It was more a matter of wondering why she was so personally distraught over Marjorie's death. She acted as though she had lost her dearest friend, which, of course, wasn't true.

I was relieved when the local police inspector arrived, accompanied by two young constables in uniform. Marshall, the butler, brought them to the library. The young police officers took positions at opposite ends of the room as the inspector assumed a stance in the middle. He was a little man, no taller than five feet six inches, which, I reasoned, accounted for his habit of moving up and down on his toes. He wore heavy laced boots and a well-worn red plaid outdoor jacket over an ill-fitting and wrinkled suit that had a distinct green cast to it. He held a notebook to his chest as he continued to rock up and down.

"I am Inspector Montgomery Coots, in charge of Crumpsworth. Miss Ainsworth has been killed, has she? Where might the body be?"

"Upstairs, in her bedroom," Jane Portelaine said. She stood with Jason Harris behind a large oak table.

Coots turned at the sound of her voice. "Miss Portelaine, isn't it?"

"Yes, I am Jane Portelaine, Marjorie Ainsworth's niece."

"I take it you found the body," Coots said.

"No, I did," I said from my chair, causing him to have to turn again.

"And who might you be?"

"My name is Jessica Fletcher, Inspector. I'm an old friend of Marjorie Ainsworth and was invited here as a weekend guest."

"American, I can hear."

"Yes, I am from the United States."

"You flew all the way here to attend a party?"

"No, you see . . ." Bruce Herbert interrupted to explain who I was and why I was there.

"A mystery writer." He took in the others: "Is that the case with all of you?"

"No," said Herbert, "we are all involved—*were* professionally involved with Marjorie Ainsworth."

"Excuse me, Inspector, but don't you want to see the body before we get into this kind of questioning?" Clayton Perry asked.

Coots fixed him with a hard stare. "I think I'll be the judge from this point forward, sir, of how we proceed with investigating this case. You are?"

Perry told him.

"Well now, where is the body?" he asked imperiously. He was a dislikable man, filled with pomposity. His left eye twitched, and he had a habit of moving his nose as though a foreign object were lodged in it.

Jane came around the table and said, "Come with me, Inspector."

Coots said to his men, "Stay here and see that no one leaves." He asked the room, "Has anyone left since the body was discovered?" We assured him no one had.

"Household staff?" he asked Jane.

"All present and accounted for," she said.

"Well then, let's proceed."

After Coots and Jane left the room, Archibald Semple, who'd resumed drinking upon being summoned to the library, started pacing, drink in hand. He said, "What we have here is right out of the cozy school of murder mysteries, it seems to me. It may be irreverent for me to be speaking this way at such a time, but Dame Agatha could not have created a more perfect setting or assembled a more fitting cast of suspects."

"This isn't the time to be discussing fictitious murders, Archie," Strayhorn, the critic, snapped. "We have a real murder here on our hands, and not only have we lost a treasured friend and colleague, the world has lost the sort of talent that comes along only once in a lifetime."

I was tempted to shout, "Bravo!"

I looked over to where Renée Perry sat hunched in a chair, her sobs soft and steady. Her husband, the patrician Clayton Perry, stood next to her but offered no solace—did not touch her or try to comfort her in any way. My attention then shifted to the table, where Jason Harris casually perched on its corner, his eyes fixed on the high ceiling, a cigarette dangling from his lips.

I asked, "Did anyone see or hear anything last night?" Everyone shook their heads and said that they hadn't. Harris did not bother to respond. "Mr. Harris, did you see or hear anything last night?"

He turned slowly and removed the cigarette from his mouth. The ashes fell to the rug, and he ground them in with his shoe. "No," he answered.

Sir James Ferguson sat in a corner of the room shaking his head and muttering over and over, "Can't be, it just can't be. It was obviously someone from the household staff. No one in this room would have had any reason to kill Marjorie. Who hires the staff here? Whoever that person is hired Marjorie's killer."

"Not necessarily," I said. "It could have been"—I took in everyone quickly before ending with—"anyone in the house or, for that matter, someone who entered from outside."

"Good point, Mrs. Fletcher. Perhaps we should check for broken glass, footprints in the soft soil outside the windows," Semple said as he refilled his drink.

"I think that would be for Inspector Coots to accomplish," I said.

"He doesn't look too swift to me," William Strayhorn said, "a typical bumbling country copper who'll undoubtedly muck things up and make it difficult for higher-ups to do their jobs."

As much as I agreed with him, I found myself mildly resentful of his characterization of Coots. Our local sheriff back in Cabot Cove, Morton Metzger, would certainly never win awards for investigative brilliance, yet he was a hardworking and competent law enforcement officer. He'd also become a dear friend.

"I think we should solve this thing ourselves instead of waiting for that inept little man to drag things out," Semple said. "This was obviously the work of an intruder, a demented one to boot. He enters bent upon thievery, steps into Mar-

jorie's room, wakes her, and in order to keep her from scream-
ing, rams a dagger into her chest." This set off an argument
among Semple, Strayhorn, and Clayton Perry which,
blessedly, came to an abrupt end when Coots and Jane Portelaine returned.

"Bloody nasty way to go," Coots said, resuming his stance
in the middle of the room. He still held the notebook close to
his chest, as though it were a prayer book from which he
would deliver a sermon. I noticed something else, however:
a gold chain dangling from his fingers glittered in the light
from a nearby lamp. I sat forward and squinted to make sure
it was what I thought it was. Indeed. My gold pendant, the
one Frank had bought for me in a beautiful little jewelry shop
in Mayfair. "Excuse me, Inspector Coots, but I believe you
have something of mine."

He looked at me over his shoulder, a snide grin on his
face. "Then you admit it's yours."

I stood. "Admit it? Of course I admit it. Why shouldn't I?"
I quickly explained the origins of the pendant. "Where did
you get it?"

"Beneath the victim's bed, that's where."

I thought back to having discovered the body and the
sound of something metallic being kicked by my slipper. Had
I been wearing it when I went to Marjorie's room in response
to the sounds I'd heard? Absolutely not. I never wore jewelry
to bed, particularly that piece of jewelry. I don't think a night
had passed since Frank bought it for me that I didn't carefully remove it at the end of an evening and place it in a
small, velvet-lined box that I reserved specifically for it. That
meant . . .

"Do you usually wear jewelry like this to bed, Mrs.
Fletcher?" Coots asked.

"I never wear jewelry to bed, Inspector, particularly that
piece."

"Then I assume you are acknowledging the fact that when you went to Miss Ainsworth's room in your nightclothes, you were not wearing it."

"Of course."

"Which means that it must have fallen to the floor by her bed prior to *that* visit to the room by you."

Everyone in the study stared at me. I knew precisely what Coots was getting at: if the pendant had been dropped in Marjorie's bedroom prior to my discovery of the body, it could have been dropped by the person who killed her. Possibly me.

Coots was still looking at me over his shoulder, the same defiant, cocky smile on his face. I said flatly, "I assure you I did not visit Miss Ainsworth's bedroom anytime prior to my having discovered the body."

Coots lowered the notebook, opened to a blank page, took the stub of a pencil from his pocket, licked the lead, and made notes, glancing at me a few times for effect. I sat down again and decided I would say nothing more.

Coots set up a system of interviews with each person in the house, using the dining room for this purpose. Simultaneously, an ambulance arrived from the district infirmary, along with an elderly gentleman who was introduced as the district coroner. Two medical aides removed Marjorie's body under his supervision—after Coots had made certain that his officers had taken photographs of the bedroom and made notes of its physical condition. I happened to be nearby when this conversation was going on, and asked Coots if he intended to take fingerprints and to check the exterior of the house for signs of a break-in. He wasn't subtle in letting me know his displeasure at my interference, although later, at dawn, he went outside and personally inspected the exterior of Ainsworth Manor.

By the time the sun was up, casting merciful light on what had been a gloomy night, a succession of people arrived at the house. One was a young woman who was the editor of the Crumpsworth *Gazette*, as well as a stringer for the London *Times*. She questioned everyone she could corner, including Mrs. Horton and the kitchen staff, Marshall, a few of the guests who agreed to be interviewed, and, finally, Inspector Montgomery Coots, who needed no urging from her.

Eventually, after all of us had been interviewed by the inspector—my interview took only five minutes, which was considerably shorter than all the others; any significance eluded me—we were allowed to leave with the provision that we stay in Great Britain until further notice. This brought forth a protest from Clayton Perry and Bruce Herbert, both of whom said they were due back in New York immediately following the opening session of the ISMW, which I was to address as the keynote speaker. Their pleas fell on deaf Coots ears, although he promised to attempt to expedite his investigation of them to accommodate their plans.

He said to me, "You'll be here all week, I understand."

"Yes, I'm to attend the entire conference at the Savoy. Surely I'll be free to return home after that."

"We'll see, we'll see," he said, bouncing on his toes.

"About the pendant, Inspector. It means a great deal to me, has considerable sentimental value. When will it be returned?"

"Hard to say, hard to say. I'd say it's vital evidence, wouldn't you?"

"I don't see why, although I won't argue with you. By the way, Inspector Coots, will there be an . . . investigation by a body . . . well, how can I say it, a body of greater authority than your agency here in Crumpsworth?"

"No need for that. Scotland Yard, you mean? A waste of time, if you ask me. The yardies won't bother coming in on this one, I can assure you. They know my reputation. No, it will remain a local matter right here in Crumpsworth where it belongs."

His little speech caused my heart to sink. Surely, I reasoned, the brutal murder of the world's leading mystery writer could not be left to a local inspector in a town the size of Crumpsworth. At least, I fervently hoped that it wouldn't.

Wilfred, Marjorie's chauffeur, drove what could be called the American contingent back to London. I shared the Morgan with the Perrys and Bruce Herbert. We said little during the hour's drive. Now that phase one of the investigation was over, the profound sadness of the event had settled in, and I found myself crying for the first time since discovering the body. Perry, who sat next to me, put his arm over my shoulder and said, "Yes, Jessica, it is a dreadful blow to all of us. It must be even more horrible for you since you shared the same talent as that wonderful woman. You do realize, of course, what ramifications this will have for you as a writer."

I pulled a handkerchief from my purse and dabbed at my eyes. "No, I'm afraid I don't have any idea what you mean."

"Well, it seems to me that Jessica Fletcher must now accept the torch."

"The torch?"

"Yes, professionally speaking, of course. I would say that Jessica Fletcher, by virtue of Marjorie Ainsworth's death, is now the world's leading writer of the murder mystery."

"Oh, I think that's overstating it," I said. "No one could ever . . ."

"Clayton is right," Bruce Herbert said. "Think about it, Jessica. You not only sell millions of copies of your books worldwide, it was you who discovered the body of your dear friend and colleague. You might need some good advice on how to handle the media attention."

He pulled a business card from his breast pocket and handed it to me. I took it, the insensitivity of the act beyond my comprehension, so much so that I could say nothing critical of it. My only words were "Thank you. I can't believe this has happened."

/ / /

If I had trouble believing the events at Ainsworth Manor, the next day's edition of the London *Times*, as well as a barrage of news items over the BBC, made a believer of me. Not only was the murder front-page news—as expected—Inspector Coots was quoted at length:

> Obviously, Jessica Fletcher, the American writer who discovered the body, must be considered a prime suspect. A gold pendant that had been given to her by her late husband—bought in London, I might add—was found under the bed of the deceased. Since Mrs. Fletcher discovered the body in her nightclothes, she obviously wasn't wearing any gold pendant or any other jewelry. It doesn't take a genius to wonder why that pendant ended up in that bedroom. The fact that Mrs. Fletcher will now replace Marjorie Ainsworth as the top mystery writer in the world leads to some interesting speculation, I'd say. Yes indeed, I'd certainly say that as a veteran investigator of crimes large and small.

The lovely, old, and gentle Savoy Hotel now became a buzz saw of activity. The press waited outside for me to show my face, and my phone kept ringing. I stopped answering it and had all calls impounded by the hotel operators, calling down hourly to have them relayed to me.

I sat in my suite for the rest of the day, exhausted but unable to entertain even the thought of sleep, my throat dry, tears flowing and ebbing, leaving a salty taste on my lips.

After hours of this nightmarish existence, I was informed of a call that had been made to me that I immediately returned. Amazing, today's satellite systems; my call to Cabot Cove, Maine, went through in seconds, and I was hearing a familiar and welcome voice, my good friend, Dr. Seth Hazlitt. "Seth, it's Jessica."

"Jessica, how are you? We've heard. We've *all* heard. It's the lead item on every television newscast, and on every front page in the country, I suspect. Are you all right, Jessica? It must have been dreadful, what you've gone through."

"Yes, Seth, it's been a very difficult time. There are dozens of strangers wanting to talk to me. I hear strange voices and see strange faces on the television. There are words being written about me that I hate, that bear no relationship to reality at all. It's so wonderful to . . . to touch base with something I know, something real." I broke down completely, the sounds of my anguish transmitted thousands of miles from the Savoy Hotel in London to a small, modest home in the small, modest town of Cabot Cove, Maine.

"The press has been all over town, Jessica, dubbin' around lookin' for dirt."

"They're all over the hotel here, too, Seth. I hate it. I'd give anything to be in Cabot Cove."

"Why don't you come on home then?"

"I can't. I have to make my speech, and there are other things I'm involved with at the conference."

I could almost see him shaking his head at me. He said, "Ginny made up a big batch o' Bakewell Cream biscuits today, Jessica, and delivered me some. I wish you were here to share them."

I smiled. "Save me some, Seth. I'll be home the end of the week."

"I wish you'd make it sooner, though I know you well enough, Jessica, to know your stubborn side'll dictate things. Most important, you take care of yourself, and you call if you need anything, anything at all, you heah me?"

"Yes, I hear you loud and clear, Seth. Thank you. I'll call again. I promise."

"Be sure and do that, Jessica. By the way, before we get off, any ideas on who killed Ms. Ainsworth?"

"No. The prime suspect seems to be me, but that will change. Frankly, Seth, I haven't given it much thought."

"But you will, won't you?"

"I'm trying not to."

"Whatever you do, do it carefully. 'Bye, Jessica. Everybody's askin' for you here."

I didn't want the call to end, but it did. I returned a few calls to friends from ISMW and tried to concentrate on the notes I'd been making for my speech. It was a losing battle, and I allowed fatigue—emotional and physical—to win out. I fell asleep in my chair, the taste of Bakewell Cream biscuits very real in my mouth.

Chapter
6

I managed a few hours of sleep after talking to Seth, then called down to get the latest batch of messages.

There were dozens, virtually all from the media, and two placed by a woman named Maria Giacona. The operator said that she had not stated her business, only that it was urgent she speak with me.

I asked the operator to connect me with the assistant manager, a pleasant young man who'd been gracious from the moment I arrived. When he came on the line, I asked whether it would be possible for me to have dinner downstairs without confronting members of the press.

"Of course, Mrs. Fletcher. There's still an assortment of them about, but we're keeping them in a designated area. Just let me know what time you wish to dine and I'll come to personally escort you."

"Thank you, that's very kind."

"Are you sure you wouldn't rather dine in your room?"

"No, I'm beginning to develop a case of cabin fever."

"Pardon?"

I laughed, and it felt good. "An American term meaning

I've been in one confined space too long. No, I think I would enjoy dining in the restaurant."

"Then, that's what it shall be. Do you prefer the Grill or the River Room?"

As much as I loved the River Room, this was not the night to step back into a world of memories, as pleasant as they might be. I opted for the Grill, and he made a reservation for me an hour from then.

I picked up the phone and returned Lucas Darling's calls. He answered on the first ring. "Jessica, Jessica, good Lord, Jessica, what a dreadful thing you've been put through. Bad enough someone murdered Marjorie, but to be the one who discovered the body. You must be shaken to your very core."

"I was, Lucas, but I'm feeling better now. You had suggested in the taxi that we sit down and have a long, leisurely dinner and discuss *Gin and Daggers*. I'd like that very much." Before he could say anything else, I added, "I've made a reservation downstairs in the Grill. Will you join me?"

"Of course."

"Fine. The assistant manager is bringing me downstairs in case there's a reporter lurking in an alcove. I'll tell him I'm being joined by someone and you can meet me in the restaurant."

"Count on my being there, Jessica, and don't you worry. This will all subside."

"I certainly hope so."

"Jessica."

"What?"

"This business about your gold pendant. Are they actually accusing you of . . . ?"

"We can discuss that at dinner, Lucas." I quickly hung up.

I was given a prime corner table, for which I was grateful. Members of the press were not the only ones I had to avoid; my picture had been large enough in the papers for three-quarters of London to recognize me. I hoped that wouldn't happen, and shifted in my chair so that I offered my profile to people at adjacent tables. There were only a handful; it was early for the main dinner crowd.

Lucas arrived a few minutes after I'd been served a glass of white wine. He wore a dark gray suit and black bow tie. "I got here as fast as I could, Jessica. The things people are saying are despicable."

"You look as though you're in mourning, Lucas," I said.

He crossed his hands on his chest and adopted a horrified expression. "Hardly," he said, "and I would suggest you not make light of it, either. The murder of Marjorie Ainsworth, and you being the one who found the body, is the biggest news here since the Profumo scandal."

I laughed away his comparison, even though I knew he was probably right.

We ordered smoked salmon as an appetizer. After it was served, and Lucas had had his Pimm's Cup, he asked me to fill him in on what had happened at Ainsworth Manor. I accommodated him in exquisite and probably unnecessary detail. He hung on every word, his face a succession of over-blown expressions. Finally I sat back and asked him what he thought.

"I would say, Jessica, that we have to look for a motive."

"Lucas, I'm not asking your thoughts on solving the murder of Marjorie Ainsworth. That's for the authorities. I'm asking what your advice would be concerning me. Should I stay and deliver the speech?" I realized how academic that question was. I was prohibited from leaving Great Britain by Inspector Coots. Still, there was the possibility of canceling any public appearances and hiding until my name had been struck from the suspect list. No, I knew myself too well. I could never bear that sort of existence.

"Of course you'll give your speech. The press coverage will be incredible."

"That's what I'm afraid of, Lucas."

"Don't be. The society can use the exposure."

My expression of shock was genuine. "Lucas, how can you say something like that at a time like this? Marjorie Ainsworth has been murdered, in cold blood."

He slumped back in his chair and pinched his nose. "I know, I know, so dreadful, but I am a realist." He sat forward again, elbows on the table and said earnestly, "Jessica, do you remember my book *Poison Alley*?"

"Yes, of course. You gave me an autographed copy." He'd written his one and only murder mystery over ten years ago. It wasn't very good, and once the critics were finished panning it, it took all the starch out of him. He'd never written another word, contenting himself to rub elbows with mystery writers through ISMW.

"The key clue in *Poison Alley* came out of the deceased's will, remember?"

"Yes."

"That's where I'd start if I were investigating this case. Marjorie must have had a will. Maybe she cut somebody out of it."

I almost welcomed the diversion of the attractive young woman standing just inside the entrance to the Grill. I'd heard Lucas go off on tangents like this, and I found them trying. He saw me staring across the room—which was now filling up—and turned in the direction of my gaze. He snapped his head back at me and said, "Who's she?"

"I don't know, but she certainly knows who I am."

He again looked in the direction of the young woman. Then, to me: "She's carrying a large handbag. I don't like this."

I took my eyes off her and asked him what he meant.

"Do you realize that half of London probably thinks you murdered Marjorie Ainsworth? It's like murdering the Queen Mother, for God's sake. Someone might want revenge."

I again looked at the young woman, who was slowly heading in our direction. "Oh no," I muttered under my breath, my eyes on the large, cheaply embroidered purse she held against her stomach. Maybe Lucas was right. I braced myself. When she reached the table, I had a chance to get a better look at her. She was absolutely beautiful, olive skin framed by long, thick black hair that fell casually to her shoulders. Her features were Middle Eastern, Lebanese perhaps, or possibly Spanish or Italian. No matter; her face was out of a beauty magazine. She wore a mauve dress that reached her ankles. It was cut moderately low and, whatever fabric it was made of, followed every contour of her lithe young body with military precision.

I smiled at her.

"Mrs. Fletcher?"

"Yes." I looked across the table. Lucas was poised to attack. "May I help you?"

"I hope so. No, I'm sure you can. That's why I've been trying to call you. My name is Maria Giacona." So much for guessing at her national origin. Her father, if the name meant anything, was Italian.

"I'm afraid this is not a good time, Ms. Giacona. I'm having an important coversation with my colleague."

"Yes, I see that, and I apologize for interrupting. I don't wish to be a problem, but it is imperative that I have a chance to speak with you, if only for a few moments." There was only a trace of accent to her words. She'd obviously lived in an English-speaking country a long time.

Lucas said to her, "Can't you see Mrs. Fletcher is busy?"

She bit her trembling lower lip and turned her head away from us. I half stood and put my hand on her bare arm. "Please, Ms. Giacona, I'll be happy to talk with you, but could I suggest we make an appointment, perhaps later this evening or tomorrow? I promise I'll honor whatever arrangements we make."

She slowly turned her head and looked at me with large

brown eyes that seemed filled with pain. "Do you mean that?" she asked.

"Of course I mean that. I always keep my word. Would you like to have breakfast tomorrow morning?"

"Breakfast? Well, I . . ."

"Please, I'll be happy to have breakfast with you. But would you mind telling me very quickly what it is we'll be discussing?"

Her purse started to slip between her hands and stomach, sending Lucas to his feet. She grabbed the purse before it fell to the floor, looked at Lucas until he slowly sat down with an embarrassed expression on his face, then said to me, "Mrs. Fletcher, I want to speak with you about Jason Harris and Marjorie Ainsworth."

Although I assumed there was something she wanted to discuss about the Ainsworth murder, I didn't expect Jason Harris to be part of it. I was almost overwhelmed with a temptation to excuse myself from the table and to find a quiet spot in the lobby where I could hear more from her. Instead, I repeated my invitation to meet for breakfast.

"Would you mind if we met somewhere else?" she asked.

"No, I suppose not. What do you suggest?"

"Do you know Speakers' Corner in Hyde Park, near Marble Arch?"

"Yes, I do. I've spent some pleasant Sunday mornings there."

"Could we meet there, say, at ten? I will be near the speakers from South Africa. They always draw the biggest crowds."

"All right, I'll be there."

She thanked me, nodded at Lucas, and crossed the room with a sensuous sway out of a commercial for a Caribbean paradise.

"What do you think?" Lucas asked me, his eyes wide.

"I don't know what to think."

"Jason Harris."

"Do you know him, Lucas? I mean, before I mentioned his having been at the house, and his relationship to Marjorie?"

"I don't know him, Jessica, but I certainly have heard of him. There was a lot of consternation when Marjorie started playing mentor to him. I did a little checking, He's what I suppose could be termed a 'failed poet,' a bright but misdirected talent."

"He said so little at the party. Has he had anything published?"

"Not that I know of, unless he's been in some of those small literary quarterlies."

"How does he live?"

"Probably by getting into the good graces of people like Marjorie Ainsworth. You know the type. Users, low-lifes who pretend to be artists, and who prey on the need of true artists to share something of their talent with the less fortunate."

I suspected he was basically right in his evaluation, although I also recognized it was presumptuous of me. Obviously, Marjorie saw something worthwhile in Jason Harris and was willing to share her knowledge with him. Was Maria Giacona his lover? Funny, but I'd immediately assumed she was.

My mind raced as we perused the menu in search of a palatable main course. I wasn't hungry, but I knew Lucas was. He had a voracious appetite.

What would Maria Giacona tell me in the morning—that she had information incriminating Jason Harris in Marjorie Ainsworth's murder? Or would she present some defense of him in anticipation of his being charged with the killing? What a silly game, I told myself as I returned my attention to the menu. Those questions would be answered tomorrow, and there was little sense losing a night's sleep by speculating.

I ordered creamed Finnan haddie garnished with a poached egg. Lucas went for London beef that was sliced tableside. A platter of boiled vegetables accompanied both entrées, prompting him to say, "We British can do anything with boiled vegetables except digest them."

I sensed that a few people recognized me as Lucas and I left the restaurant, but no one said anything—hooray for British reserve. Lucas walked me to the elevator.

"You shouldn't stay alone tonight, Jessica."

"Don't be silly, I'll be fine. I'm over the initial shock. I want to concentrate on my speech, and on being helpful to anyone seeking to solve Marjorie's murder."

"You don't understand, Jessica. A national treasure has been murdered, and the way the press has painted it—including that idiot Coots from Crumpsworth—you're being pointed to as the prime suspect. I'll stay with you. There's a couch and two rooms. I promise I won't . . ."

I laughed with genuine affection for him, took his hands in mine, and said, "Lucas, you are a sweet man and I sincerely appreciate your concern for me. But, believe me, I don't need anyone. I'll see that the door is securely locked. The way I feel now, I'll sleep through anything, including an all-out assault by the Household Guards."

He reluctantly accepted my rejection of his offer, kissed me on the cheek, and said he was only a phone call away.

"I take comfort in that, Lucas. Thank you for joining me for dinner. Oh, by the way, we never did get into a discussion of *Gin and Daggers*."

"Yes, there were too many other things. We'll catch up with that tomorrow. Your plans?"

"I don't have any aside from meeting Ms. Giacona, but I suspect they'll develop. There are people who've called me today whom I really should see, old friends, even a relative or two. Let me play it by ear. I'll call you when I'm back from Hyde Park."

"I'll go with you."

"No, you won't. It might hinder the conversation."

"I'll stay a discreet distance away, behind shrubs, or in disguise."

I was adamant in dissuading him, and rode the elevator confident that I had. I locked the door to my suite and closed the drapes, turned on the TV, and caught the tail end of an interview with Inspector Montgomery Coots at his Crumpsworth office. What I heard and saw was enough:

". . . I'll be spending considerable time in London investigating Miss Ainsworth's murder. I've developed a series of solid leads, and the people of Great Britain can rest assured that whoever did this dastardly thing shall pay for it, and soon. I stake my reputation on it."

I didn't go to bed right away. Instead, I sat up and made a list of everyone who'd been at Ainsworth Manor, and assigned to each of them a motive. When I was finished, and was about to call it a night, I called the hotel operator for any recent messages. Along with more press calls, there was another call from Cabot Cove, this one from Sheriff Morton Metzger. I was tired, but called him back at his office, where it was late afternoon.

"Jessica, this is Morton."

"I know that, Morton. You called."

"Yes I did, Jessica. Seth told me he'd talked to you."

"That's right."

"Just remember one thing, Jessica. I'm always available in case you need me."

"That's good of you, Morton, but I don't see what you could—"

"That fella Ted Koppel from television is going to do a whole program about this, Jessica."

"He is?" One of the calls had been from a producer at ABC-TV in New York.

"Not only that, a paper from New York, the New York

Post, has you on its front page. A real rag, if you ask me, but the people who wrote the story almost say flat out that you were the killer. Now, I know that—"

"Morton, nothing can be done about such reporting. I didn't kill anyone, especially my friend Marjorie Ainsworth. I'm exhausted, and am about to go to bed. I really appreciate your concern, but—"

"Just remember what I said, Jessica, about bein' ready to help. I got a book out o' the library today about the British justice system. If you need me over there, I'll be prepared. I got vacation coming and—"

"Thank you, Morton. Good night. Please give my best to everyone."

I gently replaced the phone in its cradle. They were all such good people back in Cabot Cove, true friends I could count on. But as I got under the covers and turned out the light, I knew that whatever was to happen over the ensuing days would be very much my problem, and mine alone. That was not a particularly comforting thought with which to go to sleep, but it was the best I could do.

Chapter
7

 I woke early, threw back the drapes, and allowed a brilliant burst of sunshine to enter the suite, hoping it was symbolic of what the day would be like.

The early morning news on BBC Radio brought me back to reality. Funeral plans had been announced for Marjorie Ainsworth. The service would be held on Tuesday in a small church in Crumpsworth, at Marjorie's request. The announcement was made by Jane Portelaine. I was to give my keynote address to ISMW the night of the funeral.

I took a long, leisurely shower, enjoyed the toast and coffee I'd ordered through room service, and dressed in a camel's-hair skirt, white button-down blouse, heather sweater, and brown tweed sport jacket and made sure I wore sensible walking shoes.

I was about to leave the room when I remembered that the press was laying siege. I called my assistant manager friend, and was assured that he could spirit me from the hotel through a rear entrance that few people, including veteran members of the London press, knew about. Ten minutes later he had me two blocks away and was helping me into a taxi.

I was pleased that Maria Giacona had suggested Hyde Park

instead of breakfast in the hotel. I'd wanted to spend Sunday morning at Speakers' Corner anyway, and this would allow me to indulge that plan, while also hearing what Ms. Giacona had to say. Frank and I had spent two Sunday mornings at Speakers' Corner and had not only found the experience fascinating, but were both struck with the real meaning of free speech it represented.

My driver let me off at Marble Arch, which was built originally as the main gateway to Buckingham Palace but, because it wasn't broad enough for royal coaches to pass through, was moved in 1851 to its current site. I stood for a few minutes after he drove away, and took in the broader scene in front of me. Again, as would happen countless times during this post-Frank trip to London, I was bombarded with memories that, while pleasant, carried with them a parallel sadness because they could never be repeated.

It wasn't difficult to find the South African rally that Maria had mentioned. It dominated the corner and, as opposed to most of the other speakers who had to shout over competing noise, featured a fiery young black man with a microphone and amplification system.

I stood at the rear of the crowd and looked for Maria. I didn't see her. As I started to wonder whether I was the victim of a time-consuming practical joke, a voice behind me said, "Mrs. Fletcher."

I turned and looked into Maria's dark eyes. No wonder I hadn't seen her; she was dressed very differently from last night. This morning she wore jeans and an army surplus camouflage jacket over a black turtleneck, and her hair was pulled into a French braid. No makeup.

"I was beginning to wonder whether you'd be here," I said.

"I've been here for a while. I was watching you."

"You were? Why didn't you just come over to me?"

"I don't know. Maybe it's because I wanted to gain a better

sense of the person I was going to confide in this morning. I certainly know you by reputation, and I've read some of your books, but dealing on a personal level is another matter. Wouldn't you agree?"

"Yes, I would."

She suggested we walk to the Serpentine. As we walked, and talked, I was increasingly impressed with her. I liked her, which would make things easier, no matter how startling or unpleasant her message.

We chose a bench in the shade of a huge sycamore tree. She sat hunched over, and peered with intensity out over the lake. Whatever it was she was about to tell me meant a great deal to her. She was taut, coiled, and evidently going through an internal debate either about whether to tell me anything at all, or about how to word it.

I tried to help her. "Ms. Giacona, you wanted to talk to me about Marjorie Ainsworth's murder, as well as Jason Harris."

She slowly turned her head and narrowed her eyes. "Mrs. Fletcher, I must first say that I do not wish to offend you or your friend, Marjorie Ainsworth. I know you were close to her, and that her death must be a shock to you, especially the circumstances of it."

"Very true."

"I do not share that closeness with her, but I do share such a closeness with another person who is being hurt by this."

"Jason Harris?"

"Yes."

"I can imagine. From what I understand, Marjorie had taken him in as a pupil of sorts. He certainly couldn't have had a better teacher, and losing such a mentor must be difficult."

Now her soft brown eyes were tempered with a discernible anger. It was almost frightening, so abrupt was the change. She said in measured tones, "It is not losing Marjorie Ainsworth as a teacher that is upsetting to Jason, Mrs. Fletcher. It is losing credit for his wonderful work that is so painful to him, and to me."

I processed what she had said, then asked, "What is your relationship to Jason Harris?"

"We are lovers."

"I see." I asked what she meant by his having lost credit for work he'd done.

"I suppose there is no sense in trying to say this gently, Mrs. Fletcher. The fact is that Jason wrote *Gin and Daggers*."

If she intended to bring about a physical reaction from me with her bluntness, she'd succeeded. My heart tripped, and I looked away from her.

"Mrs. Fletcher."

"Yes?"

"What I say is the truth."

"I'm not debating whether you're being truthful for now, although I don't know what the truth actually is. A much larger question at the moment, Ms. Giacona, is why are you telling me? Do you expect me to do something?"

The softness in her eyes and face returned. Was it deliberate, a good actress changing emotions on cue? I couldn't tell. All I knew was that her face was an expressive instrument, and I was responding to its shifts in mood.

"I want you to speak on Jason's behalf."

"To whom?"

"To the world."

"The *world*?"

"Those in publishing, critics, the press."

"Ms. Giacona, I could never do that."

She sighed and looked at the ground.

"Let's say what you've told me is true and, I repeat, I don't know what the truth is. But, let's say I did know for certain that Jason wrote *Gin and Daggers*. Marjorie Ainsworth was a dear friend. I would never do anything to sully her reputation."

"What about Jason's reputation, Mrs. Fletcher? Is it fair that his talent goes unrecognized, unrewarded?"

"I suppose not, but . . . was he paid to write the book?"

"A pittance."

"Does he share in its success, monetarily, I mean?"

"No."

"He was a writer for hire, then."

She looked at me quizzically.

"It's a term used in publishing. It means that he performed work, was paid for it, and has no further claim on that work."

"In terms of money, yes. In terms of fairness, no. He's not looking for more money, Mrs. Fletcher. I know he wouldn't take money if it were offered, and he would be very angry if he even knew I was speaking to you about this. Jason is . . . he's very shy and unsure of his talent. He would be content to have the world never know that he's written this wonderful book that the critics have acclaimed. I am different. I love Jason very much and am determined that the world know what a fine writer he is."

"That's admirable, Ms. Giacona. Tell me, was there a written agreement between Jason and Marjorie?"

She shook her head. "I told him he should demand such an agreement, but he didn't want to upset her."

"I don't think she would have been upset. She was a very fair person."

It was more a snort from her than a laugh. "It is good to feel that way about a dead friend. Others do not feel that way about Marjorie Ainsworth."

I debated asking how much of *Gin and Daggers* Jason had actually written, how Jane Portelaine fit into the picture, whether Marjorie's publishers and agents knew of the arrangement. I decided to, but didn't have the chance. Maria stood and looked down at me with angry eyes. "I have always heard about Jessica Fletcher being a good person, as well as a talented writer. I know you are a good writer, but as for the other attribute, I—"

I stood, too, and said, "Ms. Giacona, I think you have now gone a little too far. You expect me to stand up and proclaim that Jason Harris wrote *Gin and Daggers* when, in fact, I have no idea whether he did or not."

"If I prove it to you?"

"Proof? You said there was no written agreement."

"There is another way. Jason saw to that."

"I thought he didn't care."

"He doesn't. What he did was not deliberate but can be used now that she's dead."

I took it that she was glad Marjorie Ainsworth had died. I asked her to explain further.

"Jason used many things from his own life in *Gin and Daggers*, such as names of old friends and deceased family members. He gave some characters traits that come directly from himself. No one except Jason would have known those things, certainly not Marjorie Ainsworth."

"That's very interesting. I've read *Gin and Daggers*. Could you point out those things to me?"

"Not at this moment."

"Why not?"

"Because I do not know what they are."

"Ms. Giacona—"

"Please, allow me to finish. I know Jason included those things, because he told me he did, but he never told me exactly what they were."

"Then *Jason* would have to tell me."

"He would never do that. He made notes about them on the original manuscript."

"Have you seen the manuscript?"

"No, but I now know where it is. I would never have come to you unless I could show the manuscript to you."

"With Jason's permission, I assume."

"Without it. He wouldn't approve."

"That wouldn't be right."

"Is it more *right* that he goes unrecognized while someone else takes credit for his work?"

I turned and looked over the lake. A distinguished British couple pushing a baby carriage strolled past us, followed by two punk rockers, the girl's hair a shocking pink, the boy's hair orange, the two of them wearing matching black leather jackets with spikes.

"All right," I said. "When will you show me the manuscript?"

"Tonight? I know that Jason will be out. You could come to his flat."

"What time?"

"Eight. He'll be leaving at seven." She gave me an address on Pindar Street, near Liverpool Street Station. "It's on the third floor," she added. "I'm afraid there's no lift."

"The exercise will do me good, Ms. Giacona. I suppose that's all we need to talk about this morning."

"Except to say that I am sorry for having been . . . how shall I say it . . . for having been harsh in my words."

"No apologies necessary. This has been a stressful time for everyone. Shall we share a cab?"

"No, I am to meet someone and I'm already late. Thank you, Mrs. Fletcher."

She walked quickly along the edge of the lake and disappeared around a small building. I lingered at Speakers' Corner for a half hour before hailing a taxi and returning to the Savoy, where I took the list I'd made the night before and wrote next to Jason Harris's name:

Obviously will derive tremendous benefit from Marjorie's death. Now free to take credit for *Gin and Daggers*, with Marjorie not here to defend herself.

Chapter
8

I called downstairs to the hotel operator and was given six messages that had been left that morning.

A few were from media; the others were from Sir James Ferguson, the theatrical producer; Clayton Perry, Marjorie's American publisher; Count Antonio Zara, Marjorie's brother-in-law; and George Sutherland, who, the operator said, was a chief inspector from Scotland Yard.

I returned the call to Sutherland first and was put through immediately.

"Mrs. Fletcher, it's good of you to return my call on Sunday."

"Well, sir, you called me on Sunday. Besides, I would never hesitate to return a call to a chief inspector from Scotland Yard."

"Good of you to say so, Mrs. Fletcher. It won't come as any surprise that I'm calling about the unfortunate demise of Marjorie Ainsworth."

"No, of course not. How may I help you?"

"I'm not quite sure, but I would appreciate the opportunity to explore some possibilities with you." His voice was deep and resonant. I assumed he would be English, but a Scottish burr made the point that his roots were farther north.

"Anything you say," I said.

"Would you have some free time this afternoon?"

"I'll see to it."

"It would be my pleasure to treat the eminent Jessica Fletcher to tea, if you wouldn't think it too personal."

I wasn't sure whether it was too personal or not, but it really didn't matter. I accepted his offer, and we agreed to meet at Brown's Hotel, between Dover and Albemarle streets, in Mayfair. I'd had tea at Brown's during one of my previous trips to London and remembered how delightful it had been.

I next returned Clayton Perry's call, which was answered by his wife, Renée. She didn't sound especially pleased to be hearing from me but, I reasoned, she probably wasn't pleased to be hearing from anyone at that moment. Her husband came on the line and said pleasantly, "How are you holding up, Mrs. Fletcher?"

"As they say, as well as can be expected. You?"

"Aside from not liking the feeling of being captive, I suppose things could be worse. The reason I was calling was to invite you to dinner with us this evening."

I'd almost forgotten about my eight o'clock meeting with Maria Giacona at Jason Harris's flat. "That's very kind of you, Clayton, but I'm afraid I have other plans."

"I'm sorry to hear that. I think it might make a great deal of sense for us to get together to talk about this terrible incident on two levels." He paused, and then added, "Not only should we put our minds together where the murder of Marjorie Ainsworth is concerned, but I think you and I might find it mutually profitable to talk business."

"I hardly think Marjorie's death should trigger a burst of free enterprise." I knew it sounded harsh, but it represented what I felt.

He seemed taken aback at my words, but only for an instant. He changed the subject and, after five minutes of general banter in which I finally agreed to find some time during the coming week to spend with him, we ended the conversation.

I reached Sir James Ferguson at his home, which, he told me, was in the elegant Belgravia section of London. He sounded nervous, although it might have been nothing more than a hesitant speech pattern. He had trouble getting to the point of his call. Finally, when he did, he said, "I was wondering if you would consider being my dinner companion at a party I am to attend this evening."

Unlike the offer of tea from Chief Inspector Sutherland, there was no doubt that Ferguson's invitation was purely personal. I was flattered by it, and there was a certain appeal in it, but I told him I couldn't because of previous plans. Ferguson sounded profoundly disappointed, and I quickly soothed him by saying that I would enjoy seeing him another time while in London. He seemed buoyed by my words, thanked me profusely for returning his call, and we ended the conversation by saying how we mutually looked forward to seeing each other at the opening session of the International Society of Mystery Writers.

My return call to Count Antonio Zara resulted in a succession of unanswered rings, at which I was not disappointed: grateful is more like it.

Ten minutes later, I heard what sounded like a scuffle outside my door. I looked through the peephole. There was considerable movement, which made it difficult to identify who was involved. Then I saw Lucas Darling's face; it suddenly blurred into only one of his eyes as he pressed it against the door. "Lucas?" I said in a loud voice.

"Don't open the door, Jessica, they've followed me."

"Who followed you?"

"The vultures from the press, damn them. They're parasites, bloodsucking leeches."

A female voice shouted, "Please, Mrs. Fletcher, just give us five minutes with you to ask some questions." Other voices, some male, some female, joined in the request.

I went to the phone and called the assistant manager's office. He wasn't there, but I told a young woman that I needed security at my room immediately. Within minutes guards appeared and escorted the intruders away, including Lucas. "Jessica!" he yelled. I quickly opened the door and shouted, "*He* can stay," pointing at Lucas. The press threatened to break away from the guards, but Lucas was quicker. He sprinted to my door, and as two reporters made a dash in my direction, I slammed the door and secured the lock.

"Bastards," he said.

"It was inevitable that they would get up here, Lucas," I said. "I was just thinking before you arrived that I really should hold a press conference and get rid of them once and for all."

His look was sheer horror. "Don't you dare, Jessica. They'll tear you apart, quote you out of context. You'll end up portrayed as a vicious, greedy, and insane murderess."

I laughed and sat in a chair. "No, Lucas, I'm not afraid of that." What I didn't say was that I wasn't about to spend the rest of my time in London sneaking out back doors wearing black wigs, garish makeup, and an Arab costume rented from a theatrical supply house.

Lucas sat in a matching chair and said, "We can discuss this later. First, tell me what happened in the park today. What did she have to say?"

I'd been debating whether or not to tell anyone about my conversation with Maria, and as I sat across from Lucas, I reached a decision—I would *not* tell anyone, at least not now.

I made up a story for him: Maria was upset at the possibility that her lover, Jason Harris, might be considered a suspect in Marjorie Ainsworth's murder, and wanted me to know that

Jason had been devoted to Marjorie, not only as a protégé, but personally as well. Lucas's screwed-up face indicated that he either didn't believe me or was scornful of the sentiment expressed by Maria about Jason Harris. "Poppycock," he said with finality.

"I haven't made a judgment about Jason Harris or anyone, Lucas; I'm just telling you what we talked about."

He narrowed his eyes and cocked his head. "Are you telling me the truth, Jessica? It seemed to me that the young woman had much weightier things to discuss than that."

I shrugged. "I'm meeting with a chief inspector from Scotland Yard this afternoon."

That took his mind off my meeting in the park. "Who is he? Why does he want to see you? Is he dealing with you as a suspect?"

"No, I don't think so. Frankly, I'm pleased that Scotland Yard is involved. I would hate to think of that dreadful little man Coots remaining in charge of the investigation. Don't you agree?"

"Yes, of course. You're going to the Yard?"

"No, as a matter of fact we're having tea at Brown's Hotel."

"That's highly unusual."

"I think it's simply courteous and nice. Besides, I would love a chance to have tea at Brown's again."

"It isn't what it used to be since Trusthouse Forte took over."

"Well, I'll certainly see, won't I? What are your plans for the afternoon?"

"I was going to spend it with you discussing the opening session and going over your speech. I assume you've decided to incorporate some comments about Marjorie's murder."

I nodded.

"It's very important that what you say reflects the true sentiments of the society as a whole."

I looked at him quizzically.

"Don't misunderstand, Jessica, but this entire matter is very sensitive."

"Everyone seems to have sensitivities that must be reckoned with while, of course, poor Marjorie's sensitivities are no longer an issue. All right, Lucas, I'll be happy to go over my speech with you and to discuss the opening session, as long as we leave time for me to meet the inspector for tea."

"Would you like me to come with you when you meet him?"

"No."

"Jessica, I know you have a reputation for going things alone, but it isn't the smartest approach considering the circumstances."

"Lucas, I will keep that firmly in mind. Now let me get my speech from my briefcase and we can spend a pleasant hour going over it."

I've never been one to define handsomeness in men and beauty in women, believing that those things emanate from inside. But, by any standards, Chief Inspector George Sutherland was a handsome man. I judged him to be six feet four inches tall, and pegged his age at fifty, although my second estimate boosted it to fifty-five. He had brown hair with a tinge of red in it, and with a healthy crop of gray at the temples that added distinction. His face was large and lined, but his features were fine. There was an unmistakable kindness in his eyes, which were the color of Granny Smith apples. He wore a dark brown tweed jacket with leather patches at the elbows, a pale yellow V-neck sweater, white shirt, brown tie, and beautifully creased tan pants. Dark brown boots that came up above his ankles looked expensive.

I sat across a small table from him, sighed, and looked around the beautiful room. "It's just as I remembered it," I said. "A friend of mine told me he'd assumed everything had changed since it had been taken over by Trusthouse Forte. I don't see any changes." I looked at him. "Do you?"

"No, I can't say that I do. I've had an affinity for Brown's since moving here from Edinburgh, and it seems to have stayed a steady course since I first set foot in here fifteen years ago."

"That's comforting."

"That's England."

We ordered full tea service and, after some preliminary chitchat, he said, "Well, Mrs. Fletcher, I would be delighted to hear from you about what happened at Ainsworth Manor."

My first reaction was that this was the beginning of an interrogation. I was a suspect. But the easy way he said it, and his seemingly sincere interest in what my perceptions were, put me at ease. I quietly, and as concisely as possible, told him the events as I'd witnessed them that fateful night. He was a good listener.

When I was finished, and we'd selected crustless finger sandwiches from a silver tray, he said, "Mrs. Fletcher, I am well aware of your reputation in the literary field. I have also heard from sources I can't quite remember that you don't confine your solving of mysteries to the printed page."

I laughed. I blushed, too.

"Now that the Yard is involved with the murder of Marjorie Ainsworth, and I have been put in charge of the investigation, I'm eager to get to the first step."

"Which is?" I asked, biting into a cucumber sandwich.

"Seek help."

I smiled, and it turned into a laugh. "That sounds like a very sensible first step to me."

"It's always worked for me. At least it buys me a few days to think while my 'help' gets the ball rolling."

"I have to admit I'm pleased that you and Scotland Yard are involved, Inspector Sutherland. Frankly, I was dismayed that this brutal murder of a friend and a revered writer would be left in the hands of . . ."

He took me off the hook. "Mrs. Fletcher, it's admirable that you don't wish to be harsh on Crumpsworth's Inspector Coots, but your unspoken instincts are correct. Inspector Coots . . . well, how shall I say it? . . . Inspector Coots is . . . the inspector of Crumpsworth."

I laughed. "Your discretion is admirable, too, Inspector Sutherland. I get the picture."

"Yes, well, with that out of the way, although I must say Coots is *not* out of the way—he insists upon continuing his investigation and is entitled to do that—let me ask my first helper her thoughts on the murder of Marjorie Ainsworth."

"I take it, then, that I am your helper, not a suspect."

"Despite what the papers say, you are not a suspect on *my* list, Mrs. Fletcher. But, as I told you before, I do need help. You were there and obviously have a trained eye. Tell me, what is your response to the possibility raised by Coots that the murderer might have been an intruder from outside, and not one of the weekend guests?"

I thought for a moment before saying, "Highly unlikely to me. An intruder, unless a bumbling one, would not choose a night when the house was filled with guests to break in. No, I think the killer was someone who was in the house by invitation."

"Are you ruling out household staff, then?"

"No, by 'invitation' I mean someone who was expected to be in the house, either as a guest or because they were employed."

"Care to venture a guess?"

"No."

"Surely, Mrs. Fletcher, you must have had some thoughts about people attending the party. Let's begin with the most basic question. Who would gain from Marjorie Ainsworth's death?"

I thought of Lucas Darling and his comment about Marjorie's will. "What about her will?" I asked.

"Aha, a good question. Her solicitor is to deliver it to me in the morning. That might shed some light on motive. Financial gain always heads the list."

"I'd not put it at the top, although it certainly would rank high."

"What would be above it?" he asked.

"Pride, I think, possibly followed by lust and, in third place, money."

"Interesting, Mrs. Fletcher. Let us put the will and the question of money aside for the moment. Whose pride at the party would have been enhanced by having Miss Ainsworth dead?"

Jason Harris immediately came to mind, but I decided not to bring him up. I said, "I don't know, Inspector Sutherland; perhaps someone who was in trouble and might be bailed out by Marjorie's death." He said nothing, but it was plain he was waiting for me to come up with a name. I was caught in an internal debate between wanting very much to be of help to him, yet not wanting to point fingers at anyone. I thought of Clayton Perry, Marjorie's American publisher, who was rumored to be in serious financial difficulty, but that would be a matter of money, not pride. I said, "I hope you don't think me uncooperative, Inspector Sutherland, but I think it would be terribly premature for me to speculate on people I met for the first time at Ainsworth Manor. You understand, I'm sure."

"I must. You said lust ranked second on the list of motives. Somehow I can't see where that would enter the picture."

"Because Marjorie was . . . old?"

He smiled. "I suppose so."

"You're right, unless the lust had to do with being free to pursue a lustful venture once she was out of the way."

"Interesting," he said. "Was someone there that weekend who would fall into that category?"

I shook my head. "Not that I know of. I'm not being evasive, but I don't know enough about anyone who was there to make such a judgment."

Sutherland took a notebook from his breast pocket, flipped to a page he was looking for, and held it away from him. He was farsighted; I wondered why he didn't put on glasses. Vanity? That would have disappointed me. He did not seem to be a vain man. I was pleased when he reached into his pocket, pulled out a pair of half-glasses, and brought the notebook closer to his eyes. "Tell me about Miss Ainsworth's niece, Jane Portelaine."

"I really don't know what to say about Jane. She's been devoted to her aunt for many years, and Marjorie always acknowledged that, right up until the end. She's a seemingly cold and unhappy woman, but that's a value judgment that I promised years ago not to make about people." I paused and waited for a reaction. There was none. "There was a certain tension between Jane and her aunt," I said. "I can't deny that. Are you looking at Jane as a suspect?"

"No, just curious. She seems so obvious, but that's because that type of woman, in that sort of situation, is always obvious. A red herring, I think you mystery writers call it."

"Yes, we do. Every good mystery will have a red herring or two."

He suddenly sat up in his chair and took on an animation that had not been there before. He asked, "Do you know the origin of the term 'red herring,' Mrs. Fletcher?"

"No, I don't."

He seemed pleased that he could explain it to me. "It goes back to the seventeenth century, perhaps even earlier. Animal activists who were dismayed by the senseless killing of foxes for sport would smoke herrings, which turned them red, and then drag them through the fields. The smell of the fish was so strong that it disguised the foxes' scent—making it possible for them to beat a hasty retreat while packs of confused hunting dogs sniffed around in circles. It was a simple and effective ruse.

"That's fascinating. I will now inject red herrings into my books with greater respect."

"The business of your necklace, Mrs. Fletcher, about which so much has been made in the press. You obviously dropped it when you discovered the body."

"No, I don't think I did. I would have heard it drop. The only sound I heard was when I kicked it under the bed. It obviously was there when I entered the room."

"Do you have an explanation for that?"

It was the first question that sounded like a question to a suspect. I said, "I have no idea how it happened, although I did leave my bedroom prior to going to sleep. I went to the bathroom for about ten minutes. It's possible someone came into my room during that period, took the necklace, murdered Marjorie, and, in the process, dropped it."

"Deliberately, of course."

"Of course."

"Perhaps the intruder theory isn't so farfetched. A thief enters the manor, goes to your room first, and takes your necklace, goes to the next room—I understand your bedroom was next to Miss Ainsworth's—proceeds to steal from that room, is startled by Miss Ainsworth awakening, drops your necklace in the confusion, and, in order to silence Miss Ainsworth, rams a dagger into her."

I shook my head. "No, Inspector Sutherland, I think that *is* farfetched. I believe someone placed my necklace there to cast suspicion on me."

He nodded and finished his tea. "Mrs. Fletcher, I have found this to be extremely interesting and pleasant. You are . . . well, may I say, you are an intelligent and attractive woman."

My blush was slightly deeper this time. I simply said, "Thank you."

"I was quite serious when I said I was looking for help. I know that you have been restricted to Great Britain, at least for a period of time. I would be most appreciative if you would use some of that time to confer with me, to give me the benefit of your insights. I was not at the manor when Marjorie Ainsworth was killed. You were. In effect, you could be my eyes there, which would be especially helpful considering that your eyes are obviously observant."

Was he out to flatter me, or did he mean it? It didn't matter. Either approach brought about in me the same pleasant sensation. I assured him that I would be available, if he needed me, at any time.

We stood on the pretty street in front of Brown's Hotel. He took my hand in both of his and said, "Thank you for a most pleasant afternoon, Mrs. Fletcher. You'll be hearing from me soon."

We looked at each other and waited for the other to make a move in the opposite direction. I believe he did so out of a sense of chivalry; the awkward situation demanded it. I watched him walk away, and was struck by his gait. Some people walk with confidence and purpose; others amble, which belies their basic modest nature. He certainly fell into the latter category. He looked back once; I waved, then turned and walked in the opposite direction until rounding the corner.

It wasn't until I had returned to the Savoy and had settled in an easy chair near the window that the warm feelings I'd experienced since leaving Brown's were pushed aside by a sudden recognition that I might have had tea with an extremely skilled interrogator. Had he found me as attractive as I perceived, or was it his way, was it his technique of drawing me into his confidence?

"I think I am a suspect," I said aloud as I picked up the phone to order coffee from room service. "I really think I am, and this time it isn't some Napoleonic inspector from Crumpsworth, it's a top investigator from Scotland Yard."

Chapter
9

I left the Savoy in plenty of time for my eight o'clock meeting with Maria Giacona at Jason Harris's flat.

"Number 17 Pindar Street," I told the cab driver, a ruddy-faced gentleman who smelled of too liberal a splash of after-shave lotion. "I'm told it's near Liverpool Street Station. I really don't have more information than that, I'm afraid."

He turned and laughed. "No need for more information, ma'am. I know Pindar Street. We'll be there shortly, depending upon the bloody traffic."

I sat back and smiled in the taxi's spacious rear compartment. Of course he knew where Pindar Street was; London cab drivers know their city better than any other drivers on earth.

He chatted amiably as we headed for our destination. "What an interesting area of the city," I said. "There are so many parts of London I've never seen."

"Some not especially worth seeing," he said. "We're coming into the Liverpool Street Station area now. Many changes going on, ma'am, but it's still a grotty neighborhood. Lots of young people moving in 'cause the rents are low, struggling artists and writers and the like. They all used to live on Grub Street, were called Grub Streeters. There's no Grub Street any longer." He pointed to what looked like an iron Gothic cathedral. "That's the Liverpool Street Station, ma'am, and next to it is the Great Eastern Hotel. Not much on amenities, but quite a bargain, I hear."

I was glad I was staying at the Savoy. There was something ominous about the area surrounding Liverpool Street Station, although the streets themselves—residential buildings of varying sizes and shapes dotted with small restaurants and shops—were pleasant enough.

Pindar Street was tiny and slightly curved, running between Norton and Appold, not far from Finsbury Square. We stopped in front of Number 17, four stories tall and, I judged, classical in its architecture, although it was difficult to see much because the street was dark. The only light in the building came from two windows on the top floor.

As I paid the fare, the driver said, "You ought to be careful on the streets, ma'am. There's been some nasty incidents of late."

I thought of Lucas's same admonition and decided to heed the advice of both. "I won't be here long," I said. "A brief visit with an old friend."

"Well, enjoy your stay in London."

I stood on the sidewalk and watched him drive off, wondering whether I should have asked him to stay until I was safely inside. I suddenly felt isolated and alone. The only activity on Pindar Street seemed to be a small Chinese takeout restaurant on the far corner, its yellow light spilling out onto the pavement in front of it. I then became aware of the faint sound of music coming from one of the buildings near me, dissonant string music with steady, underlying drone tones, accompanied by complex cross-rhythms played on *tablas*, hand drums used widely throughout the Middle East, India, and Africa. East Indian, I decided, and cocked my head to listen better. I'd introduced an East Indian detective in one of my earlier novels and had steeped myself in the music and culture. Obviously, a mixed ethnic neighborhood, immigrants making their way in a strange city.

I climbed three cement steps to the front door of Number 17, took a tiny flashlight from my bag, and used it to search for the names of occupants, perhaps buzzers. I found neither. Maria had said it was on the third floor, but how could I let her know I was downstairs? The outside door would certainly be locked. I pushed it; it swung open with a groan. So much for that theory.

I stepped into the dark foyer and looked up a narrow flight of stairs to the first floor, reminding myself that in Europe I was standing on the ground floor; one flight up was the first. A low-wattage bare bulb spilled eerie light over the landing and a portion of the stairway.

I slowly began to climb, my steps deliberate, my eyes and ears at full alert. I reached the first-floor landing, paused, and continued up until reaching the top floor—the third. There were two doors off the landing. Neither had a number. One was painted a glossy fire-engine red, the other a dull black. I recalled that the light from the building had been on the left side as I faced it, which would put it behind the black door. I knocked, and heard someone move in the room. I knocked again, and was aware of further movement. Maria Giacona opened the door. She looked a wreck. Tears had carried whatever eye makeup she wore down her cheeks. Her hair had the look of having had too many fingers run through it too many times.

"He's gone," she said.

"Jason?"

"Yes."

We looked at each other until I asked, "May I come in?"

Her response was to open her eyes wide, turn to the interior of the flat, and raise both arms. "He's gone," she said again, this time her words accompanied by tears. She slapped her hands to her sides and walked into the cluttered and cramped living room. I followed, leaving the door open behind me. It looked as if someone—probably Jason Harris—had frantically pulled things from shelves and drawers, or as if someone had entered the apartment desperately searching for something. The room was a shambles, clothing tossed everywhere, books piled haphazardly on shelves and the floor. The few pieces of stuffed furniture were ripped and faded. Light from a streetlamp was virtually stopped at the windows by layers of grime and nicotine.

"You said Jason was leaving at seven," I said as pleasantly as I could. "What makes you think he's 'gone'?"

She turned and glared at me, anger etched on her face. "He took the manuscript. The manuscript is gone, and so is he."

I started once again to rationalize why Jason might not be there, but decided it was a fruitless exercise. There was no dissuading Maria at this moment, so intense was her upset. "Was this the only copy of the manuscript?"

"Yes."

"No one made a photocopy?"

"I told him . . ."

"No matter," I said. "Obviously a manuscript was delivered to Marjorie Ainsworth's publisher, probably more than one."

"But Jason made his notations only on the copy he kept."

I was torn between sitting down and continuing the discussion, and getting out of Jason's flat as quickly as possible. I opted for the latter course of action. "Why don't we go get a bite to eat and talk about this some more? I know you said Jason is reluctant to do anything about his alleged authorship of Marjorie's book, but maybe we can convince him otherwise. Please, don't misunderstand. I'm not suggesting that I would do anything along the lines you suggested in the park this morning, but I would be interested in finding out to what extent he did contribute to the novel. The three of us could sit down and discuss it."

She shook her head with vigor, sending thick black hair whirling about her. "It is not that easy, Mrs. Fletcher. I don't think . . ." She broke down now into heavy sobbing and sat on the edge of a frayed love seat. "Something dreadful has happened to him. I just know it."

I sat and put my arm about her. "Maria, there's no reason to say that. I'm sure Jason is perfectly all right and will return tonight. We can continue with this in the morning." I stood. "In the meantime, I really think we should leave and have a cup of coffee or tea. I noticed a Chinese restaurant on the corner. Perhaps—"

"Just leave me alone," she snapped.

"If you wish. I certainly didn't mean to impose upon you. If you'd like to talk again, call me at the Savoy." I walked to the door, stopped, turned, and looked back at her. She was still sitting on the love seat, crying. What a volatile, emotional young woman, I thought. I turned to leave. "Oh my God!" I gasped. The man was huge. He filled the doorway. He had a long, matted gray beard and a bird's nest of filthy gray hair. He was obviously drunk; his slurred speech confirmed that. "What are you two duckies up to?" he asked.

I tried to catch my breath as I said, "You startled me. Excuse me, I was just leaving."

He looked past me to Maria and said, "What'd the bastard do, Maria, take his hand to you again?"

Maria shook her head without looking up. "He's gone," she said, her words barely audible. I repeated to the large man that I wished to leave. He scowled at me as he stepped back unsteadily and grabbed the railing of the stairs for support. I didn't say anything to Maria as I left, did not repeat my suggestion that she call me at the Savoy. I descended the stairs, slowly at first, picking up speed as I approached the ground floor. I stepped outside and took a series of deep breaths. It had been cool in London since my arrival, perfect early September weather. Now the humidity had begun to increase and I felt choked by it. A thick fog had developed in the short time I was in Jason's flat.

I walked with haste toward the Chinese restaurant on the corner, my heightened awareness causing the sound of my heels on the pavement to be louder than was the fact. I looked in the window and saw a few young people seated at two small tables. A Chinese man and woman were behind a counter. I wanted a cab. I looked for a telephone in the restaurant, but saw none. I took in the four corners of the intersection. No familiar red British phone booth on any of them.

I started walking in the direction of Liverpool Street Station. Surely there would be taxis waiting there. The closer I got, the more alone I felt, even though there were people on the street, small groups, mostly young, the majority obviously not native-born. I forced myself to slow down, and to respond more realistically to my surroundings. There was nothing threatening about the people I passed. For the most part, they looked like everyday folks going about their business.

I felt better after a couple more blocks and even considered stopping into one of the small, intimate restaurants for something to eat. No, I decided, I would wait until I got back to my hotel.

I paused at a corner. To my right, a block away, was what appeared to be a main thoroughfare. I started in its direction, then realized that the block I had to travel was particularly dark. It occurred to me for a fleeting moment that I should return to the better lighted corner from which I'd come, but the allure of the traffic and lights on the larger street was too compelling.

I reached a point approximately halfway along the street when I became aware of the presence of something—or someone—behind a tall pile of packing crates to my right. I froze; the presence was confirmed by the movement of a ten-foot shadow on the wall, followed by the person who'd cast it. He was young, and very punk. A wide streak of vivid pink ran through the middle of his Mohawk-styled blond hair from front to back. His acne was terminal. Three long silver earrings dangled from his left ear, and he was dressed in a black leather jacket with silver studs. He said in a distinct Cockney accent, "'Ere we go, give it to me now." He stepped directly in front of me and grabbed the lapel of my raincoat. My bag hung on my right shoulder. I tried to yank free, but his other hand fastened on the strap of the bag and spun me around. I fell heavily to my knees, pain immediately radiating to my brain. Still, I continued to hold on to my handbag and started yelling.

He cursed and gave a final tug on the strap, pulling it from my shoulder.

"Stop!" I shouted as he took off on the run. I saw him disappear around the corner and realized it was futile to pursue him. Actually, it was foolish of me to have fought him at all. I'd established a habit years ago of keeping anything of value like credit cards, cash, and airline tickets in a small leather pouch around my waist whenever I was in a big city. My handbag contained nothing but cosmetics, my small flashlight, and two ten-pound notes.

I stood and gently touched my kneecaps. The stockings on both were torn, and one knee was bleeding. I stumbled to the larger street, where two black London cabs waited at a corner. I opened the door of the first, said, "Savoy Hotel, please," and collapsed on the back seat.

"You all right, mum?" the young driver asked.

"Yes . . . no, I'm not. I've just been mugged."

"I'll get a bobby," he said.

"No, please, just take me to the hotel. I'll notify the police from there."

My assistant manager friend was in the lobby when I arrived. I explained to him what had happened, and he paid the taxi driver.

As I crossed the lobby, two young reporters who'd been sitting in a corner sprinted toward me. "Mrs. Fletcher, would you give us a few minutes for some questions?"

I couldn't help but smile. There I was, my knees bruised and bloody, my stockings torn, lucky to have escaped with my life (the driver had told me so at least six times), and they wanted to interview me for a story. I shook my head and walked toward the elevators.

"Mrs. Fletcher," the assistant manager called. "Please, let me escort you to your room."

No hotel room in my memory ever looked as pleasing and welcome as mine did at that moment. The assistant manager assured me that the police would be notified immediately, and he ordered a light dinner for me from room service.

I knew I wouldn't be able to take a nice, soothing bath until the police had called, and I didn't want to be in the tub when the food arrived, so I stayed in my clothes until those things happened. The police were cordial and courteous enough, but I sensed a weariness in their taking of my statement over the phone. The assault on me was obviously not the only crime they had to worry about that Sunday evening in London.

My bath felt heavenly, and I applied bandages to the knee that had bled. I sat in a nightgown, robe, and slippers and nibbled at my dinner. I was hungry, yet had little interest in eating. I'd spent time in many major cities and had never come close to being mugged. Now, it had happened to me for the first time, and in London, of all places.

"Stupid," I said to myself as I got up from the rolling table and looked out the window. "You asked for it, Jess," I added in a louder voice.

I called the hotel operator for messages. There were the usual assortment of media people trying to reach me. The only caller not identified as someone from the press was named Jimmy Biggers. His message indicated that he was a private investigator, and that it would be very much to my advantage to talk to him. I thanked the operator, noted the numbers she gave me, and went to bed, the face of that young mugger hovering over me until sleep wiped him away.

Chapter

10

My knees ached when I awoke the next morning. So did the shoulder on which I'd carried my handbag. But, overall, I felt pretty good, especially considering what might have been.

The phone rang a few times while I was in the shower. I called the operator and was told that Lucas Darling had called twice; Scotland Yard Chief Inspector George Sutherland once; and private investigator Jimmy Biggers had tried to reach me again. It then dawned on me that this was the day of the dinner to kick off the conference of the International Society of Mystery Writers, and that I was to give my address. In the bustle of things, I'd completely forgotten about that, and my heart tripped as I now thought of it. You'd better get rolling, I told myself.

The phone rang again. This time I instinctively picked it up. "Hello," I said.

"Jessica, it's Lucas. You answered your own phone."

"Purely involuntary, I assure you. I suppose we ought to get together and talk about this evening."

"Of course we should. You have a major speech to give."

"I know, and I'm beginning to wish I didn't. Are you free for lunch?"

"I kept it open, hoping you and I could meet. How are you?"

"With the exception of being mugged last night, fine."

He gulped. "Who, where, when, why?"

I laughed. "You left out 'What?' Not to worry, Lucas, I'm all right."

"I told you to be careful," he said sternly.

"Yes, and I should have listened. I promise you I will from this moment on. Where are we having lunch?"

"I was leaning toward the Connaught, or Le Gavroche, but we won't have time to linger, so I thought a pub was probably more sensible. The Victoria, on Strathearn Place, Bayswater, is pleasant. I won't have a chance to pick you up at the hotel. Noon?"

I'd written down the name of the pub and its address, and told him I'd be there on time.

I returned the call to George Sutherland at Scotland Yard. "Mrs. Fletcher, how are you?"

"Fine, thank you."

"I received a report about what happened to you last night. Dreadful shame."

"My first and only mugging," I said. "It was terribly upsetting at the time, but I'm feeling better today." Why would he have received a report of a run-of-the-mill mugging in a city the size of London, I wondered. I asked him.

"Insightful of you to question that, Mrs. Fletcher. The fact is I have made it known to the authorities that I have a special interest in Jessica Fletcher, and that I am to receive any news regarding you during your stay."

I didn't know whether to be flattered or concerned. I decided not to pursue the matter further. I knew what his response would be, flattering undoubtedly, but hardly telling. I asked, "Anything new on Marjorie Ainsworth's murder?"

"As a matter of fact . . ." Was he going to finish what he'd started to say? I hoped so. He did. "Miss Ainsworth had two Spanish gardeners working on the grounds. One of them tried to sell a wristwatch to a jeweler in Crumpsworth. It belonged, it turns out, to Miss Ainsworth."

"That's very interesting," I said, "but it wouldn't necessarily mean that he killed her. He obviously had access to the house and might simply have picked it up from a table where Marjorie had inadvertently left it."

"My sentiments exactly, but you did ask if anything was new, and I'm afraid that's all I have to offer at the moment."

"I'm sorry. I didn't mean to be discourteous."

"Mrs. Fletcher, I seriously doubt whether you even possess the capability of being discourteous. I would like to 'touch base' with you again, as I believe you say in America. Would it be possible for me to drop round sometime later this afternoon?"

That sounded pleasant, but I knew the day was going to be frenetic because of the opening of the conference. I said, "Inspector Sutherland, I would love to meet with you again, but I wonder if we could make it another day, perhaps tomorrow. The conference I came to attend starts this evening, and I am the opening speaker. You can imagine the case of nerves I'll develop as the day progresses."

There was that warm, gentle laugh again. "Yes, I can well understand. I've faced many difficult situations in my life, including hardened criminals hell-bent on doing away with me, and seldom flinched. But having to get up and speak to a group of people would reduce me to jelly, I'm afraid."

I doubted that, but it was good of him to sympathize. I promised I would call him the next day.

The Victoria Tavern, a tall and typically high Victorian structure, lies between the intersection of Bayswater Road and Edgware Road, an area sometimes known as Tyburnia. It's surrounded with large, elegant mansions, most erected during the 1840s.

Lucas was there when I arrived; he was always on time and usually early. He'd secured a small table off to the corner in the restaurant portion of the pub called "Our Mutual Friend."

"What a lovely pub," I said as I joined him.

"A real favorite of mine," he said. "Look." He pointed to a far wall. "Not long ago they restored a painting on that wall and discovered it was a valuable portrait of a long-deceased member of the royal family. The owner presented it to the Queen, and it's now part of the royal portrait collection."

"How generous," I said.

"For an American perhaps," he replied. I let the comment pass. "Well, tell me all about this vicious assault on you."

There wasn't much to tell, but I gave him as much detail as possible, knowing he thrived on such things. When I was finished, he asked if anything was new in the Ainsworth murder. I told him of my conversation with Inspector Sutherland, and about the arrest of the Spanish gardener.

"What a break," he said.

"I don't think so. As I told Inspector Sutherland, the gardener might have picked it up anywhere in the house. It doesn't necessarily have a connection with the murder."

Lucas thought for a moment before saying, "You're absolutely right, Jessica. The thought of Marjorie Ainsworth being murdered by a common laborer is too dismaying to contemplate. It has to have been done by someone with better credentials than that."

I couldn't help laughing at the pomposity in what he'd said. "I'm famished," I said.

Later, after I'd consumed a lunch of Scotch eggs—hard-boiled eggs wrapped in saveloy, a highly seasoned sausage —and Lucas had put away a ploughman's lunch (he insisted we order a glass of Tusker Bitter and Wethered Bitter, and do a taste test; he swore the Wethered was better, although I couldn't discern any difference), I asked him whether he'd ever heard of a London private detective named Jimmy Biggers.

You never had to wonder what Lucas Darling was thinking. His face was like a television screen, his thoughts playing on it in Technicolor. The mention of Mr. Biggers's name brought forth an expression of horror usually reserved for the discovery of corpses.

"You do know him."

"Oh, Jessica, of course I know him. Why do you mention him?"

"He's called me at the hotel a couple of times."

"Don't call him back."

"Why not?"

"Because"—he leaned closer and whispered conspiratorially—"Jimmy Biggers is not famous in London, Jessica. He's *infamous.*"

"Really? Sounds intriguing."

"He's a rotter who operates barely on the side of the law."

"Tell me more."

"Jimmy Biggers . . . Well, do you remember the murder a year or two ago of the professor at Cambridge?"

I shook my head.

"He was one of Cambridge's most esteemed and revered professors of ancient Greek literature. His name was Pickings, Sir Reginald Pickings. They found him lying face down along the bank of the river that runs through town. He'd been badly bludgeoned. The Cambridge police came up empty-handed, and the crime went unsolved for months. Then the university quietly hired Mr. Biggers, and he sussed the culprit in less than a week."

" 'Sussed'?"

"Suspected—identified the student who'd murdered Sir Reginald and who, by the way, had been involved in a nasty homosexual relationship with him. Biggers is not a shy man. He milked that case to the limit, had his picture in every newspaper almost daily for two weeks."

"I'm impressed. Maybe he could be helpful in solving . . ."

That look of horror came over Lucas's face again. "Marjorie's murder? Out of the question. Forget it. The man's friends are prostitutes and yobs—"

" 'Yobs'?"

Lucas sighed and said, "Oh, Jessica, I really must give you a course in British slang. Thugs. Yobs are thugs."

"Thank you for the translation."

"My pleasure." He looked at his watch. "We must go." He placed money on the check, stood, took his umbrella and raincoat from where he'd hung them on a coat tree, and was at the door before I could even gather my things. He'd hailed a taxi by the time I joined him outside, and we headed for the Savoy.

"How is your speech shaping up?" he asked.

"I really haven't given it much thought, but I intend to devote the afternoon to that."

By the time the cocktail party preceding the ISMW dinner had started, I was fully prepared for the evening ahead. I walked into the party and was struck immediately with how different this meeting was from previous ones. The differences involved two things. First, the number of people far exceeded that of any previous convention. I couldn't be sure whether it was because more members were in attendance, or whether the ranks had been swelled by the number of media people present. There were television cameras—something I'd never seen before at these meetings—and a horde of print journalists circulating through the room. The minute they saw me come in, they converged. "Please, no, I really have nothing to say about Marjorie Ainsworth's unfortunate death. I have a speech to give tonight and would like to focus my attention on that. Please, try to understand." They were, as media people tend to be, unwilling to abide by my wishes, but I brusquely walked through the cluster they'd formed around me and went to the bar, where I ordered a ginger ale. I was nervous enough without having to worry about the possible effects of an alcoholic beverage.

The second thing that was different was the intensity in the room. Mystery writers, like most writers, tend to be a low-key species. Previous meetings of ISMW had always been characterized by a quiet, introspective atmosphere. Not tonight; there was a sense of urgency that was almost palpable, undoubtedly caused by the presence of so many media people and the meaning of Marjorie's untimely and brutal death. I was also acutely aware that I was indeed the center of attention, and probably would be for the rest of the night, not because I was making a speech, but because of the circumstances surrounding my relationship with Marjorie and my having found her body. It was too late to wish those things away, and I didn't try.

"Jessica, how good to see you again," Clayton Perry, Marjorie's American publisher, said. He was standing with a glass of tonic water in his hand, his wife, Renée, at his side.

"Such excitement," I said.

"Certainly not unexpected," Perry said. "How are you holding up?"

"Fine . . . I think. You?"

"Oh, we're doing quite nicely," Renée Perry said. "If one is to be detained anywhere, I can't think of a more pleasant place than London."

I looked past them to where a knot of journalists had cornered someone. My eyes widened. "Isn't that Inspector Coots from Crumpsworth?" I asked.

The Perrys turned. "Yes, it is," Clayton Perry said. "I understand he's here by invitation of the society."

"Why would the society invite *him*?" I asked.

Perry shrugged and sipped his drink. "You know Lucas, Jessica, he's absolutely thrilled at the publicity the society is receiving this year. Having Coots giving out his pompous statements to the press from the convention will undoubtedly secure more newspaper space, and time on television."

"Excuse me," I said, moving away from them to where Lucas was in an animated conversation with Marjorie's American agent, Bruce Herbert. Listening in on what they were saying was Marjorie's British publisher, Archibald Semple, and a man I did not recognize. He was short and slender. Multiple tufts of carrot-red hair sprouted from his head, as though planted there. His suit was an iridescent black. He wore a yellow shirt and narrow black tie. As I approached, I noticed his face was heavily freckled. I also observed a bulge beneath his suit jacket that could be nothing but a revolver.

"Aha, Jessica, your ears must be burning," Herbert said, enthusiastically shaking my hand. "You've been the subject of an interesting discussion here."

"I hope the words were kind," I said.

"More than kind, Mrs. Fletcher, glowing." Semple said. He, too, took my hand but, unlike the agent's, his hand was cold and codlike.

"Jessica, allow me to introduce you to Mr. Biggers."

"*Jimmy* Biggers?" I asked.

"Yes, and I don't blame you for not returning my calls. I wouldn't have." He smiled, exposing a set of teeth that leaned toward the color of his shirt. A cigarette dangled from the fingers of one hand; a lot of nicotine had stuck to those teeth.

"Quite an interesting cast of characters has been assembled here this evening," I said. "Usually the only ones who attend are ISMW members."

"Yes, a motley crew indeed. I do hope you'll give me a few minutes of your undivided attention when the dinner is over, Mrs. Fletcher," Biggers said.

I wasn't sure whether I would or not, so I said nothing.

"Jessica, Archibald and I have brainstormed a wonderful idea for you," Herbert said.

"Oh? Tell me."

"What would you think of writing a nonfiction book about the murder of Marjorie Ainsworth and the eventual resolution of the case?"

I looked down into my glass and thought for a moment, then looked up and said, "I think it's a dreadful idea."

"Why?" Semple asked. "Who better to do such a book? We all know that the minute her murder has been solved and the trial concluded, a dozen writers will turn out purple prose about it. As one of Marjorie's close friends, you would certainly do it with more sensitivity, more compassion."

"It's really worth considering, Jessica," Bruce Herbert said.

"Well, I . . . Yes, I will consider it. Thank you for thinking of me."

A dinner bell struck by Lucas, and sounding more like the bell announcing the beginning and end of rounds in a boxing match, heralded that we were to go into the main ballroom for dinner, and for the evening's presentations. I was relieved; all I wanted to do was to find some time alone and mentally prepare myself. Fortunately, I was seated on the dais with Lucas, and with members of that year's slate of ISMW officers, none of whom seemed interested in discussing Marjorie with me.

Lucas welcomed everyone and suggested we enjoy our meal before the "important and fascinating presentations begin."

The meal was splendid, as it always was at these yearly gatherings. Lucas's penchant for good food was as well known as his zealous championing of the society, and he always saw to it that the chef, no matter which the hotel, was inspired to reach beyond the typical meeting fare. We began with oysters and caviar in Champagne sauce, went on to truffle-scented chicken consommé, and a choice of Dover sole sautéed with leeks or rack of lamb with stewed shallots for the main course. The most delicate raspberry and lemon sherbert I had ever tasted was the dessert.

Lucas stood at the microphone and said, "Ladies and gentlemen, fellow authors, friends, I welcome you here tonight for the opening of what promises to be the most interesting and successful ISMW conference in our history. I'm sure you all approve of the dinner that was so caringly and expertly prepared by the glorious staff of the Savoy." There was applause. He rubbed his hands and announced with considerable glee, "It is time to commence the grisly business at hand." He gave me an embarrassingly flowery introduction.

I stepped to the microphone and looked out over the crowd. I spotted him immediately in the far right-hand corner of the large room: Chief Inspector George Sutherland. It seemed as if every law enforcement agency and individual involved with the Marjorie Ainsworth murder had been invited to attend, and to hear me speak.

I'd rewritten my speech to include opening remarks about Marjorie, about the dreadful thing that had happened to her, and about how we would all miss her presence as both a person, as well as a professional inspiration for every writer of the genre. I got through that portion nicely, although I did have to fight back a tear or two. Then I launched into the major thrust of my remarks, which dealt primarily with the unparalleled popularity of the murder mystery in today's fiction marketplace, and how it had crossed over the line from genre fiction into the mainstream of literature. I had sprinkled many examples throughout my notes and, as I progressed, found myself becoming more comfortable, more at ease, and actually enjoying the experience.

Until . . .

It happened so fast, without warning. The man wore a black raincoat and tweed cap. He burst from behind swinging doors that led to the kitchen, and carried the longest sword I had ever seen. It was held in both his hands and was pointed directly at me. He yelled as he ran toward the dais, "You killed the Queen, you killed the Queen. . . . Death to the Queen killer!"

I stood frozen at the podium. A few people reached for him, but he was moving too fast, passed right by them, the sword held high, a maniacal look in his eyes.

Jimmy Biggers stuck out his foot from where he sat, tripping the man, the sword flying in one direction, he the other. Biggers was on him in a second, twisting his arms behind his back and yelling for help. It was Montgomery Coots who was first at the scene, but he seemed unsure of what to do. Then two young men in business suits jumped up from a table and raced to where Biggers held the attacker down. One of them pulled out handcuffs from beneath his jacket and secured the crazed man's wrists behind his back.

There was bedlam in the room. Lucas came to my side, grabbed both my arms, and led me to my seat.

"What happened?" I asked.

"A madman, demented, hell-bent on killing you because he thinks you murdered Marjorie."

"Good Lord."

"I told you it could happen, Jessica, just as I told you to be careful on the streets of London."

We all watched as the two plainclothes policemen led the man from the room. He continued to yell over his shoulder that I had robbed Great Britain and the literary world of Marjorie Ainsworth. It was a great relief to have him out of the room, his irrational threats suddenly muffled by the slamming of a door.

Once a relative calm had returned, I was urged to continue my speech—which I did, reluctantly, and with considerably less enthusiasm and confidence than before.

When I was finished, Lucas outlined the program for the rest of the conference. There were to be seminars on new forensic techniques, weapons, surveillance apparatus, poisons, police procedure, and everything else of which the working mystery writer likes to keep abreast. There were also to be talks on more esoteric subjects, such as the future of the murder mystery, historical perspectives, and evaluations of new works by a reviewing panel.

A coffee reception followed the dinner, and a receiving line of sorts was formed, with me at its head. It was an awkward situation, but I did my best to get through it, shaking too many hands, smiling too much, saying too often, "Yes, it was startling." I was relieved when it was over and I could mingle freely.

"Excellent speech, Mrs. Fletcher," Inspector George Sutherland said. It was good to see him, and I told him so.

"Dreadful incident," he said. "The city is crawling with daft people like that. Sorry one of them had to decide to do away with you."

I laughed nervously. "I'm just pleased that he didn't accomplish his mission."

"So am I. Might I get you a coffee, or would you prefer to slip away from your adoring public for a drink at the bar?"

The latter sounded appealing, and I graciously accepted, asking, though, for ten minutes before leaving. I walked over to Jimmy Biggers, who was talking with a contingent from the Dutch chapter of ISMW.

"Mr. Biggers, I owe you a debt of gratitude. I saw how you stopped him."

He excused himself from the Dutch writers, and we moved a few feet away. "Mrs. Fletcher, will you give me a half hour of your time?"

"Now? I'm afraid I'm—"

"Mrs. Fletcher, I would never think of interfering with your responsibilities tonight. Could we meet tomorrow?"

"Yes, I suppose so, but what do you wish to meet about?"

He displayed his yellow teeth and said, "Marjorie Ainsworth, of course. I think you could use the services of someone who knows London as I do, its underbelly, its dark corners. I have some definite ideas on her murder and would like to share them with you."

His Cockney accent was charming, and went with his physical appearance, which, I knew, represented stereotyping on my part. Cockneys don't have a *look*; they simply happened to be born within hearing distance of Bow Bells, the bells of St. Mary-le-Bow Church in Cheapside.

"I'd also like to discuss that fellow over there with you," he said, pointing to Montgomery Coots.

"Why?"

"He's a nasty chap, and he's fixated on you, Mrs. Fletcher, as a suss."

"Suspect," I said, remembering Lucas's language lesson. "Preposterous."

"Maybe so, but not to be taken lightly."

I remembered what Lucas had said about Biggers's reputation but, at the same time, I was eager to talk with him. We agreed to meet in the Grill for lunch. Then I remembered that Marjorie's funeral was the next day. "Mr. Biggers, I'm afraid I couldn't possibly meet with you tomorrow. I'll be attending Marjorie Ainsworth's funeral in Crumpsworth."

"The day after then?"

"Call me, Mr. Biggers. I'm sure we can arrange something."

"I certainly will, Mrs. Fletcher. Cheerio!"

I spent the next hour with the same warm feeling I'd had when Inspector Sutherland and I had tea at Brown's. He was charming, and although I reminded myself on more than one occasion that he was investigating Marjorie's murder, the ambience he created made it difficult to dwell upon such thoughts. We talked about many things, none of them having anything to do with crime. He told me his background—born in Wick, on Scotland's uppermost shores; father was a commercial fisherman, herring mostly, until the herring virtually

disappeared; a harsh life in a harsh place, but a loving family.
He'd received a degree in psychology from the University of
Edinburgh, joined the Edinburgh police force, married a
woman from London, transferred to the London MPD, then
moved over to Scotland Yard. His wife had been killed in a
car accident some years ago.

We left the Savoy bar and stood in the lobby. "Good night,
Mrs. Fletcher. It is always a pleasure."

"I might say the same thing, Inspector."

"I saw you speaking with Jimmy Biggers."

"Yes."

"He's notorious, you know, definitely *aff the fuit*."

"Pardon?"

A big smile. "An old Scottish expression for morally unfit.
Just be careful, that's all."

"I will. Thank you for the warning, Inspector."

"Call me George, please."

"If you'll call me Jessica."

"I assume your friends call you Jess."

"Yes, my . . . *close* friends do."

"And I? Shall it be Jessica or Jess?"

"Whatever pleases you."

"One thing, before we end this evening. It seems to me it
might be a good idea for me to assign permanent protection
for you while you remain in London."

"Oh, Inspector . . . George, I don't think that's at all necessary."

"May I be the judge of that, Jessica?"

"Yes, if you wish."

"Good. I'll arrange it. Thank you once again for sharing
some time with me. Good night . . . Jess."

Chapter

11

 "Unto Almighty God we commend the soul of our sister departed, Marjorie, and we commit her body to the ground. . . ."

Mother Nature had not been kind to Marjorie Ainsworth on the day she formally departed this earth. A heavy rain fell, and a scolding wind whipped it about, giving credence to claims of experiencing "horizontal rain" in Great Britain.

Everyone who'd been at Marjorie's house the weekend of her murder was present for the funeral, with the exception of Jason Harris. I'd hoped that he would surface, if only to pay his final respects to the woman who'd given him the benefit of her experience and talent. But he hadn't. As I stood in the downpour wiping tears from my eyes, I wondered whether Maria Giacona had been right, and that her lover had, in fact, met some nasty fate.

The simple wood coffin containing the body of the world's greatest writer of mysteries was slowly lowered into the soggy earth. The rector of the Crumpsworth church sprinkled clumps of mud over it as it disappeared from the view of the mourners. "The Lord be with you," he said.

"And with thy spirit," a few people muttered.

"Let us pray. Lord have mercy upon us."

"Christ have mercy upon us."

"Lord have mercy upon us."

The press had been restricted to a cordoned-off area a hundred feet from the graveside. Young men from the congregation held large black umbrellas over those in attendance, which included not only those who'd been at Ainsworth Manor, but faces that had now become disconcertingly familiar—Crumpsworth Inspector Montgomery Coots, Chief Inspector George Sutherland, and, most surprising to me, the private detective Jimmy Biggers.

I looked up to the road where hundreds of spectators, restrained by uniformed Crumpsworth police, looked on. Were they avid readers of Marjorie's books, townspeople who'd lost a local celebrity, the curious, the macabre? What did it matter? She was gone.

"Excuse me a moment, Lucas," I said, heading for Jane Portelaine, who was slogging through deep muck to the road where cars were parked. Lucas and I had shared a limo from London.

"Jane," I said.

She snapped her head in my direction and looked at me with what I could only read as anger.

"I was wondering if . . ."

"She would have enjoyed this weather, wouldn't she?" she said, continuing to move her booted feet through the glop. "She loved the rain, loved darkness."

"She had the soul of a mystery writer," I said. "I was surprised not to see your friend Mr. Harris here."

Jane stopped abruptly. She looked at me with those same tempestuous eyes and said, "Mr. Harris is not a friend of mine, and I don't know why you would raise his name to me."

I suppose my face reflected the surprise I felt. I said, "I thought you two were close. At least, it seemed that way on the weekend. I don't mean to offend but—"

"Mrs. Fletcher, my aunt is dead. That carries with it a certain finality, including the right of those close to her to enjoy their privacy. I am being curt, I know, but consider the circumstances."

She'd lost the one person who had been a constant in her life for many years, and I admonished myself for being insensitive. Still, I was determined to pursue what I'd been thinking ever since I left the hotel that morning. "Would it be possible for me to visit the manor again while I'm still in London?" I asked.

"What for?"

"Oh, I don't know, just the need to touch Marjorie's surroundings once again before going home."

"I can't imagine why you would want to do that, but I suppose . . ."

I took advantage of this apparent weakening. "Could I stop by now?"

"No, that would be quite impossible."

"Well, perhaps another day?"

"I suppose you could call me, Mrs. Fletcher. I will do what I can to accommodate you."

I watched her continue walking to the road where Wilfred, their faithful chauffeur, opened the door for her. I assumed he would close it behind her, but Constable Coots climbed in after her, and the door was closed once he was inside. Strange, I thought, that Coots would ride to and from the funeral with someone who was obviously a suspect. Then again, it might represent a certain brilliance on his part. Stay close: that often paid off when investigating murder.

I'd reached the road and was approaching my limo when Sir James Ferguson, the producer of Marjorie's *Who Killed Darby and Joan?*, came up behind me.

"Sir James. What a horrible day to bury someone."

"Yes, Mrs. Fletcher, although I vividly recall a scene in one of Marjorie's early novels in which the murderer was identified at just such a burial. Do you remember it? It was called *Murder and Other Inconveniences*."

"Of course I do, but it hadn't occurred to me to make the connection. How are you, Sir James?"

"Quite well. I still wish to find quiet time to spend with you while you are here in London. I have some things to discuss with you."

"Sounds terribly weighty."

He broke into a smile; he had a wonderfully pleasant face. "Nothing of the sort, although I think we might benefit from a frank discussion about the possibilities of who murdered our dear friend and colleague. No, I just thought that you and I might find some common ground on a personal level, some pleasant dinner conversation, perhaps a spin around the dance floor at the Dorchester or Savoy, whatever would make the world's most famous mystery writer happy."

"You're very flattering," I said. "Yes, I would enjoy that. Please call."

"I certainly shall. How long since you've seen *Who Killed Darby and Joan?*"

"A few years."

"Would you enjoy seeing it again? Somehow I find watching the play puts me in touch with Marjorie. I suppose that will become increasingly important now that she's no longer physically present."

His comment touched me.

"Shall we go together? As the producer, I have two of the best seats in the house reserved for me at each performance. I would consider it a great privilege."

"Sir James, I have no idea of my schedule for the rest of this week. I have responsibilities at the convention, and there are so many people I must see while here. But, of course, I would love to accompany you to the play if I can work it out."

He swallowed his disappointment and looked up into the

gray sky, then back at me. "The gods are not happy that she's gone."

As I walked to my car, Inspector Sutherland of Scotland Yard nodded. That was all—a simple, unsmiling nod. I joined Lucas in the back seat and said to the driver, "Please take us into Crumpsworth."

"Why are we going *there*?" Lucas asked. "I have to get back to the convention."

"It won't take long, Lucas. Indulge me a half hour." I looked through the rear window as we pulled away and saw Sutherland still standing in the rain, his eyes fixed upon us. A strange change in him, I thought. What could have caused it?

We reached the center of Crumpsworth within a few minutes and circled the small main square until I spotted a shop whose sign read JEWELRY. "Stop here," I said. Then, to Lucas: "Won't be a minute."

He followed me out of the car—of course—and we entered the tiny shop. A wizened little old man wearing a jeweler's loupe and a green eyeshade looked up. "May I help you?" he asked in a shaky, raspy voice.

"Yes. My name is Jessica Fletcher. I was a close friend of Marjorie Ainsworth."

"Oh. Just come from the planting, have you?"

"Planting? Yes, she's been buried. I understand one of her gardeners tried to sell you a watch belonging to her."

"That's right. Those bloody foreigners'll steal the gold from your teeth."

"Yes. . . . I also understand you turned the watch over to local authorities."

"Coots. I gave it to Coots."

"How did you know it belonged to Ms. Ainsworth?"

"I fixed that watch before, I did. Saw whose it was right off."

"That was very astute of you."

A smug smile came to his lips.

"Is the man who tried to sell it to you in jail?"

"Should be. You'll have to ask Coots about that. I told the other bloke this morning the same thing."

"Other bloke? Who might that have been?"

"Read his name yourself." He pointed to a business card on top of the glass display case.

JIMMY BIGGERS
PRIVATE INVESTIGATIONS
Discretion Assured.

"He moves fast," I said to Lucas.

"Let's get out of here," Lucas said.

"Yes, I'm ready." I thanked the jeweler and we headed for London.

My thoughts during the ride were divided between the conversations I'd had that morning at the burial and trying to shake off an intense chill. My raincoat, good as it was, had merely strained the rain. My feet were soaked; all of me was wet, and I looked forward to a hot bath.

"Mrs. Fletcher, we have messages for you," the desk clerk said as I asked for the key to my suite. I wasn't surprised; I'd never had so many people trying to reach me at once in my life.

She handed me a pile of telephone message forms, and I skimmed them. There were many familiar names written on the small slips of paper, but one message caught my eye. It was from my dear friends from Cabot Cove, Dr. Seth Hazlitt and Sheriff Morton Metzger. The message read.

Arriving by Pan Am World Airways at eleven tonight at Heathrow Airport. Will arrange own transportation to hotel. Please don't wait up for us.

"I can't believe this," I said to Lucas. I handed him the paper.

"Who are these people?"

"Very good friends from home."

As we rode the elevator to my floor, I suffered mixed emotions. On the one hand, the idea of seeing familiar faces from Cabot Cove was as welcome as roses in May. On the other hand, my life seemed to have become so complicated since arriving in London that having more players involved was overwhelming.

We were no sooner inside the suite than Lucas said, "I found out more about that lunatic who attacked you last night."

"Really? Tell me."

"A certifiable madman. He attacked the London postmaster two years ago when he suggested the color of post boxes be changed. They let him go because he was obviously so demented that he couldn't be held responsible."

"That sword looked serious enough to me," I said.

"He's fruity, that's all. I consider your friendship with Jimmy Biggers to pose a greater threat."

"My friendship? I haven't established a friendship with him. We've agreed to meet, that's all. How did you know about that?"

"I have my sources. Keep your distance from him, Jessica. He's nothing but trouble."

I put my hands to my temples and said, "I know, I know, Lucas, and I promised I would heed your advice after what happened to me the other night on the street, but you can't preclude me from making contact with people."

"You're willing to risk your life for that principle?"

"Risk my life? Lucas, I don't wish to discuss this any further. I would like to attend some of the seminars and displays that are going on in the hotel. What are your plans?"

He sighed and huffed. "My plans were all carefully scheduled weeks ago, and on paper. The funeral has disrupted them. I might as well accompany you to whatever it is you decide to do. Damn, Jessica, things have gotten bloody wimpled. I detest complication."

"Well, you don't have any choice, do you? I need a hot bath to get rid of this chill. Shall we meet downstairs in an hour?"

"I suppose so. Why did you want to stop in that shop in Crumpsworth?"

"I was curious, that's all."

"I thought since you'd become so chummy with that Scotland Yard inspector, you'd be up on the latest through him."

I was becoming increasingly annoyed with Lucas, and my face reflected it. He grinned sheepishly and said, "You have that good hot bath, Jessica. See you at the weapons display in Room 707 in an hour."

I sank into the hot water foaming with bubbles and let out a long sigh, my tensions evaporating as the warm water worked its magic. My body felt instantly better, but I couldn't shut off my mind. Most of all, I wished Frank were alive. I missed him every day of my life, but there were times when that desire became acute, and this was one of them.

The phone rang. I was glad I wasn't in the living room to answer it. It rang again. And again. Someone was persistent in trying to reach me.

Fifteen minutes later, wrapped in a luxuriant terry-cloth robe provided by the hotel, I padded barefoot into the living room. The phone rang again.

"Mrs. Fletcher, it's Maria Giacona."

I hadn't left Jason Harris's flat with especially fond feelings for her, mitigated, of course, by having learned that he was known to have beaten her. "Yes, Ms. Giacona, what can I do for you?"

"Mrs. Fletcher, I'm terribly sorry for the way I acted at

Jason's flat. I was upset and . . ." Her voice lightened. "No excuses, I was simply rude, and I apologize."

I sat on the bed. Her apology, sounding sincere, alleviated the annoyance I'd felt. I thanked her for her apology and asked whether she'd heard from Jason.

"No, I haven't. I know you went to the funeral. He wasn't there, was he?"

"No, he wasn't. Are you at his flat now?"

"No, but I'm about to go there. I thought I'd tidy up in anticipation of his return."

Apparently she'd brought her emotions under control. "You will call me if he comes home?" I said.

"Yes, of course. Mrs. Fletcher, when Jason *does* come home—and I know he will—I hope you and I can resurrect our plan to sit down together and discuss the work he did on *Gin and Daggers*."

"Of course, provided I'm still here in London. I plan to be here only through this week."

She laughed. "If he isn't back by then, I will really worry." Not that she hadn't already. "Sorry to trouble you, Mrs. Fletcher. You are obviously a good person, and I appreciate the interest you've shown."

"That's quite all right, Ms. Giacona. Thank you for calling."

The weapons display was fascinating, although I have always tended to look for less violent methods of doing away with victims in my books. Guns and knives certainly have their place in murder mystery fiction, and I'm sure there is a legion of readers who prefer some gore in their reading, but I've always been more comfortable with a more genteel approach. Very much like Marjorie Ainsworth, I thought. Still, there were times when a piece of destructive hardware was much needed, and I browsed the display with interest—and horror at what the real weapons could do to real people.

More interesting to me, however, was an array of methods to do away with someone that had nothing to do with triggers and bullets and blades. A London pharmacist who'd been a member of ISMW for many years, and who'd been a consultant to many British mystery writers, had not only created a remarkable display of poisons but, in conjunction with a leading cookbook author, had developed a series of recipes perfect for delivering these lethal chemicals to intended victims—only in books, of course.

I listened to a heated debate between a German psychologist turned mystery writer and a stout Canadian woman who'd written dozens of novels featuring a disgraced Royal Canadian Mounted Policeman, over the reasons that food often plays such a large role in mystery novels. She: "Having a fascination with, and skill at preparing food gives a hero or heroine a worldly sophistication." He: "*Unsinn!* It all has to do with sex. There is no sex in murder mysteries. Food is the substitute. For each missing kiss or embrace, there will be an extra *Brathandl!*"

I noticed as the day wore on that fewer members of the press hung around the hotel, and I enjoyed an accompanying feeling of freedom. But, as when one jinxes a trip by commenting on how smoothly it's gone just before a tire blows out, and the engine suddenly seizes, my pleasure was short-lived.

It happened at five o'clock as I sat in the lobby with other American writers attending the conference. I was in the process of retelling the German writer's analysis of food and murder mysteries when Lucas came up to us. "Jessica, I must speak with you immediately."

Lucas was always so dramatic, and most times it stemmed from his personality, rather than from an event he was about to report. Still, you never knew. I followed him to a corner.

"You haven't heard?" he said.

"I suppose not. What haven't I heard?"

"Marjorie's last will and testament. It's to be officially read and released tomorrow, but a few reporters were tipped off about its major provisions."

"And?"

"She left a fortune, millions of pounds."

"I don't wonder."

"The report didn't mention specific numbers. Most of her estate, as I understand it, is to be used to establish Ainsworth Manor as an international research facility for mystery writers."

"How wonderful," I said.

"Her niece, Jane, gets some."

"I would certainly hope so."

"Household staff is in for a share."

"I wouldn't expect less of Marjorie than to reward them."

"And, according to the report, she left a sizable portion to you."

I was speechless.

"Did you hear me, Jessica?"

"Yes, I think so. *Me?*"

"You."

"I can't imagine why."

"It doesn't matter, Jessica. Do you realize what that means?"

"It means . . . I would never accept it. I don't need money. I'll simply donate my share to the study center that obviously meant so much to her."

"Jessica."

"What?"

"Her will. Motive. They'll say you had a motive to kill her."

I guffawed.

His face was dour. "I'm serious, Jessica."

"Well, I'm certainly not, and I—"

Six reporters, followed by a camera crew from the BBC,

entered the lobby and headed straight for me. "See you later, Lucas," I said, walking quickly to the elevators while Lucas shouted for calm. Ten minutes after I'd reached my suite, Lucas arrived.

"I took care of them," he said. "I gave them a statement."

"What did you say?"

"You'll see on the telly."

An hour later, a BBC anchorman said in a deep voice: "The contents of the late Marjorie Ainsworth's last will and testament were revealed today, twenty-four hours in advance of the formal reading of it." He went on to say what Lucas had told me downstairs.

Then Lucas's face filled the screen. "Ladies and gentlemen, it is only fitting that this news be announced on the second day of the annual meeting of the International Society of Mystery Writers." He'd gotten in the plug; he was beaming as we watched the newscast together.

"The world-famous writer, Jessica Fletcher, who delivered our keynote speech last night, and was the target of a madman's attack, has no comment at this time about having been named in Marjorie Ainsworth's will. She is overcome with shock and gratitude to her dear and departed friend and will make a statement later."

"Lucas," I said, "this is—"

"Sssssh," he said, holding his finger to his lips.

Montgomery Coots's face replaced Lucas on the screen. He'd been videotaped on the road in front of Ainsworth Manor.

"First, I wish to announce that the foreign gardener arrested for attempting to sell a watch belonging to Marjorie Ainsworth has been released. He has an ironclad alibi, which I personally confirmed. Of course, with the release of the deceased's will, focus must be on those who benefited financially from her death. I make no accusations, but the British people have my word that this heinous crime will be solved."

"This is dreadful," I said when the report was over.

"Don't worry, Jess, I'll make sure this is handled properly," said Lucas.

"Lucas."

"What?"

"Play cribbage with me."

"Cribbage? At a time like this?"

"Especially at a time like this." I removed a small cribbage board from my briefcase and set it up.

"Jessica, this is . . . mad."

"No, Lucas, what's going on downstairs and on television is madness. Cribbage is sanity, my kind of sanity. When Frank was alive, and when there was pressure in our lives, we played cribbage, or some other game. I nearly always won, and felt better. Sit down and cut the cards to see who goes first, and not another word about anything except the game."

Chapter

12

"You're in uniform," I said to Morton Metzger, sheriff of Cabot Cove. He and Seth Hazlitt had called my room upon their arrival, and I'd suggested we meet in the bar.

"Yes, Jess, I am. This is no vacation. I'm here on official business."

I turned to Seth, a familiar warm smile on his face. "Seth, how wonderful to see you." I kissed him on the cheek, did the same to Morton.

"Well, Jess, Mort and I spent considerable time chewin' it over, and it seemed like the only sensible thing to do was to climb on an airplane and get here fast as possible. We've been hearin' terrible things back home, includin' about that fella who went haywire and tried to kill you. Never heard of anything so lackin'."

"Yes, it was quite an experience, although he really didn't have much of a chance to get to me with so many people in the room."

"Still, Jess, it caused Seth and me to think we'd better help our good friend," said Morton, "no matter how far away she is. Must be fright'nin' bein' here in a strange country."

I laughed. "It isn't strange at all. After all, we came from here."

"You'd never know it by listenin' to that cab driver we had. I only understood every third word."

"Yes, sometimes they speak quickly, but it *is* English."

I was exhausted; it was one o'clock in the morning, London time. For them it was eight in the evening, and they looked ready for a night on the town. They insisted upon buying me a drink, and I filled them in on everything that had happened since my arrival. They listened intently, interrupting only with an occasional grunt or nod. When I was finished recounting my tales of woe, I asked them what their plans were for the next day.

"To be with you, Jess," Seth said. "That's why we came."

I shook my head and said with conviction, "Oh no, I'll be extremely busy with the convention, and I insist that you two spend the day sightseeing. London is a remarkable city, and to fly all the way here and not see as much of it as you can would be a crime." This was debated for a few minutes until Seth finally said, "All right, Jess, but only tomorra, and we're goin' to keep in close touch. Right?"

"Absolutely. Now this lady needs her beauty sleep." I stood.

"You do look a mite fatigued," Morton Metzger said. "Want me to escort you to your room?"

"No, thank you, Morton, that won't be necessary. Tell you what. You go off on a good day's sightseeing tomorrow, and I'll meet you right here in this same bar for a drink at five o'clock."

"Fair enough," said Seth.

"Buy yourself a good map and a guidebook. Be sure to see the Changing of the Guard, Westminster Abbey, and try to fit in the Tower of London."

Seth smiled. "I brought some good walkin' shoes. Looks like they'll get considerable use."

"I hope so," I said over my shoulder as I headed for the elevators. "Walking is the best way to see London."

I started to undress the minute I reached my suite, but was stopped by the ringing of the telephone. Who would be calling at this hour? Must be Seth or Morton with some last-minute comment or question. I picked up the phone and was confronted with a hysterical Maria Giacona. "Please, calm down, Maria, or I'll never understand what you're saying."

It took her a moment to muster enough composure to speak with some clarity. When she did, her words cut into me like a stiletto. "Jason is dead, murdered," she said. I sat heavily on the bed and asked her to give me more details.

"They found him in the Thames, off Wapping Wall, near the docks."

"Maria, I am so sorry. How did it happen? Any idea of who might have done it?"

"No, I just heard. I'm at Jason's flat. The police called looking for a family member, and I happened to be here. I wish I hadn't been."

"It must have been a dreadful shock. What do you intend to do now?"

"I don't know. I shouldn't be calling you this late, but I didn't know who else to turn to."

I felt the ambivalence one always feels in such a situation, flattered to be important enough to a person to be the one to whom they turn in time of trouble, yet wishing you weren't.

"Maria, why don't you come here to the hotel."

"Oh, Mrs. Fletcher, I couldn't . . ."

"No, I insist. Obviously, there will have to be a trip to the police, but it doesn't have to be now, at this hour. I would feel much better if you were here. Spend the night if you wish. The living room has a lovely pull-out couch."

She uttered a few further protestations, then agreed.

By the time she arrived, it was almost three in the morning, and I was exhausted. Simultaneously, my adrenaline was flowing at an accelerated pace, and I wouldn't have been able to sleep whether she arrived or not.

As I waited for her, I thought about the location she'd mentioned, Wapping Wall. I remembered it, of course, as a setting in Dicken's novels, a densely populated waterfront cut into many pieces by narrow, twisting alleys, long sets of stone steps, and a succession of docks, including Execution Dock where condemned pirates and thieves, including Captain Kidd in 1701, were left for the tide to wash over them three times. It was, in Dickens's time and probably long after, a sinister area of London where crime and criminals ruled.

I had no idea what the area was like today, but had a feeling I would soon find out.

Maria and I sat in the living room. She was now more composed, although she occasionally lapsed into quiet sobbing. She knew nothing more than what she'd told me on the phone.

"I assume they identified him from objects in his pockets," I said.

"Yes."

"Will you . . ." I hesitated before completing my sentence. "Will you have to identify the body, Maria?"

She shook her head.

"Who will? Does he have family here in London?"

"Yes, a stepbrother."

"Is he a writer, too?"

"No. He's a talent agent."

"Really? Does he handle big stars?"

"No. I mean, I really don't know. I know very little about him. His name is David Simpson. Jason and he haven't had much to do with each other. I suppose it would not be an overstatement to say that they dislike . . . disliked each other."

The next time I checked my watch, it was 4 A.M. "Would you like something to eat?" I asked. "I'll order it up."

She went through a mandatory "Oh, that isn't necessary," then quickly agreed that food would be welcome. After room service had delivered club sandwiches and coffee, I asked Maria about herself, her life, what she aspired to.

"I'm an actress," she said.

"How wonderful. I have great respect for people possessing that kind of talent. Have you appeared in anything in London?"

"Oh no, nothing that impressive yet. I've been in some smaller productions. I toured Ireland and Wales two summers ago with a troupe."

"That must have been fun."

"It didn't pay much, but I learned a lot."

"You're a beautiful young woman, Maria. Have you thought of films?"

She smiled. "Of course I have. Every actor or actress does. I'm afraid I haven't made much headway in that direction, but I keep trying."

"That's the spirit. It's so difficult making a living as a performer. Lord knows where most people find the perseverance and patience to continue."

"Like writing," she said.

"Yes, very much like writing. I was fortunate to have a loving and supportive husband who made sure the refrigerator had food in it while I tried to sell my stories." I laughed. "I still have a wonderful drawer filled with rejection slips. I treasure those. Somehow they mean more than the letters I've received praising what I've done, and announcing a publication date for my newest book. Does that make sense?"

"I think so, although I would love to receive such a letter informing me that I'd been selected for a major role at the Old

Vic." She sat back and her eyes misted. "My God, Mrs. Fletcher, it just hit me full force that Jason will never receive such a letter. He was so talented, and it will never be recognized." She started sobbing. I sat beside her and put my arms about her, pulled her to me and held her close, murmuring over and over, "I know, I know, I know."

After she'd calmed down, I suggested we catch a couple of hours' sleep before the sun came up. The couch was already made up. I gave her a spare nightgown, suggested that she try to get some sleep despite the fact that this horrible thing had happened, and went to the bedroom where I lay awake for an hour. Was it reasonable to assume that whoever killed Jason Harris also killed Marjorie Ainsworth? Possible, certainly, although as hard as I tried, I could not come up with a link. I also had to admit to myself that if pressed to name the person most likely to have murdered Marjorie, it would have been Jason, based on nothing but pure intuition. Now he was dead, a corpse dragged from the river Thames. Of course, that did not rule out the possibility that he had killed Marjorie, and had met his own fate for some reason totally unrelated.

I wondered whether Jane Portelaine had heard about Jason's demise. She'd certainly dismissed him at the funeral, but that didn't necessarily represent her true feelings. Was she disengaging from him for my benefit? Possibly. Her denial of friendship with Jason certainly hadn't held water with me. Their relationship, on whatever level it was conducted, was blatantly self-evident during the weekend at Ainsworth Manor.

"We'll see, we'll see," I said softly to myself as I rearranged the pillow beneath my head. Then I sat straight up. Wapping Wall. Yes, I knew it from reading Dickens, but I'd also been made aware of it more recently—in the past day or two, in fact.

I turned on the light and went through my purse until I

found Jimmy Biggers's business card. Sure enough, his office was located on Wapping Wall.

I returned to bed and, after my going through a series of relaxation exercises, beginning with my toes and ending with my eyes, sleep finally arrived.

Chapter

13

I'd no sooner gotten up and dressed when the phone rang again. "Mornin', Jess. Seth. Sleep well?"

"Good morning, Seth," I replied, my head still foggy from lack of sleep.

"Mort and I are gettin' ready to see the town. Thought you'd like to have breakfast with us."

"Seth, I . . ."

"You all right, Jess?"

"Yes, but I was up very late last night. Something has developed that I must take care of this morning."

"That so? Can we be of help?"

"No, I don't think so, but thank you for offering." Then, without thinking, I proceeded to tell him about Jason Harris's murder, and Maria Giacona sleeping in my living room.

"That sounds mighty serious, Jess. We'll be right up."

"No, Seth, I—"

"No arguments, Jessica Fletcher." He hung up.

I went to the living room and wakened Maria. "You'll have to get up now, Maria. Two male friends of mine are on their way here."

She disappeared into the bathroom, and I hastily put the

bed linens back in order and folded up the couch. It had no sooner snapped into place when there was a knock on the door. I opened it, and Seth and Morton walked in. Seth was dressed in a handsome tan poplin suit and wore his walking shoes. Mort was in his Cabot Cove sheriff's uniform. He had changed shirts, however. Last night it was tan; this morning it was blue.

"I really don't know what you can do," I said. "Ms. Giacona is in the bathroom, and I intend to escort her to the police station."

"Jessica, I know you are a woman who has traveled the world, and who feels very comfortable with crime, but there is no substitute for a professional talking to a fellow professional," Mort Metzger said.

"What do you mean?" I asked.

"If there is any trip to be made to the London police, I will make it with you. After all, I am a law enforcement officer. I speak their language. Trust me, Jessica. It's a good thing I'm here." Seth glanced at him and frowned. "That *we're* here," Morton added.

After Maria had finished getting dressed, I introduced her to my friends from Maine, and the four of us went downstairs for breakfast. Seth insisted upon putting the check on his room tab. When he saw the amount, and calculated pounds to U.S. dollars, he remarked, "I could feed a family of four for a month back in Cabot Cove for this money."

"Hotel breakfast," I said lightly. "Come on, let's go."

Like all London cab drivers, ours this morning was steeped in the history of the city. He pointed out to us the National Museum of Labour History, which, he said, memorialized the strivings of common men and women for a better life. He also pointed to a fascinating church, St. Paul's Shadwell, that had been built to minister to sea captains, including Captain Cook.

"Everything's so old," Morton Metzger said, his tan Stetson pulled down low over his eyes as he peered through the taxi's window.

Eventually, after our mini-tour of the Wapping district of London, we pulled up in front of the Metropolitan Special Constabulary, Thames Division, established in 1798 and responsible for patrolling fifty-four miles of the river with its thirty-three police boats.

I looked at Maria. "Are you up to this?" I asked.

She'd been extremely quiet the whole morning, saying virtually nothing. She looked at me with those huge brown eyes and forced a smile onto her pretty lips. "Yes, I suppose I have to be."

A sergeant at the front desk asked who we were.

"My name is Jessica Fletcher, and these are my friends," I said. "This young lady was a close personal friend of someone you found in the river last night, a young man by the name of Jason Harris."

The sergeant licked his thumb and turned pages in a book. "Yes, he's in the book. What's your business?"

"Well," I said, "this young lady, whose name is Maria Giacona, received the phone call at Mr. Harris's flat last night. They were . . . well, they were very close, and we felt that you would probably want her to personally identify the body."

The sergeant glanced down at the page in front of him, looked up, and said, "That's already been done."

"It has?"

"Yes, ma'am."

"Who, might I ask, identified the body?"

"Not for me to say."

"Sergeant, is there a detective or an inspector with whom we could speak about this matter?"

"Any of you family?" the sergeant asked. He was a slight man with thin black hair; a wavy scar on his upper lip formed a horizontal *S* over his mouth.

"No, no family, but someone who was very close to the deceased. Please, Sergeant, can't you show a little consideration for this young woman who has lost a loved one?"

He looked at each of us, then punched a button on a telephone console. "Inspector, there's four people out here inquiring about the floater last night." He listened to what the person on the other end of the line said, then hung up. "Okay, you can go back and see Inspector Bobby Half, down the hall, third door to the left."

Three of us started toward the corridor, but Mort Metzger lingered. He put his hand across the desk and said, "Sheriff Metzger, Cabot Cove, Maine. Here on official business."

The desk sergeant looked at Metzger's hat, then his uniform. Morton's hand continued to dangle over the desk. The *S* above the sergeant's mouth wiggled. He limply shook Mort's hand.

"Come on, Mort," Seth said impatiently.

Unlike the desk sergeant, the inspector was a big man. He had the rugged, leathery look of a commercial fisherman, which, I reasoned, resulted from having spent his career squinting against the sun's reflection off the water of the Thames. His hands were hamlike, calloused, and covered with scratches, nails grimy. His face was round, like a Halloween pumpkin, all the features barely protruding from the surface.

I went through my introduction again. This time, however, Morton insisted upon injecting himself into the middle of things. "Sheriff Metzger, Cabot Cove," he said, shooting his hand at Inspector Half.

"That so?" Half said. "Where might Cabot Cove be?"

"Maine, Inspector," I quickly said, moving to put myself between them. I told him of Maria's relationship with Jason Harris and expressed surprise that the body had already been identified. I asked by whom.

"His half brother, stepbrother, something like that. Came in a few hours after we dragged him out of the river."

"David Simpson," I said.

"That was his name."

"He was certain it was his stepbrother, Jason Harris?" I asked.

"Hard to be certain about a body like that. His throat had been slit from ear to ear, it had, and his face pretty badly battered in. Frankly, I couldn't tell him from Winston Churchill. A bloody mess, that's what he was, and floating in the river didn't help."

"Then how could his stepbrother make a positive identification?"

"Who knows? He didn't have any hesitation, and that was good enough for me." He looked at Maria. "What were you, his girlfriend?"

"Yes."

"And you want to see the body?"

"I . . . no, I suppose after what you've said, it would be better if I didn't." She started to cry.

"Inspector, it seems to me there are certain procedures here that should be followed," Sheriff Metzger said with considerable profundity.

"You're the sheriff of where?"

"Cabot Cove, Maine. You see, I flew here on behalf of Mrs. Fletcher, who, I am sure you know, is one of the world's most distinguished writers. She also was the person who discovered the body of Marjorie Ainsworth."

Morton's comment obviously meant something to the inspector. He smiled—actually, more of a simple parting of the lips—and extended his hand to me. "You're the one I've been reading about. Pleased to make your acquaintance."

"Likewise," I said.

Inspector Half seemed unsure of what to do next. He sat behind his desk and rolled his fingertips on its surface. "Happy to oblige you folks," he said. "If you'd like to see the body, you're welcome."

Maria turned and walked to the door. "I don't want to see him," she said.

"Let's go," Seth Hazlitt said.

"*I* would like to see the body, Inspector," I said.

"Jessica—"

"I would like to see the body."

The Inspector stood. "I warn you, it isn't a pretty sight."

"I assure you you won't have a fainter on your hands," I said.

The Inspector and I went to a small morgue set up at the rear of the building. Through the window, the Thames rolled by. There was a considerable amount of commercial activity on it, and I couldn't help but wonder what it had looked like two or three hundred years ago when pirates plied its waters. I didn't have much time to contemplate history, however, because before I knew it, Inspector Half had pulled out a body drawer from the wall and had flipped the end of a sheet that covered a corpse's face.

I quickly turned away. It wasn't recognizable as a human face, nothing but a gruesome mass of black flesh, no nose, no eyes, just a fetid blob. Look at it, Jessica, I told myself. You asked for this.

I forced myself to look once again at what the inspector had exposed. "Thank you," I said. "That's sufficient."

By the time we reappeared in the lobby of the constabulary, word had gotten out who I was. Inspector Half personally escorted us to the front door. The desk sergeant asked timidly, "Could I have your signature for me kids, Mrs. Fletcher?"

Half gave him a stern look. "If she wouldn't mind, Inspector," the sergeant said.

I quickly scrawled my name on the piece of paper he held out, thanked them once again, and walked out onto the street.

"Why did you have to see the body?" Seth asked. "It's nothing for a lady to see."

"Seth, *someone* had to look at the body. Frankly, I was surprised you didn't come with me. As a doctor, you've seen enough corpses."

"Yes, but I couldn't have been of any help. I never met the young man when he was alive."

"Well, I did."

"Was it as terrible as he said it would be?" Maria asked.

I solemnly nodded and avoided her gaze.

"Who could have done such a thing?" she asked.

"I don't know, Maria, but we'll try to find out."

"Must be near lunchtime," Morton Metzger said. "I'm hungry."

"It's only eleven o'clock," Seth said.

"My body is all turned around," Morton said. "Jet lag, I guess. What say we find ourselves a place to get a snack, just to tide us over till lunchtime."

I wasn't particularly hungry after viewing the remains, but I wasn't averse to a cup of tea. We looked down the length of the street and saw a pub at the far corner. "Let's go there," I said. "We can call a taxi after we eat."

The pub was called the Red Feather. We looked through the window. It seemed pleasant enough, somewhat run down, but weren't most neighborhood pubs? The others started in. I stepped back to take in the entire building, which was only two stories tall. Then I noticed a small sign next to the door:

JIMMY BIGGERS
PRIVATE INVESTIGATIONS

We settled at a table in the main room and ordered Devonshire ham and Stilton cheese sandwiches. I asked the owner where Mr. Biggers's office was; he pointed to a set of stairs to the rear.

"Is he up there now?" I asked.

"Probably asleep. He works nights most times, and sleeps the day away."

"Do you think he would mind being awakened by an old friend?"

"I didn't know he had any old friends, new ones either."

I waited until we finished our sandwiches and tea before going upstairs. I knocked.

"Who in hell is it?" Biggers shouted.

"Jessica Fletcher," I yelled with equal volume.

There was cursing and the sound of furniture being bumped into before Biggers opened the door. His hair went in a dozen directions, and there was a healthy growth of stubble on his cheeks. He wore an old flannel bathrobe riddled with cigarette burns.

"Sorry to have woken you, Mr. Biggers, but I was in the neighborhood and thought I'd stop in to say hello."

"That so? Wouldn't expect to see you sightseeing Wapping Wall."

"One of my favorite places," I said.

He yawned and scratched his belly through a gap in his robe and pajamas. "I intended to call you today," he said.

"I'm downstairs with friends," I said. "We've finished eating, but if you'd like to join us, we can have another cup of tea, or a beer."

"I might do just that, Mrs. Fletcher. Give me a minute."

He took five minutes to join us. Obviously, showering upon awakening wasn't part of his morning routine. He'd tried to tame his hair but without much success. There were still sleep granules in the corners of his eyes. I introduced him to the others.

"What brings you to this neighborhood?" he asked.

"An unfortunate circumstance," I answered. I told him about Jason Harris, and how Maria was Jason's closest friend.

"Friend?" he said, grinning. "If that's all he saw in you, miss, he was a bloody fool."

Maria didn't know what to do, so she looked away. I was embarrassed, too, but tried not to show it. Biggers asked some questions about Jason Harris, which I deftly avoided. I was aware that Morton Metzger was taking in Biggers with narrowed, questioning eyes. He didn't say anything, but his stare became unsettling. I decided it was time to leave, thanked Biggers for allowing me to barge in on him as I had, and said we'd be in touch.

"Anytime, Mrs. Fletcher," he said, standing and pulling out my chair. "It's a grotty neighborhood, but I call it home, have for many years. You ought to come back just for a social visit some time."

"I might take you up on that, Mr. Biggers. Good day."

When we returned to the Savoy, I suggested that Morton and Seth try to salvage some of the day for sightseeing. They reluctantly agreed, and we reconfirmed our plans to meet for a drink at five in the Thames Foyer bar.

Maria and I went up to my suite.

"I really must be leaving now, Mrs. Fletcher. Thank you so much for all you've done. You're a very kind person."

"No need to thank me, Maria. You've been through something dreadful."

"Mrs. Fletcher, could I ask you something?"

"Of course."

"How terrible did he look? I mean . . ."

"I won't mince words with you, Maria. It was a horrible sight. Frankly, I had no idea whether it was Jason or not."

Her eyes filled up, and she quickly left the room.

Chapter

14

Lucas had wanted me to take part in a panel discussion on creating believable female detectives in fiction, but I begged off, agreeing instead to join one the next morning on the relative merits of small-town settings versus big cities.

I couldn't get the vision of the battered face I'd seen in the Wapping police headquarters out of my mind, nor could I ignore Maria's comments about Jason Harris's stepbrother, David Simpson. I've always prided myself on my ability to maintain order in my life. Like any writer who's made a living at it, discipline has been the key, and I've had to be a disciplined person.

There are times, however, when, hard as I try, I am drawn to something like a moth to a summer candle. That's what was happening as I mulled over the circumstances of Jason's death. How had the police known to contact David Simpson in the middle of the night? I should have asked that. Perhaps Jason carried a card that indicated in the event of emergency, his stepbrother was to be called.

Each time I raised a question—and answered it—I was dissatisfied with my reply.

I went through the London Yellow Pages until I came to the Talent Agent section, which told me to look at Booking Agents. I did, and found an agency in the listing: Simpson Talent Bookers, located on Dean Street, in Soho. I noted the address and phone number on a piece of paper and decided I needed a leisurely walk in London to help clear my mind. It might as well be to Soho. Besides, I've often found that simply dropping in on someone can be more effective than trying to arrange a meeting in advance. Sometimes it works, sometimes it doesn't, but it was the approach I decided to take.

It was a lovely afternoon as I strolled the streets of Soho. It had, like New York's Times Square, deteriorated because of a proliferation of striptease clubs and sex shops, but they seemed relatively innocuous in the daylight. Unlike the case with Times Square, legitimate business hadn't fled the area, and Soho was still filled with quaint restaurants, fascinating newsstands, and boutiques.

I stopped in at St. Anne's Church, bombed during the war, its tower and clock now faithfully restored. Behind it, in simple graves, were buried Dorothy Sayers, a churchwarden and no relation to the writer, and the *other* Hazlitt, William, no relationship to my friend Seth.

I stopped for tea at the York Minster Pub, known as the French Pub because its owners are probably the only French pub owners in all of Great Britain. Frank and I had enjoyed a beer there before going on to hear jazz at Ronnie Scott's club on Firth Street. Afterward we'd had a scrumptious dinner in the Neal Street Restaurant; I could almost taste the grilled calf kidney I'd had that night, and a dessert I have never experienced again called tiramisu. Those were good memories but, because they could never be repeated, there was also a sense of sadness as I stood in front of the restaurant and looked through the window at the very table we'd shared.

Enough of that, I told myself, continuing my walk. I lingered in Soho Square, then went to Dean Street and looked for the address of Simpson Talent Bookers. I found it easily enough; it was above a strip club called Nell Gwynne's. If the lurid photographs in the window were any indication of what went on inside, it was not a place I was likely to frequent.

I walked up a narrow set of stairs to the floor above the club. The door bearing the name of the agency was open, and I went inside. It was a waiting room, with cheap red and yellow vinyl chairs lined up along the walls, a few occupied by young women dressed either in trendy outfits or in jeans and T shirts. A middle-aged woman with orange hair and long red fingernails tipped with black sat behind a desk reading a magazine. She glanced up, and went back to her page. I approached her and said pleasantly, "My name is Jessica Fletcher. I would appreciate having a few minutes with Mr. Simpson, if he's available."

She looked up, shifted gum from one side of her mouth to the other, pointed to a chair, and said, "Wait your turn."

I cocked my head, was about to say something, then simply followed her instructions and sat, the new handbag Lucas had bought me at Harrods on my lap.

Ten minutes later, a door opened behind the receptionist and a handsome young man stood in the doorway. He wore gray slacks, an expensive, custom-tailored burgundy blazer with gold buttons, a white silk shirt, and a variegated ascot of primarily burgundy and blue. Black hair was carefully arranged on his head. His features were chiseled, and while he certainly was good-looking, there was a discernible cruelty to his mouth.

He looked around the room (undressed everyone is more like it) until his eyes rested upon me. He shook his head and said, "Sorry, I don't have anything for you today."

I got up and approached him, smiled, and said, "Mr. Simpson—"

"Look, I don't know what your gimmick is, but you're a

little long in the tooth for what I have open. Sorry, I'd like to help you out but—"

"Mr. Simpson, I am not here looking for a job as a stripper. My name is Jessica Fletcher, and I would like to speak with you about the death of your stepbrother, Jason Harris."

His expression changed now. He narrowed his eyes and asked, "What are you, a wopsie?"

"I don't think so, but if you would tell me what that means, I might reconsider."

He shook his head. "A policewoman?"

I laughed. "Heavens, no, I am not a policewoman, although I have known some. I am a writer of murder mysteries. I was one of Marjorie Ainsworth's good friends and was unfortunate enough to have been the one to discover her body. I have been in touch with your stepbrother's companion, Maria Giacona." I was pleased he gave me the time to get all that out.

"Look, Mrs. Fletcher, you can see I'm busy. I've got jobs to fill tonight and not enough birds to fill them."

"I can see you're busy, and I don't wish to intrude for more than a few minutes. Couldn't you find those few minutes for me?"

He said to the others in the room, "Are you all available tonight?"

There was a chorus of "Yes."

He said to his receptionist, "Carmela, send these two to Joey over at Raymond's. Then get on the phone and see who you can hustle for these other openings. Come on," he said to me. "Five minutes, no more."

His office was larger than I thought it would be. The walls were covered with the sort of photographs that adorned the windows downstairs, only some of them were much bigger, life-size. In one corner of the room was a small circular platform. Spotlights covered with blue and red gel were trained on it. I assumed that was where young women auditioned for him, to stretch the use of the word. The thing about the office that gained my immediate attention, however, was the overpowering combination of perfume, cologne, makeup, and incense that burned in a bowl on his desk.

"Okay," he said, "what is it you want to talk to me about?"

"As I said, I wanted to discuss Jason Harris's murder. I understand you were called in last night to identify the body."

He sat back in a chair and looked at the ceiling. "Christ, that was something I didn't need. I couldn't believe what they'd done to him."

"Yes, I know, I saw the body this morning."

He sat up straight. "Why did *you* look at his body?"

"Because I was with Maria Giacona. I took her to the police station this morning. She was, as you can imagine, terribly upset."

"Yes, I dare say she would be. They'd been lovers for a while. You met Jason?"

"As a matter of fact, I did, at Marjorie Ainsworth's house the weekend she was killed. Actually, I was to meet him again at his flat. Maria wanted me to talk to him about an allegation that he'd played some part in helping Marjorie Ainsworth write her latest novel, *Gin and Daggers*."

His laugh was small and unpleasant. He lighted a cigarette, drew deeply on it, exhaled the blue smoke into the room—adding yet another odor—and said, "Mrs. Fletcher, Jason didn't help her. He wrote the whole bloody thing."

"I can't believe that," I said.

"Believe what you want, but it's true. I told him he was daft to do it, that he ought to cut himself a better deal, get some kind of credit or at least get a piece of the action. He didn't listen to me. She paid him a bloody pittance to lend his talent to that book, and look where it got him. He's dead, nobody will ever know what a good writer he was, and her estate will make millions off his hard work. I think that stinks, Mrs. Fletcher, and I don't mind telling you that."

"If what you say is true, Mr. Simpson, I can understand your anger—and Maria's too—but whether he did as much with the novel as you claim remains to be seen, at least for me. Under what circumstances did you and Jason become stepbrothers?"

"Simple. Jason's father, an American, married my mother, a Brit."

"And where are they?"

"Both dead, an automobile accident in the States."

"No other family on either side?"

"I have cousins scattered about, but Jason had absolutely no one else. That's why he carried a card indicating that if anything ever happened to him, I was to be called."

"Of course. I'd already assumed that. Were you and Jason involved professionally, in a business sense?"

Simpson looked around his office and laughed. "Jason get involved in this business? No, he stayed far away. We kept our relationship purely social."

"You were good friends, then, as well as stepbrothers."

"Yes."

I thought of Maria's comment about them not liking each other.

"You don't benefit from any success his writing might achieve, do you?"

"Hell, no. Why do you ask that?"

"I don't know. I suppose I'm trying to find out as much as I can about Jason, about his life. Maria tells me that Jason used a number of names and incidents from his own life in *Gin and Daggers* as a way of proving his involvement with it. She says he made notations on the pages of the manuscript, but the manuscript seems to be missing. You wouldn't have a copy of it, would you?"

Simpson shook his head. The door opened and his receptionist said, "I've got a couple more out here."

"Yeah, one minute, don't let them get away." He said to

me, "I'm afraid this is all the time I have, Mrs. Fletcher. It gets this way every afternoon. More clubs open up and need talent, and I make a living providing it."

"Judging from the number of such establishments I've seen in Soho today like the one downstairs, you must be kept very busy. Are they . . . I mean, do you only supply striptease artists?"

"We don't call them that anymore. They're exotic dancers."

"Exotic. Of course. They certainly are."

"I also book ethnic musical groups. If you ever need the best Greek or Arabic band in London, give me a call."

"I will, although I don't think I'll be in the market for that in the near future." I stood and extended my hand. "Thank you, Mr. Simpson. You've been very gracious."

"No problem, Mrs. Fletcher. I'll tell you one thing."

"What's that?"

"That if you want to do something worthwhile in this world, let it know that my brother wrote *Gin and Daggers*."

"I'll certainly think about that. Thank you again."

As I crossed the waiting room, two girls who looked hardly older than teenagers giggled. I stopped, looked at them, and said with as much dignity as I could muster, "I have a gimmick."

I decided to continue my leisurely stroll rather than return right away to the Savoy. Eventually I drifted into neighboring Mayfair, whose quiet elegance contrasted sharply with the more frenetic pace of Soho. I would have attempted to walk back to the Savoy, but I was running late for my drink with Seth and Morton. Besides, as sensible as my shoes were, my feet were beginning to feel the effects of the pavement.

"Well, Jessica, what kind of day did you have?" Seth asked as we sat in the Thames Foyer bar and sipped drinks.

"Absolutely lovely. I took the afternoon to be by myself and to walk around London. Do you know what was especially wonderful? No one recognized me, not a soul."

Morton made a gagging sound.

"What's the matter?" I asked.

"This isn't a martini."

I looked at Seth, and we both started to laugh. I should have warned Morton that when a martini is ordered in London, you generally get a glass of vermouth. The fact that he had specified a dry martini only meant that the vermouth poured over the ice cubes was of the dry variety. "You have to ask for a martini *cocktail*," I said, feeling slightly superior at that knowledge. We motioned for a waiter and put in the new order.

"Tell me what you did and saw today," I said to them.

"Morton wanted to see if we could get a tour of Scotland Yard, but I convinced him we ought to seek out a little more culture while in London. We spent the afternoon at the British Museum."

"Isn't it marvelous?" I said.

Morton, who obviously had not found an afternoon in the sprawling British Museum to be his cup of tea, shook his head and said, "You've seen one museum, you've seen them all, Jess." He looked at Seth: "I wouldn't mind seeing that famous wax museum they've got here in London."

"Madame Tussaud's on Marylebone Road," I said. "I've been there. It's interesting, but I wouldn't put it high on my list of priorities."

After discussing other possibilities for them to visit the next day, they asked what I was doing for dinner. I told them I was free. "Tell you what," I said, "I'll dream up a place for dinner and make a reservation for seven. We'll meet here in the lobby at six-thirty." I had La Tante Claire in mind, a restaurant I'd heard so much about over the years but had never had the opportunity to visit. I also knew it was small and had probably been booked for weeks. I said to Morton as we walked from the bar, "Morton, you will have to change out

148

of your uniform and put on a suit. You did bring a suit with you?"

"Of course I did, Jess, but like I told Seth, having me in uniform will keep us out of trouble on the streets, keep the pickpockets away."

"What a . . . splendid idea. See you at six-thirty."

I called La Tante Claire. "My name is Jessica Fletcher," I said, "and I was wondering whether you could accommodate three people this evening at seven."

"Jessica Fletcher, the famous writer?" he asked in a French accent.

"Yes."

"We keep one table open until six for important customers, Mrs. Fletcher. It is for you, of course."

"Well, I . . . that's very nice of you. Thank you . . . very much."

Morton had changed into a nice brown suit, white shirt, and tie. Seth was his usual well-groomed self; he was always dressed properly, even to go to his driveway in the morning to pick up the newspaper.

We climbed into a cab and told the driver to take us to La Tante Claire, on Royal Hospital Road. I was feeling very relaxed. Lucas had called as I was getting ready for dinner to admonish me for spending so much time away from the ISMW conference. I tried to explain that circumstances had changed, and that they would dictate, to some extent, how I spent the rest of my week. I sounded forthright and full of conviction, but I knew he was right. I promised that I would try to focus more on the conference in the days ahead.

As the cab pulled away from the curb and headed for the Strand, I noticed a large automobile, whose lights had been on, make a three-point U-turn and fall in behind us. It was a Cadillac, originally white but now battered and discolored. It had caught my attention because of its size; you seldom see automobiles like that on London streets. Then, as we happily talked about the gastronomic treat awaiting us, I completely forgot about it.

We pulled up in front of La Tante Claire. Seth, who was now adept at handling British currency, paid the driver, and we moved toward the door of the restaurant. I glanced back; the large white Cadillac had pulled up behind cars half a block away, and the lights had been turned off.

"Strange," I muttered.

"What?" Morton asked.

"Nothing. Come, let's enjoy a wonderful meal together."

"Thank you for accommodating us at the last minute," I told the maître d'hôtel.

"My pleasure, Mrs. Fletcher," he said in his charming accent. "I have been following events surrounding you very carefully. By the way, my wife has read all the French translations of your books."

"How flattering."

"I had one delivered to me when I knew you would be dining with us. I thought perhaps . . ."

He obviously wasn't sure whether he was out of place to be requesting an autograph. He wasn't, of course, and I told him I would be happy to inscribe the book to his wife.

We were shown to what was obviously a prime table. There were only a dozen of them, and ours was in a corner, offering an unobstructed view of the beautiful room, basically white, with some blond wood, blue curtains, lavender-gray armchairs, and portraits of lovely ladies on the walls. The maître d'hôtel handed us expensively printed menus. He also handed me a copy of one of my novels that had been translated.

"What is your wife's name?" I asked.

"Nicole."

I wrote a long inscription, tossing in an occasional French word that I happened to know, and handed it back to him. He beamed and told me his wife would be extremely pleased.

"I don't understand this menu," Morton said.

"Neither do I," I said, "but I intend to fake it."

Seth laughed. He spoke serviceable French, and we allowed him to translate for us, although he did need the help of a waiter on a few items. I knew that Morton would have preferred a steak house where he could order mashed potatoes and corn on the cob. Instead, we had scallop and oyster ragout studded with truffles as an appetizer. "The monkfish with saffron, capers, and celery root sounds wonderful to me," I said. Seth decided to be adventurous and try the fillet of hare with bitter chocolate and raspberry sauce. We both looked at Morton, whose face was screwed up in debate with himself. He decided on lamb with parsley and garlic, and asked timidly, as though he expected to be attacked for asking, "Do you have any mashed potatoes?"

"*Oui.*"

We had a wonderful meal together. Being with them represented something familiar and solid to hold on to, and I reveled in the laughter, the gossip about people in Cabot Cove, and Seth's and Morton's reaction to my recounting again everything that had happened since arriving in London.

We all enjoyed crème brûlée and petits fours with coffee to end the glorious meal, and Morton proclaimed the mashed potatoes the best he'd ever eaten.

When we stepped outside into the clear, fresh air, I breathed deeply and said, "Let's take a walk. I'm in the mood."

We started arm in arm down Royal Hospital Road, almost giddy enough to break into a song and dance. I didn't tell them that my reason for wanting the walk had nothing to do with a need to exercise off some of the dinner. I was aware the moment we had come out of the restaurant that we were being watched by a man across the street. He stood behind the white Cadillac, and I couldn't see him well enough to determine anything about him.

I led the trio around a corner, stopped, and said, "Indulge me a moment. Keep walking. Don't look back. Just keep walking. I'll catch up with you in a second."

They looked quizzically at each other, but did what I asked. I stepped behind a wall that defined the property of a large house and waited. I saw my friends continue up the street, then heard footsteps rounding the corner, stopping for a second, then moving at an accelerated rate. The minute the feet passed me, I stepped out and said, "Excuse me, are you following us?"

Jimmy Biggers turned and looked at me.

"Mr. Biggers, what a pleasant surprise," I said.

"Mrs. Fletcher, I . . ." He smiled and shuffled from one foot to the other. "I was just out taking a walk in the neighborhood."

"I would think your neighborhood walks would take place in Wapping."

"Well, nice to change the scenery every once in a while. What are you doing here?"

"We had dinner at La Tante Claire. Didn't you notice?"

"No, I just got here."

"My friends from Maine and I are taking a walk. We'll probably end up in some pub or hotel bar, extending the evening. Would you care to join us?"

By this time Seth and Morton had decided they'd gone far enough and were on their way back to where Biggers and I stood.

"Are you all right, Jess?" Morton asked, placing himself between Biggers and me. "You're the fella we met this morning in that Red Feather pub," he said.

"Right you are, mate," said Biggers.

I announced my plans for the rest of the evening and suggested we move on.

"No argument from me," Morton said. "I get the creeps out here on the street at night."

"You should have worn your uniform."

"That's what I said, but you told me to wear a suit."

"And you're a darling to do it for me. What do you say we find an archetypal British pub and have ourselves a shandy for a nightcap?"

"What's a shandy?" Seth asked.

"Half a bitter, half lemonade," Biggers said. "Come on, I'll drive us to one of my favorites."

Our vehicle was, of course, the battered white Cadillac.

"We're on Wapping Wall," I said after we'd driven for fifteen minutes.

"Right you are, Mrs. Fletcher, my neighborhood. I feel comfortable over here." We pulled up in front of a pub called the Prospect of Whitby. "The manager's a chum o' mine," Biggers said as he held open the door for me. "I think you'll enjoy it."

Because the pub sat directly on the Thames, and because it dated back to the sixteenth century (the area on which it sat was once known as the "hanging dock," where the infamous Judge Jeffreys would approve of the bodies of his victims hanging in chains, and then enter the tavern to feast), it was dripping with atmosphere and packed with customers, most of them American.

Biggers was greeted warmly and we were led to a scarred table in the darts room. A bouncy, pleasant young waitress, who threatened to burst through her white blouse, gave Biggers a kiss on the cheek and asked what we would be having.

"Friends from America," Biggers said. "Let's give 'em a taste of the good stuff, best bitter for everyone."

"I thought you'd be taking us to the Red Feather," I said.

"Have to admit I'm partial to it, Mrs. Fletcher. Never see a tourist there, but I thought you'd enjoy this place. Lots of postcards sent back to the States from here."

Biggers proved to be an amiable and entertaining drinking companion, although Morton Metzger didn't seem to be enthralled, judging by the perpetual sour expression on his face. Seth, on the other hand, seemed to be enjoying the little Cockney private detective, and they were soon talking, laughing, and slapping each other's backs like old fraternity brothers.

Eventually, after the third round of best bitter had been served (I'd switched to a shandy because I knew I couldn't handle another straight beer), I brought up the subject of Jason Harris's murder.

"Nasty business, that," Biggers said. "Learn anything startling at the coppers this morning?"

"No, just what I mentioned to you at the Red Feather."

"What did that sack o' manure Simpson tell you?"

"Simpson?" I sat back and scrutinized him across the table. "How did you know I saw David Simpson?"

"Me gut told me."

"You've been following me all day, Mr. Biggers."

"Just the latter part of it," he said, "after you woke me up and I put me act together. Simpson's no good, a slimy one, if you catch my drift."

"Because of the business he's in? Yes, I would agree."

"More than that. He's connected."

"Connected? You mean with organized crime?"

"That's what I mean. Tell me, you seem to have become a mother hen of sorts to the Giacona girl."

"Oh no, but I do feel sorry for her. She's a nice person."

"Is she now?"

"Yes . . . she is."

Seth and Morton listened closely to our conversation.

"Mrs. Fletcher—can I call you Jessica?—I had a fling with a bird named Jessica once, lovely thing, but mean-spirited when she drank."

"Yes, call me Jessica."

"All right then, Jessica, you might ask Miss Giacona about David Simpson."

"She's already spoken to me of him. He's her dead lover's stepbrother."

"That may be true, Jessica, but Simpson was also her lover."

"The two of them?"

"Not at once." He laughed loudly, and we all smiled. "She did a bit o' dancin' for Mr. Simpson and he took a shine to her, sort of a favorite."

"She was a stripper . . . exotic dancer?"

"Good, too, real popular. Beautiful bird."

"Yes, she is."

"Yup, David Simpson and she had quite a fling. She didn't mention that to you?"

"No, she didn't."

"Probably a bit embarrassed. More bitter?"

"No, I think it's time we leave."

I insisted upon paying the check, and Biggers drove us back to the Savoy.

"Thank you for escorting us," I said. "It's been a pleasant and educational evening."

"My pleasure, Jessica." He said to Seth, "Enjoyed your company, sir." And to Morton: "I'm really a likable chap once you get to know me."

"I like you."

"Yeah, well, good night, everyone. Sleep well. See you soon."

"I *don't* like him," Morton said as we entered the hotel.

"I do," said Seth.

I said, "I'm not sure whether I like him or not, but I have a feeling I'm going to learn a lot more from him before this little London escapade is over."

Chapter

15

I had trouble falling asleep after returning from the evening with Seth, Morton, and Jimmy Biggers, and turned to *Gin and Daggers*, which I read for nearly two hours before drifting off.

I wasn't reading for pleasure this time; my first read had provided that. This time I concentrated on characters and events that might possibly link up with people and episodes from Jason Harris's life. It was an impossible task. How could I know whether the name given to a certain character had relevance where Jason was concerned? I also knew that if Jason had included real names, it would have violated a steadfast principle of Marjorie Ainsworth's—that real names never be used in any novel. Some authors will inadvertently, or deliberately, name characters after people they know, either because the name comes easily to them, or because they wish to give a friend or family member a special treat while reading the book. Not Marjorie. She considered that practice to be patently amateurish, and it didn't take much to get her up on her soapbox on the subject.

My meeting with Jason's stepbrother, David Simpson, had

been entirely too cursory, and I decided to contact him again. Had Simpson read either the manuscript or the finished book? If so, he probably had some inkling as to which references Jason used to establish his authorship—provided he had lent a creative hand to it. I still had my doubts about that, although I had to admit to myself that after reading a major portion of *Gin and Daggers* for the second time, I could certainly discern a change from the Marjorie Ainsworth writing style with which I was so familiar. Yes, it was possible that another hand had played a part in writing the book. That didn't mean, however, that it was Jason Harris's.

I thought about Marjorie's failing health over the past few years, and how she had dictated a great deal of her correspondence to her niece, Jane. I'd once tried dictating one of my own novels and had found the process excruciating. Not only that, what came out in the transcription of the tapes was a markedly different style from when I sat at my trusty typewriter and pecked away word after word, sentence after sentence. I did, of course, heavily edit the transcript of the dictation, which brought the finished manuscript into line with my hunt-and-peck style. Even then there was some change. Could this explain the difference in *Gin and Daggers*? Perhaps. The only person who might provide insight would be Jane Portelaine, and based upon my brief exchange with her at the cemetery, I doubted whether she would welcome such a conversation with me. But she had suggested I call her if I wished to spend time at Ainsworth Manor before returning to Cabot Cove, and I intended to take her up on it.

My first thought upon awakening the next morning was Maria Giacona. Was Jimmy Biggers telling the truth about her life as an exotic dancer and her affair with Jason's stepbrother? I suspected he had been truthful, and it perplexed me. I wanted to call Maria, but I had no idea where to reach her. She'd never given me an address or telephone number, aside from Jason's flat, and I doubted whether she would be staying there. But on the chance that she might, I went to the London telephone directory looking for a Jason Harris. No listing; he had either not had a telephone or had requested he be excluded from the book.

I made my usual list of what I intended to accomplish that day: call on David Simpson, and stop by Jason's flat in the hope that I might catch Maria there.

I received a call after breakfast from Marjorie Ainsworth's solicitor, a huffy man named Chester Gould-Brayton, who spoke in slow, sonorous tones. He said, "Mrs. Fletcher, it occurred to me that you might wish to be present at the formal reading of Ms. Ainsworth's last will and testament."

"I'd wondered whether I'd be invited, considering I've been included in it," I said, "but I certainly wouldn't be offended if I weren't. I don't intend to accept whatever money she's left me. I prefer to donate it to the study center that I understand is to be established with the majority of the estate."

"That, of course, is your decision, Mrs. Fletcher, although I have known more than one person who took such an altruistic stance in the beginning, then succumbed to the temptation of large money."

I was offended at his comment and told him so.

"As you wish, Mrs. Fletcher. The reading will be at four this afternoon in my office." He gave me the address.

The ISMW panel at which the relative merits of large cities versus small towns as settings for murder mysteries was discussed turned out to be, in my estimation, a monumental bore. The others on the panel tried to outprecious one another, as a certain ilk of writer is prone to do, and I found myself with little to offer. I was delighted when it ended and I could get on with the rest of my day. I was free until a dinner that night sponsored by Marjorie's British publisher, Archibald Semple. I was glad I'd been able to have dinner with Seth and Morton the previous night because I didn't see another evening together for the rest of the week.

I had a half-dozen invitations for lunch that day but politely declined all of them. Seth and Morton had left a message that they were off to do some sightseeing and shopping. I knew Seth was eager to explore the possibility of having a suit made on Savile Row. Once he saw the prices, however, I had a suspicion he would shelve the idea in favor of off-the-rack selections back in Bangor. Morton's hobby was collecting toy soldiers, and he'd heard about a shop called Under Two Flags that specialized in English and Scottish regiments. That was obviously on their agenda, too. It was good they were entertaining themselves because I'd decided that I would indeed attend the reading of Marjorie's will after taking care of the two other items on my list.

The Liverpool Street Station area was far less ominous in broad daylight. I made a point of walking up the street on which I'd been mugged and stopping on the spot where the young man had stepped out from behind the packing crates. I would probably always stop there on subsequent visits to London. "It happened right here," I would tell whomever I was with, increasing my attacker's height each time, and embellishing my fearless defense of my purse.

I entered Jason's building and went upstairs. The black door to his flat was locked. I looked through the open door into the flat across the tiny landing, and assumed it was where the man lived who had come to the door the night I was in Jason's flat with Maria. I peered inside. Aside from a few scattered pieces of furniture, it seemed to be uninhabited.

"'Ere now, what might you be lookin' for?" a shrill female voice said from the landing below.

I looked down the stairs and saw an old woman with frizzy hair and thick glasses, wearing a housedress and carpet slippers. "I was looking for . . ." I couldn't say Jason Harris. "I was looking for the young lady who was a friend of Mr. Harris."

"'Aven't seen that bint since 'e got 'is throat slit. Who are you?"

"A friend of the family. The man who lives across the hall. I met him the other night and—"

"God blind me, talkin' about the likes of him. The bugger scarpered out in the middle of the night, owes me rent, too, he does."

"I'm sorry to hear that," I said, coming down a few steps. "What was his name?"

"Maroney, if you believe 'im. Probably got 'imself a dozen of 'em. Blokes like 'im usually do. You a family friend of 'is, too? Maybe you'd like to pay up for 'im."

"No, I only met him briefly. You say Mr. Harris's friend, the attractive young woman named Maria, hasn't been here?"

"Not that I've seen, only I don't spend my day snoopin' on me tenants."

I bet you don't, I thought. I said, "Well, I think I'll leave a note on Mr. Harris's door if you don't mind."

"Harris owed me rent, too. You say you're a friend of the family? How about payin' 'is rent?"

"I'm not *that* much of a friend. Excuse me." I wrote a brief note asking Maria to call me, and slipped it under Jason's door.

I descended to the ground floor, the landlady yelling after me every step that no one had any sense of honor or decency anymore, that all she ended up with in the building was bums, and that she intended only to rent to "proper ladies" from now on. I wasn't sure how many "proper ladies" would be interested in living in that building, but you never knew. Then again, how did she intend to define "proper ladies"?

I moved on to Soho and David Simpson's talent agency. The waiting room was filled with young women of varying shades, sizes, and dress. Simpson would have no trouble filling openings for exotic dancers that night. Carmela, the receptionist, was in her usual pose behind the desk, reading a magazine and chewing gum. I asked for Mr. Simpson, and she curtly told me he was gone for the day.

"Will he be here tomorrow?" I asked.

She shrugged. "Wouldn't I like to know that? He owes me pay."

I left feeling as though I'd touched base with the Debtors' Society of London. It was three o'clock; an hour to go before Marjorie's will was read. I hadn't eaten, and stopped in the Soho Brasserie for a sandwich and soft drink, then headed for Mr. Gould-Brayton's office on Newgate Street, where the Roman and mediaeval wall dissects it.

As I entered the spacious, richly paneled, and sedate surroundings of Gould-Brayton & Partners office, I expected to see very few people. Certainly Jane Portelaine would be on hand, as might those members of the household staff who were named in the will. Instead, the conference room looked like a re-creation, minus food, of the dinner party at Ainsworth Manor the night Marjorie died. There were some notable exceptions; Jason Harris, of course, wasn't there, nor was William Strayhorn, the London book reviewer. The other missing personages included Sir James Ferguson, the theatrical producer, and Clayton Perry's wife, Reneé.

I was seated next to Count Antonio Zara, who held out my chair for me and, I suspect, had intentions of kissing my hand, which I deftly avoided by wrapping both of them around my purse.

Mr. Gould-Brayton looked the way he sounded, terribly overweight, dark three-piece suit with gold chain draped across his large belly, and rimless spectacles, and, I was certain, had bad breath, although I wasn't close enough to confirm that supposition.

My assumption that Jane Portelaine would be there had been confirmed the moment I entered the reception area. Victorian posy hung heavy in the air and dominated the conference room.

Jane sat across the large mahogany conference table from me, flanked by American agent Bruce Herbert, and American publisher Clayton Perry. Her appearance this afternoon interested me. She wore lipstick, just a touch, but surprising nonetheless. She'd done something with her hair that allowed it to fall with more softness about her face. Her nails appeared to have been freshly manicured, and a subtle rose-colored nail polish, the same shade as her lipstick, had been expertly applied. Her dress, too, was different, although not dramatically so. She wore a teal blouse and had left the top button open, of all things. A simple chain suspended the gold letters of her name above her bosom. The heavy gray cardigan sweater seemed the only throwback to how I'd always remembered her, although I couldn't see her skirt and shoes.

"Hello, Jane," I said.

She smiled at me. "Hello, Mrs. Fletcher. It's good to see you again."

What a change from our strained conversation at the graveside.

"Bloody shame we meet again like this," said Archibald Semple, Marjorie's British publisher. "We'll have a more festive atmosphere this evening at dinner. I trust you are joining us, Mrs. Fletcher."

"Yes, and looking forward to it, Mr. Semple."

Bruce Herbert, whose suit looked as though it had come minutes ago from Tommy Nutter or Henry Poole on Savile Row, leaned as far as he could over the table and asked, "Have you given any thought to the suggestion?"

"What suggestion?"

"About the nonfiction account of this tragedy."

"Oh no, no further thought at all, Mr. Herbert. It really doesn't interest me." Herbert sat back. The broad, engaging smile that had been on his face disappeared, and he cast a sideward glance at Clayton Perry, who sat in his usual bolt-upright posture, tanned hands folded neatly on the table. Perry smiled; I returned the smile.

"Well now, ladies and gentlemen," Mr. Gould-Brayton intoned, "we might as well get to this painful but necessary business." He looked across the room to where a young assistant stood at attention. Gould-Brayton didn't have to say anything to him. The young man opened the door and motioned to someone, and a young female stenographer came to a small desk at Gould-Brayton's side and poised her fingers over the keyboard of a court stenographer's machine.

Marjorie's will turned out to be novella-length. I didn't want to be impudent, but I couldn't help but smile at so many of the preliminary comments she included in it. She seemed to have used the opportunity to expound on matters dear to her, including her growing disgust with brooding, discourteous, and unpleasant young people behind shop counters; television programs that insult the intelligence of anyone with an IQ slightly above moronic; writers who use the word "enthused" rather than "enthusiastic"; frozen food; women who wear fur coats; and myriad other aspects of life she found disagreeable. Mr. Gould-Brayton was obviously embarrassed at having to read all of this. He stopped once, smiled, and said through fleshy lips, "She was a writer, after all." We all laughed nervously, and he continued, evidently content that he had sufficiently distanced himself from this client who viewed a last will and testament as more than simply a division of spoils.

"She should have videotaped this," Bruce Herbert said. "I can see her now delivering these protestations against society."

Mr. Gould-Brayton looked at Herbert, closed his heavy eyelids as though to ask whether he were through, then returned his attention to the typewritten pages in front of him.

Eventually he reached the financial portion of the will, and I noticed everyone sit up a little straighter. Gould-Brayton paused for effect, removed his spectacles and held them up to the light to ascertain they were clean enough for accurate reading, placed them on his nose, and read, " 'I have made far more money then any human being is entitled to make, and have spent very little of it, my frugality a source of constant annoyance to local shopkeepers and telephone solicitors attempting to sell me magazines that would surely go unread. Because of my lifelong dedication to cheeseparing, I am able to leave behind a substantial sum of money, most of it undoubtedly to be squandered, some of it to be used wisely only because I have taken the steps necessary to ensure that.' " Gould-Brayton looked up at us. "Any questions?" he asked.

We all shook our heads.

He continued. " 'I hereby bequeath one half of my estate, presently accounted for and to be earned through the future sale of my books, to a trust to be named the Marjorie Ainsworth International Study Center for Mystery Writers, to be housed at Ainsworth Manor, and to be stocked with every available reference source the trustees are able to obtain.' "

"Hear, hear," said Archibald Semple. "The woman was a benefactor to her profession, a saint. How splendid to have such a center here in Great Britain."

Gould-Brayton cleared his throat for order. " 'Because my niece and companion of many years, Jane Portelaine, has, at least from her perspective, given up her life for me, I leave to her one quarter of my estate, currently accounted for and to be earned in the future.' " Jane managed a smile and looked down at the table, her hands clasped in front of her.

" 'To my dear friend and American colleague, Jessica Fletcher, I leave one eighth of my estate, present money only. Her earnings in the days ahead from her wonderful works of fiction will ensure her future without any help from me.' "

I blushed and shook my head. "That is so generous, but

165

as I told Mr. Gould-Brayton, I intend to donate whatever money my share amounts to to the center Marjorie has established."

"Very generous of you, Jessica," said Bruce Herbert.

Archibald Semple's wife tapped the ends of her fingers together and said, "Bravo, Mrs. Fletcher. How typically American."

" 'Next, to my dear friend, critic William Strayhorn, who always had kind things to say about my books, the only exception being his occasional annoyance at how often I mention food in them, which, I might add, I do to substitute for the singular lack of sex in the genre—' "

I laughed; I couldn't help it. Everyone looked at me. "Sorry," I said. "Please continue."

" '. . . I leave the sum of twenty thousand pounds for the day when he is no longer able to enjoy either sex or food.' "

"Shame he isn't here," Semple said.

"Just as well that he isn't," said Bruce Herbert.

Gould-Brayton again checked his glasses for dirt, drew in a deep, rumbling breath to maintain his reading momentum, and pressed on. " 'My faithful household staff, with the exception of the newcomer, Marshall, are to be cared for in Ainsworth Manor for the rest of their days, their salary doubled from the date of my demise.' "

"It is nice to see she kept the common man in mind," Count Zara said, to which his wife, Ona, mumbled, "Let them eat cake. They don't deserve a penny."

Gould-Brayton asked his assistant for a glass of water. After he'd drunk it (the room was so quiet you could hear the liquid cascading down his throat and into his belly), he said, "There are still other disbursements to be announced. I must admit that in all my years in the legal profession, I have yet to see such provisions in any other will, although, I must admit, Miss Ainsworth was . . . how shall we say it, an unusual individual." He looked at Ona Ainsworth-Zara. "I indicated to you, Mrs. Ainsworth-Zara, that it might be less painful for you and your husband not to have attended this gathering. If you would like to leave now, I am sure everyone would understand."

"Go on, read," said Marjorie's younger sister.

"Poor thing," said the count. "She was not herself in her last days."

"I thought she was at her intellectual best right up until the end," said Bruce Herbert.

"Enough," Gould-Brayton said. "Let me proceed. 'To my younger sister, Ona, who saw fit to marry into Italian aristocracy and suffer the inevitable impoverishment inherent in such an act, I consider my debt paid. The money I have given them over the years far surpasses what my instincts would tell me to leave them after my departure from this earth. I do, however, leave to my beloved brother-in-law, Count Zara, as he prefers to call himself, a fat envelope of bills from the clothing stores, gourmet food shops, hotels, alcoholic beverage establishments, and other purveyors of the good life that he had made such generous use of. I have not paid these bills; I trust he will see to it that the debts are honored forthwith.' "

"Preposterous," Zara exclaimed, standing and slamming his fist on the table. "Those were gifts to me from Marjorie." He looked down at his wife. "Weren't they, Ona, gifts from your sister? She always told me that I was her favorite."

"Pay them, Tony, and let's get on with this bloody circus."

" 'To my loyal and accomplished American publisher, Clayton Perry, and my devoted literary agent, Bruce Herbert, I leave two things. First, the large sums of money I have loaned Mr. Perry are to be forgiven at the time of my death. By doing this, I trust the publishing house that Perry built, constantly tottering on the verge of bankruptcy and worse, will be able to sustain itself for a period of time, which means the American reading public will continue to have access to my books. Second, I forgive Mr. Herbert and Mr. Perry for all the royalties they have stolen from me over the years, and assure them that I have not instructed those I leave behind to pursue that matter with the sort of professional diligence that would undoubtedly uncover these thefts.' "

"I can't believe she wrote that," Herbert said.

"She was obviously demented when she did," Clayton Perry said, only his lips moving.

"Of course, that is what I said," the count said. "This entire will must be contested."

Gould-Brayton said, "I think I should read this next paragraph rather quickly. 'At the time these provisions have been read, I assume those in the room such as my American publisher and agent, and my beloved brother-in-law, are calling me demented and demanding that the will be contested. Good luck.' "

Gould-Brayton sat back in his tall, wide leather armchair.

"There's nothing else?" Archibald Semple said. "She didn't mention me?"

"I am just taking a breather to break the tension in the room," said the solicitor. "Shall I proceed?"

"Yes, please do," Semple said, grabbing his wife's hand and squeezing it, evidently hurting her because she made a face and emitted a tiny squeal. He let go and focused his attention on Gould-Brayton, who'd cleaned his glasses and was once again hunched over Marjorie Ainworth's will.

" 'To my friend and producer of the most successful dramatic adaptation of any of my books, *Who Killed Darby and Joan?*,' Sir James Ferguson, I leave all future royalties from that work, beginning at the moment of my death, and to last in perpetuity. It is my wish that Sir James use the extra money to foster young and deserving theatrical talent in London, although I imagine the overhead of his rather overdone home in Belgravia, and his penchant for expensive young women, will preclude that act of artistic generosity. So be it. I feel compelled to do this, although I can't possibly tell you why.' "

"Come on, come on," Semple said.

Gould-Brayton scowled at the British publisher, who laughed nervously and looked at his watch. "It's just that we have another appointment," Semple said.

"Yes, quite," said the solicitor. " 'My British publisher for many years, Archibald Semple, has undoubtedly stolen from me just as my American business partners have. I forgive him, too, and will not press the matter from the grave.' "

"That's a bloody lie," Semple said.

This time his wife took *his* hand and said, "Ssssh, Archie, your colitis."

" 'Still, Archie has displayed friendship to me over these many years, and if he has stolen from me, he has managed to do it with appropriate British reserve, as opposed to his American colleagues. Therefore, in honor of this discretion on his part, I leave him the sum of twenty thousand pounds with which to buy his wife some new and more appropriate clothing, and for him to buy a decent toupee. He may do with the balance what he wishes.' "

"She didn't have to be quite so testy about it," Semple said, sitting back relieved that he had received a decent sum.

Gould-Brayton looked at his watch. "I shan't keep you much longer. There is one final provision."

I knew that everyone at the table was trying to imagine who'd not been mentioned, positively or negatively. We all looked at the large solicitor as he read the final codicil in the will. " 'To my former lover, who shall be known only to my solicitor and executor, the most decent man I have ever known, I leave a yearly sum, to be determined by him, to ensure that he spends the rest of his days on this earth in the style to which he is accustomed. When he is no longer of this life, I look forward to once again sharing my bed with him in a higher, grander setting.' "

There were gasps around the table. "Lover? I didn't know Marjorie ever had a lover," said Semple.

"Who the hell is he?" Bruce Herbert asked.

Marjorie's sister, Ona, and her husband stood. She said, "Good day."

"Ona, do you know this lover Marjorie has mentioned?" Bruce Herbert asked.

"I know nothing of my sister's private life. Excuse us, please."

We all eventually drifted from the conference room, rode down on the elevator together, and stood on Newgate Street.

"Fascinating," I said.

"An infuriating, insulting session," Clayton Perry said. "Her nasty side certainly came out."

"I might consider libel action if I were you," Bruce Herbert said to the publisher.

"I think that's a stupid idea, Bruce."

I rode alone in a taxi back to the Savoy, Gould-Brayton's voice buzzing in my ears. I wished I had a tape recording of the reading. It was, as Clayton Perry said, infuriating and insulting to certain people. It was also devilishly typical of my departed friend.

There were a sizable number of the press waiting outside the Savoy. I walked through them saying, "No comment." The only thing on my mind was Marjorie's unnamed paramour. While I was filled with natural curiosity about who this mysterious gentleman was, my overriding thought was how nice it was that she'd had such a meaningful and close relationship during her life. "Good girl, Marjorie," I said aloud.

"Pardon?" the desk clerk said.

"I just came from a celebration of life." I said, and strode toward the elevators feeling very good indeed.

Chapter
16

The dinner hosted by Archibald Semple and his wife for selected members of ISMW was, as might be predicted, flat. The reading of the will had taken the starch out of Archie, Clayton Perry, and Bruce Herbert, and everyone went through the motions of making small talk until dessert had been consumed and we could escape. The only item from the will that was brought up was Marjorie's mystery lover. Everyone was naturally bursting with curiosity about his identity. I had mixed emotions about it. On the one hand, I would have loved to meet the man who had played such a precious role in Marjorie's life. On the other hand, it was only fitting that the world's greatest mystery writer should have a mystery lover.

As I came into the lobby looking for Seth and Morton, I spotted Jimmy Biggers seated in a chair, reading a newspaper. "Mr. Biggers, how unsurprising to see you here."

He looked over the paper, smiled, stood, and said, "I didn't want to let a day go by without making contact with you. What did you think of your friend's final wishes?"

I looked down at the newspaper in his hand: It was a late

171

evening edition, and details of the will had been hastily crammed into a box on page one. "Interesting" was all I said.

"Yes, it does open up some *interesting* possibilities, doesn't it?"

"Such as?"

"Well, a few motives came out of that reading, I'd say."

I'd thought the same thing, but really hadn't dwelled on it.

"You an' me should get together and discuss it in a little more depth," he said.

"Perhaps, but not now. I'm looking for my friends from home."

"Gone out to a gentlemen's club, they 'ave," he said.

"How do you know where they are?"

"Because they asked me for my recommendation, and I gave it to them."

"Gentlemen's club?"

"Yes, and a good one, the Office."

"Sounds like a business meeting to me," I said.

"That's the beauty of it, Jessica. Husbands call their wives and tell them they'll be late at 'the Office,' and they say it without feelin' too bloody guilty."

"I see, and what does 'the Office' offer my friends?"

"Pretty ladies, decent drinks, and a hell of a tab at night's end. I'm sure they'll fill you in on everything . . . well, maybe not *everything*."

I got his point and didn't ask any further questions.

"Excuse me, Mrs. Fletcher, I don't mean to intrude, but . . ."

I turned to face Renée Perry, who'd been at the dinner I'd come from and, as far as I was concerned, seemed to have suffered through it with even more difficulty than the rest of us. "No bother," I said.

We stepped away from Biggers.

"Mrs. Fletcher, I must talk to you."

"Fine."

"I'd like to get out of here, go where we can be alone. Would you take a walk with me?"

"Of course. Excuse me." I told Biggers I'd be gone for a while.

"Care for a male escort?" he asked.

"No, I don't think that will be necessary, but thank you for offering."

It was a balmy night, rendering Renée's fur coat superfluous. What would Marjorie have thought? My mugger of the other night came to mind, and I hoped there wasn't a team of them out this night sniffing for mink.

We walked without saying much of anything—"London is so beautiful"; "Clayton and I had tea at the Dorchester"; "They say a boat ride up the Thames is delightful"; "How unfortunate that Marjorie's death marred the conference and the week in England"—and then found ourselves in front of a small wine bar called Woodhouse's.

"Care for a glass of wine, Jessica?"

"That's a nice idea. It looks charming."

Woodhouse's was virtually empty. We settled at a table by the window and ordered individual glasses of white wine. After it was served, Renée Perry looked at me, opened her mouth to say something, then lowered her head.

"What's wrong?" I asked. "I know some of the things said today in the lawyer's office must have been upsetting to your husband, but—"

"It goes far deeper than that, Jessica."

I sat back and opened my eyes as an indication that I was receptive to whatever she wished to say next.

"Are you aware, Jessica, that Marjorie wrote a novel that was never published?"

"No, but that wouldn't strike me as terribly unusual. Most writers, especially successful ones with long careers, have early unsold works in the trunk, as they say."

She shook her head. "I'm not talking about an early work.

I'm talking about a novel that was written just before *Gin and Daggers*."

"*Before Gin and Daggers*? Why wasn't it published?"

"I don't know, but I do know it exists. The title of it is *Brandy and Blood*."

I smiled. "*Brandy and Blood. Gin and Daggers*. It sounds as though Marjorie was launching into a series at her advanced age, an alcoholic beverage in every title instead of a color, as in John D. MacDonald's novels."

"Perhaps. I don't know what her motivation was, but it was written, and never submitted to Mr. Semple, or to my husband."

"Why not?"

She took a sip of her wine and then said, "Because, Jessica, Bruce Herbert stole it."

"Gracious, that's quite an accusation. Are you certain?"

"Yes, I am. It's why he murdered her."

I suppose you could call it the "layered shock approach" —hit you with one, then quickly hit you with another. Whatever it might be called, it worked, and I was without words.

"I've considered going to the authorities, Jessica, but I'm afraid it might implicate my husband."

"How would Clayton be implicated?" I asked. "He knows about the manuscript?"

"Yes, he does. Don't misunderstand me. I'm not suggesting that he had anything to do with stealing it, but because he and Bruce are such close friends and working colleagues, Bruce naturally made him aware of it."

"Because he wants your husband to publish it."

"I'm not so certain about that, although Clayton thinks so. The fact is, Bruce Herbert will sell it to whoever will pay top dollar. He isn't what you'd call the most ethical of people."

I took another sip of wine. "How could he have stolen it, Renée? Wouldn't Marjorie have raised a beef?"

She smiled ruefully. "Exactly. That's why he killed her."

"Let me ask you something very directly, and hope for an answer containing nothing except hard-nosed fact. Are you certain, without question, that not only did Bruce Herbert steal this manuscript, but he murdered Marjorie Ainsworth, too?"

She silently stared at me before saying softly, "No. I mean, I know he stole the manuscript, but I certainly can't prove he murdered her."

I asked, "Didn't Marjorie ask him why this novel of hers wasn't being published? She obviously knew that anything she put her name on would be instantly gobbled up, if not by Perry House, then by any one of fifty other publishers."

"She did ask him, as I understand it, and he told her he considered it so special that he wanted to have time to think about the proper way to market it."

"And she accepted that?"

"Yes. With all Marjorie Ainsworth's insight and intelligence, she could be remarkably naïve and easily led."

"I see. Why are you telling me this?"

"Because I have tremendous respect for you, am well aware that you are the one person who had nothing to gain by Marjorie's death, and because not only are you recognized as a fine writer of murder mysteries; you've ended up solving many real murders yourself. Is that sufficient?"

"More than sufficient, although the compliments are hardly justified. You say I'm the only one with nothing to gain. Obviously, you're including your husband in the group who would benefit from Marjorie's death."

She'd been reticent and sedate during the conversation. My comment brought forth animation for the first time. "Jessica, my husband did not kill Marjorie Ainsworth. Bruce Herbert did."

Up until that moment I had assigned a certain credence to what she'd been saying. Now, as I looked at this beautiful and expensively dressed woman across from me, I wondered whether this pointing of fingers at Bruce Herbert was, in fact, designed to point fingers away from her husband. I couldn't ask that directly, of course, but it stayed with me as we finished our wine, she paid the check, and we retraced our steps to the Savoy.

We paused in the lobby. "I'm putting tremendous faith in you, Jessica, telling you this. Will you talk to the London authorities?"

"I don't know. I'm not sure what you've told me would warrant that."

"I only ask because I know you're on friendly terms with that Scotland Yard inspector."

George Sutherland. I'd like to have said I'd forgotten about him, but that was hardly the case. The fact was, I thought about him often, the warm and pleasant conversations we'd had, and the cold shoulder he'd given me at the funeral. I said to Renée Perry, "I'll think about what I might do with what you've told me. If I decide to do anything, I'll certainly let you know."

"I can't ask for more. Thank you, Jessica. Have a good evening."

I watched her elegant, tall figure swathed in mink cross the lobby and disappear around a bend. Was she being sincere and forthright, or was this a calculated move to establish a field in which any suspicion would be diverted from her handsome publisher husband? According to Marjorie's will, she'd accused him, along with Bruce Herbert, of stealing money from her, although she'd dismissed it in a charmingly cavalier manner. The loan she claimed to have given him was another matter. More substance to that. Depending upon how large it was, it could certainly provide motive for murder.

"Enjoy your walk?" Jimmy Biggers asked me.

"Still here? Yes, we had a lovely walk, just the thing to get over a large meal."

He smiled, narrowed his eyes, and tapped me on the shoulder with his index finger. It was a strange action for him to take; was he about to attack me, give me a push? No, it was just his way of getting my attention for what he was about to say next. "Jessica, a word of warning. You're much too visible in the way you're going about this. People are talking. You don't want to end up like Marjorie Ainsworth."

His words had their intended effect. "Do you know something I don't?" I asked.

He flashed his nicotine-stained teeth and moved his head back and forth, as he was wont to do. "Absolutely not, Jessica Fletcher, but I will tell you that I like you, have respect for you, and don't want to see you floating face down in the Thames like the Harris chap."

"How do I avoid that, Jimmy?" I asked.

"That, Jessica, is the subject of our breakfast meeting tomorrow morning."

"I wasn't aware that we had a 'breakfast meeting.' "

"I think we should. Meet me at eight o'clock at the Red Feather. They'll whip us up a proper English breakfast, and I'll tell you what's on my mind. You'll be there?"

What else could I say? "Yes."

Chapter

17

Because the Red Feather was close to the Metropolitan Special Constabulary on Wapping Wall, it was a popular hangout for police from that division. When I walked in at precisely eight o'clock the next morning, Biggers was sitting with Inspector Half and three other uniformed officers. He bounced up and met me just inside the door. "Good morning to you, Jessica, right on time. Punctuality. I like punctuality."

"I try my best," I said. "I see you know Inspector Half."

Biggers laughed. "Know 'em all, all good chums o' mine. Care to join 'em, or would you rather we take another table?"

"Whatever pleases you, Mr. Biggers. I'm here by your invitation."

"Let's find us a spot where we can talk in private." That spot turned out to be a table tucked in the darts room. Biggers ordered a full English breakfast for both of us—fresh-squeezed orange juice, porridge with cream, fried eggs, crisp bacon, well-done sausages, kippered herring, and an excellent pot of coffee.

"This is delicious," I said.

"Not quite up to the Goring, but better than most." I'd had one of the famed English breakfasts at the Goring Hotel, and the Red Feather's was almost as good.

After our plates had been cleared and the waitress poured fresh coffee, I said to Jimmy Biggers, "This has been a very pleasant start to my day. I'd like to know, though, why you invited me here. You said you had something to discuss with me."

"Simple, Jessica, I need me a client."

"Really? From what I understand, you're never without one."

"True, but I'm talking about a big client, somebody I can hang me hat on. I've always got me share of wives wanting their husbands followed, insurance fraud cases, all the run-of-the-mill stuff, but I like big cases, ones that really keep me mind working."

"You mean cases of the magnitude of Sir Reginald Pickings."

"How'd you know about that one?"

"Someone told me."

"Well, you're right."

"Obviously, the murder of Marjorie Ainsworth would qualify."

"Right again."

"I've wondered why you've stayed so close to the people involved. Frankly, I assumed you were working for someone already."

"Not yet." He stared at me.

"Are you suggesting that I hire you as a private investigator?"

"Actually, they call us inquiry agents here in Great Britain, but I like the American way. Gumshoe? That's a good one. Call me what you will."

"Mr. Biggers, I don't need a . . . gumshoe."

"Worried about the money?"

"The money? Of course not."

"No need, 'cause I'm offerin' my services off the cuff, gratis, no charge."

"I'm sorry, I don't understand."

"Let's just say I wouldn't mind bein' the investigator who helps the famous Jessica Fletcher solve the murder of the world's greatest mystery writer, Marjorie Ainsworth. From what I understand—and I've done a bit of checkin' on you—you've knocked off as many murderers in real life as you have in your books."

I laughed; I didn't know how else to respond.

Biggers nodded his head and narrowed his eyes as he said, "I'm serious."

"Yes, I can see that. Actually, I would like to help solve Marjorie's murder. She happened to be a very dear friend of mine."

He sat back and grinned. "What say, Jessica, you and me work together, figure out who killed Marjorie Ainsworth, and all I ask is for some public credit. Good for my business, wouldn't you say, to be hooked up with the likes of you?"

Somehow, what he was offering had a certain appeal. His knowledge of London, especially its less obvious aspects, would be helpful. "I'll think about it," I said.

"All right, but don't take too long. I just might end up solvin' this one on my own."

He wangled a promise from me that I would call him as soon as possible with my answer. I thanked him for breakfast, we shook hands, and he called a cab that transported me back to the Savoy. Seth and Morton were having breakfast in the dining room, and I joined them.

"Tell me all about your fling last night," I said.

Seth glanced at Morton, whose face had a slightly green tinge to it. Seth said, "We went to a very exclusive club, compliments of your Mr. Biggers."

"*Compliments* of him? He told me he'd recommended it, that's all."

"That's what I mean. Naturally, we would never have considered going to such a place if it had not been so highly recommended by a native like him."

I smiled and looked down at the table. "I won't ask any more questions," I said.

"I learned one thing," Morton said.

I looked up. "What's that?"

"There's lots of beautiful young French ladies in London who were born in Sweden."

"Where've you been this morning?" Seth asked me.

"Having breakfast at the Red Feather with Jimmy Biggers. He's made me a business proposition."

Seth frowned. "I wouldn't trust him, Jess. You're not thinking of putting up any money in some scheme of his."

"No, of course not. He wants us—him and me—to solve Marjorie Ainsworth's murder together."

"I don't like the sound of that," said Morton.

"I told him I would give him an answer as soon as I could. Frankly, I'm tempted. He seems to be a veritable fount of information, and I'd like to be on the receiving end of it."

"Jess . . ." Seth said, placing his hand on mine.

"Let's face it," I said, "I've already been sticking my nose into Marjorie's murder: one, because she was a good friend, and two, because I have been a suspect all along, and three, because obviously I was born with an extra gene that makes me the way I am." I quickly changed the subject and asked what their plans were. They said they intended to take it easy that day, which didn't surprise me, considering the way they looked after their boys' night out.

As I stood to leave, Seth asked me about the reading of Marjorie's will.

"It was fascinating."

"And she did leave you something?"

"Left me quite a bit, although I am donating it back to the

study center she created. I'll fill you in on the details later. Have to run. Enjoy your day of leisure."

I went up to my suite and picked up the telephone. There was no answer at Jimmy Biggers's office-apartment above the Red Feather, so I found the number of the pub itself and called it. He was still there; the owner put him on the line.

"You've got yourself a client, Mr. Biggers."

"Good girl, Jess. You've made a very wise decision."

"That will be determined when this is over. In the meantime, I'd like you to do two things for me. First, see if you can find Maria Giacona. Second, learn everything you can about the relationship between Jason Harris and David Simpson."

"Whoa now, slow down, I'm not sure I like havin' a woman give me orders like this."

"I thought you wanted me to be your client."

"That's right, but—"

"Well, as I've always been taught, clients tell those working for them what to do."

"Behind that pleasant, feminine façade, you are a tough duck, Mrs. Fletcher."

"Only when I'm a client, Jimmy. Will you do those things for me?"

"You bet. Just testing, seein' how far I can go. Where will you be later in the day?"

"I don't know, but you can leave a message with the hotel and I'll get back to you. Thanks again for breakfast. It was excellent."

I changed into a sweat suit and running shoes I'd brought with me and went downstairs with the intention of finding a pleasant jogging path along the Victoria Embankment on the river.

"Mrs. Fletcher," a familiar male voice said. It was Montgomery Coots, the Crumpsworth inspector.

"Yes, Inspector?"

"On your way for a run, are you?" he asked, moving up and down on his toes.

"Yes, as a matter of fact I was. Would you care to join me?"

He looked down at the suit and leather shoes he wore and said, "Afraid I'm not quite dressed for such activity. Would you spare me a few minutes before you go?"

"Of course. Perhaps you'd like to walk with me. I feel an overwhelming need to be out of doors."

We made our way around back of the hotel and headed down toward the Embankment. We stopped at a wooden bench beneath a clump of trees. Coots pulled out my gold pendant from his breast pocket and handed it to me.

"Thank you, Inspector. I was wondering whether I would ever see this again."

"Never any fear of that with me, Mrs. Fletcher. I don't lose evidence like some others do."

"Yes, I'm sure that's true. Evidence? You really did consider this evidence?"

"I overlook nothing, Mrs. Fletcher. I'm well known for that."

I smiled pleasantly. "Anything else you wish to give me, or discuss with me?"

"As a matter of fact, there is. I don't like having inquiry agents the likes of Jimmy Biggers—whom, I must say, you've been spending a lot of time with—snoopin' into my business."

"I don't know what you mean."

"Come now, Mrs. Fletcher, let's not beat round bushes. Biggers has been poking around Crumpsworth, asking questions about Miss Ainsworth and the young writer who got his throat slit." He paused a moment to gauge my reaction. "Are you aware, Mrs. Fletcher, of the reputation of Jimmy Biggers?"

"I've heard some stories about him although, I must admit, I've found him to be nothing but pleasant, straightforward, and helpful."

Coots narrowed his eyes and started his up-and-down motion again. "Mrs. Fletcher, you write about murders, I solve 'em. I suggest we keep it that way."

"I assure you, Inspector Coots, that I have no intention of stepping on your toes, but I have lost a very dear friend under tragic circumstances, and there are questions I want answered. Frankly, I don't think those questions will be answered by you."

Anger flashed across his face, and I quickly added, "Not because of any lack of competence on your part, but because some of the questions involve literary matters quite aside from murder."

"What might those 'literary matters' be?"

"I really don't think you'd be interested in them."

"Better to let me be the judge of that, Mrs. Fletcher. Like I said, I leave no stone unturned when I'm out to knock off a killer."

"Well, Inspector Coots, I can only assure you that my inquiries, in concert with Mr. Biggers, have nothing whatsoever to do with your investigation of the murder of Marjorie Ainsworth. Now I really must run, in a literal sense. We can continue this conversation if you'll join me, or we can make an appointment to continue it later on." I looked at him; he obviously wasn't about to join me, so I took off at a trot, looking back only once to see him glaring at me from where I'd left him.

I returned to my room after an hour or so, showered, and called Bruce Herbert's room. He answered, and I asked whether he was free to meet for a cocktail later that afternoon.

"Anything special on your mind, Jessica?"

"No, I just thought it might be fun as long as we're at a writers' convention to talk books. We really haven't had much of a chance to do that."

I figured he would think that I wanted to discuss his nonfiction book idea about Marjorie Ainsworth's murder, and I was obviously right. He not only accepted the invitation, he was gleeful about it.

Dressed as impeccably as ever, Herbert conducted himself with the easy aplomb I was accustomed to seeing. He ordered scotch on the rocks, white wine for me.

"So, Jessica Fletcher, let's talk books. Are you in the midst of writing another novel?"

"No, the last one was difficult to resolve and took more time than I'd anticipated. Actually, it worked out nicely. I was able to make this trip while 'between books,' as they say."

"Have you plotted your next one yet?"

"No. I decided to give my brain a much needed rest for a while. I am very much at liberty these days, and loving every minute of it."

He raised his handsome face and studied me. "Am I wrong, Jessica, in having the feeling that you might want to reconsider my suggestion about writing an account of what's happened this week?"

"Yes, and no. I dismissed the suggestion out of hand, which, I should be old enough to know, is never a good idea. I wouldn't mind discussing it further with you, although I admit that while I no longer rule it out, I have no real intention of doing it. You might say I'm in a state of ambivalence."

He smiled and visibly settled a little deeper into his chair. "Wonderful," he said. "Let me tell you what my ideas are about the book."

He presented an eloquent description of how he saw such a book taking shape. "Well, what do you think?" he asked when he was finished.

"I certainly agree with you, Bruce, that if such a book were done, the approach you suggest makes sense."

"Not only does the approach make sense; having Jessica Fletcher do it guarantees a runaway best-seller."

I smiled. "I've had a few best-sellers in my career."

"But nothing of the magnitude this would be."

I told him I would give it further thought, and sipped my wine before changing subjects. "Let me bounce an idea off *you* that I've had."

"I'm all ears."

"I've been thinking about developing a series of murder mysteries. As you might know, each of my books stands on its own. There are very few running characters, which, I always felt, made sense. On the other hand, I know how successful a well-crafted series can be, and I've been toying with it."

"Sounds like a dynamite idea, Jessica."

I laughed and took another sip of wine. "What got me thinking about this was *Gin and Daggers*."

"How so?"

"What a marvelous series it could turn into, using a gimmick similar to John D. MacDonald's—you know, the way he used color in each of his titles. We have *Gin and Daggers*, which takes place in England, of course. Now we could go on to *Rum and Razors*, set in the Caribbean. There could be *Beer and Bullets*, with Germany the location. *Bourbon and Bodies* would be another, with Kentucky as the setting. Bourbon is so American. The list is endless. What do you think?"

A certain amount of his ebullience drained from him. As I listed the title possibilities, he made a point of looking around the bar. I knew he wasn't searching for anything or anyone; he was trying to avoid looking directly at me. I kept my smile as I asked his reaction.

"It's . . . it's not a very good idea, in my opinion, Jessica."

"It worked for John D."

He shook his head. "No, that wouldn't interest me." He checked his watch. "I really have to run. I did enjoy this, though. If you'd like to put a proposal together for the nonfiction work, and give it to me, I'll be happy to submit it to publishers."

"That would make you my agent," I said.

"Exactly."

"I've never had an agent."

"It's about time you did." He reached for money, but I told him I would put it on my room tab. He was obviously anxious to get away from me, and I didn't do anything to prolong his discomfort.

As I walked back to my room, I knew I had learned something. Judging from Bruce Herbert's response, Renée Perry might have been right about his possessing an unpublished Marjorie Ainsworth novel called *Brandy and Blood*.

Jimmy Biggers called me at five-thirty.

"I understand you've been getting into Inspector Coots's hair," I said.

He laughed. "I have been spending some time in Crumpsworth lately."

"And?"

"It's a depressing little burg, if you ask me. Learned nothing except that your chum, Marjorie Ainsworth, was on the cheap, she was."

I smiled. "Yes, Marjorie was known as a frugal woman."

"She wasn't much liked in Crumpsworth."

"Yes, I've heard that, too, but that seems to have little meaning where her murder is concerned."

"Not necessarily true, Jessica. Some of the people I talked to didn't just dislike the lady, they hated her."

"That sounds unnecessarily harsh. Marjorie might have been a difficult person, but she wasn't deserving of hate."

"Your interpretation, ducks, not mine. No matter, that's what I found out."

"Well, what about David Simpson?" I asked. "Have you found out out anything on him yet?"

"As a matter a fact, Jessica, I paid him a visit this afternoon. My timing was perfect. I walked in, told that grizzling receptionist of his who I was, and that I was working for you. She started to give me a bit of her lip, she did, but all of a sudden

Simpson comes to the door and greets me like I was a long-lost rich brother."

"You must have been flattered," I said.

"Blokes like him don't flatter me, Jessica. The reason he was happy to see me was that he was about to call you, he said."

"Why?"

"'Cause he had something to give you. He give it to me to pass on."

"What is it?"

"I don't open me client's packages but, from the feel of it, I'd say it's either a big fat catalog or a manuscript."

Could it be, I wondered? Was I about to be handed Jason Harris's manuscript of *Gin and Daggers*? I asked Biggers whether Simpson had told him how he'd gotten it.

"He said it was perched in front of his office door."

"What does it say on the outside of the package?"

"It's got 'is name and address on it."

"And it hasn't been opened? How would he know to give it to me?"

"No idea, Jessica. Want me to bring it over now?"

"Yes, that would be very helpful, thank you."

"Be there in a half hour."

While I waited for Biggers, I wondered who would have sent Jason's manuscript to Simpson, why they would have sent it, and why Simpson would have been so cavalier in handing it over. Of course, I knew I was doing a lot of assuming. Maybe it was a big fat catalog. But Simpson must have opened it; there could be no other rational explanation for sending it on to me. That gave credence to the concept that the package must contain the manuscript or some other material bearing upon Jason's claim that he'd written *Gin and Daggers*.

Biggers called from the lobby and I told him to come up. He walked into the suite, the package cradled in his arms, looked around, whistled, and said, "Nice digs they put you up in."

"They've been very generous. May I have the package?"

"Oh sure," he said, handing it to me. I placed it on the desk and said, "Thank you very much for bringing this to me. We'll be in touch tomorrow."

"Ain't you goin' to open it?"

"Not immediately. I have to . . . I have to meet someone downstairs, and I'm already running late. Come, I'll ride down with you."

He obviously didn't like my approach, but had little choice but to accommodate me. I walked him to the main entrance of the Savoy and thanked him again.

"What do you figure's in that?" he asked.

I shrugged. "I'll certainly find out."

He gave me that little tap on the shoulder again, and this time I started to say, "Don't do that," when he quickly blurted, "Remember one thing, Mrs. Fletcher, you and me agreed to be partners. If there's somethin' important in that package havin' to do with Ms. Ainsworth's murder, we share the credit."

"Yes, I understand," I said. "I'll call you tomorrow and let you know what it contains."

As I watched him leave the hotel, I knew there was no need to call him to reveal the contents of the package. He already knew what was inside, and had probably looked at it with Simpson. Deciding to become involved with Jimmy Biggers might not have been the smartest decision I had made of late, and that thought served as a gentle reminder to be more on my toes when around him.

My phone was ringing as I entered the suite. I picked it up. "Mrs. Fletcher?"

"Yes."

"George Sutherland. Am I catching you at a bad time?"

"No, I just walked in."

"I've been meaning to call you, but life is so busy and . . . well, as my father used to say, the road to hell is paved with good intentions."

I laughed. My father used to say the same thing.

"The reason I'm calling, Jessica, is to invite you to dinner this evening. I know this is terribly short notice but . . ."

"Yes, it is short notice, but that happens not to matter. I am free this evening, and would very much enjoy dining with you."

There was an audible sigh of relief on his end. He said, "I have a favorite restaurant in Central Market called Bubbs that I thought you might enjoy. It tends to be somewhat masculine, but the food is quite good and I'm comfortable there."

"Then I'm sure I will be, too."

"I'm afraid I'm going to be running late here at the office. Would you consider it discourteous of me not to pick you up, to ask you to meet me there at eight-thirty?"

"Absolutely not." He gave me the address and phone number of the restaurant.

I'd no sooner hung up when Lucas Darling called. "Jessica, I have missed you so. I never have the opportunity to see you because we live thousands of miles apart, and then you come all the way to London and I still am not able to see you. I insist that we have dinner tonight. Eleven Park Walk has absolutely become the city's in place for people-watching, and I intend to treat you to an evening there."

"Lucas, that's awfully nice of you, but the last thing I want to do is watch people. I'd intended to spend the evening alone with a good book"—I glanced at the desk where the package sat—"but I've ended up with a dinner engagement with Inspector Sutherland from Scotland Yard."

"Him again."

"What do you mean, 'him again'? You sound annoyed."

"Jessica, I have been a model of patience since you arrived. I have put up with constant changes in the program schedule.

A nutter has attacked my keynote speaker with a sword, the world's most revered mystery writer has been murdered, bloody television crews keep getting in my way—not that I mind the publicity for ISMW, mind you—and, most painful, my good friend and colleague, Jessica Fletcher, has been conspicuous by her almost constant absence. I insist you come to dinner with me. Wear your finest. We'll be watched, too.''

I'd known Lucas well enough over the years to know when it was possible to turn him down, and when doing so might send him to the brink of suicide. This was one of those times when I could be adamant in my refusal and still expect to see him in the morning. He muttered a few terms of disgruntlement, made me promise that I would meet with him the following day, and hung up.

I went to the desk, tore open the package, settled in a comfortable chair beneath the room's most functional lamp, and stared down at the title page of *Gin and Daggers*. Scrawled across the top in red pen was the comment: *"Proof copy—title was mine."*

Chapter
18

I was getting out of my taxi in front of Bubbs when Inspector Sutherland came walking up the street, a newspaper casually tucked beneath his arm. "Please, let me," he said, and paid the driver. "Shall we?" He offered his elbow. I took it and we entered the restaurant. "I prefer upstairs, if you don't mind," he said. "Not as fancy as down, but more conducive to serious eating. The food is good, and plentiful."

He was greeted warmly by the host and staff, and we were settled in a corner of the upstairs dining room, the walls ox-blood red, the linen frosty white. "Wine?" he asked.

"Yes, please."

"It won't be a fancy vintage. The owners are rather bourgeois for Frenchmen in London."

He insisted I taste the wine. "Never sure what I'm supposed to look for," he said, laughing, "except a large piece of cork floating in it." I tasted and approved, primarily because I didn't see any cork.

He raised his glass. "To Jessica Fletcher, who seems to be in the midst of murder no matter where she is."

"Frankly, I could do without that characterization."

"Yes, I'm sure you could." He sat back and was the picture of the relaxed, confident man. He wore a three-piece navy blue suit, probably not very expensive, but he was a man who wore clothes nicely, off the rack or custom-tailored. "Your friend Mr. Darling convinced me to conduct a panel tomorrow for your society."

"Really? That wasn't on the schedule."

"No, a last-minute whim of his, I suppose. I thought you might join me on it."

"What's the subject?"

"Contemporary investigative techniques."

"I'm afraid I wouldn't be qualified," I said.

"I think quite the opposite. It's at eleven. Will you?"

"Yes, all right. I'm flattered. Lucas must consider having you speak to be the coup of the conference."

"He's a pleasant fellow, quite a fan of yours."

I couldn't help but wonder as we talked why his manner with me this night was so much warmer than it had been at Marjorie's burial service.

"I have something to show you that might be of interest," he said. He handed me that day's London *Times*. It was opened to the arts and entertainment section. I scanned the page; nothing jumped off it at me.

"Read the 'Book Notes' column," he said.

The column was written by William Strayhorn, the eminent London book critic. "What am I looking for in this?" I asked.

"Read a bit and and you'll see."

I took out my half-glasses and started. The item he wanted me to see was buried in the middle of the column:

Jason Harris, a heretofore unsuccessful author who was dragged from the Thames the other night with his throat slit and face battered, and who was a protégé of murdered mystery writing queen Marjorie Ainsworth, is about to find posthumous publishing success. Cadence House, headed all these years by Walter Cole, who's made his millions publishing pornography disguised as literature, has announced its intention to publish the first of four novels written by Mr. Harris before his death, and unpublished to date. Either Jason Harris has written the sort of rubbish that usually appeals to Mr. Cole, or Mr. Cole has decided to take a portion of the money he's made in the sewer and devote it to works of merit, assuming Mr. Harris has written anything of merit.

I handed the paper back to Sutherland. "Fascinating," I said. "I had no idea Jason had written four novels."

"Either he has, or there is a room filled with writers turning out prose to bear his name, and to capitalize on small mentions of his murder in the local press."

I shook my head. "That doesn't make any sense to me. Does it to you?"

He shrugged. "I'm afraid I'm out of my element when it comes to the publishing world."

"How's the investigation into Marjorie's murder going?"

Sutherland pursed his lips. "Mrs. Ainsworth-Zara, the deceased's sister, has come forward with interesting information that I wanted to share with you. I was eager not only to have you hear this information, but to benefit from your evaluation of it."

If he meant to flatter me, he'd succeeded. As with our previous times together, I could never be sure when he was being personally sincere and when he was playing the role of a smooth, skilled investigator. I decided to give him the benefit of the doubt, and asked him to continue.

"She came to me this morning. I made notes during our conversation." He pulled them from his pocket, along with his glasses.

Ona's timing was interesting, I thought. Would she have

sought out a Scotland Yard chief inspector if she hadn't been cut out of Marjorie's will? A beneficiary spurned could be every bit as lethal as a woman scorned.

He recounted for me his meeting that morning.

Ona had begun by saying, "I have spent considerable time at Ainsworth Manor over the past year or two. Despite the fact that Marjorie and I did not get along especially well, she was always gracious in allowing me extended stays at the manor. I took advantage of that hospitality whenever Antonio and I were estranged, which has been the rule rather than the exception. Antonio would remain at the villa in Capri, and I would seek solace in Ainsworth Manor. He's in Capri now."

Sutherland reminded her that leaving Great Britain violated the condition laid down that all those who were at the manor the night Marjorie was murdered remain in Britain. He placed an immediate call to institute an all-points bulletin. Not very wifely to run to the authorities to snitch on one's husband, he'd thought. He asked her to continue.

"My sister had not been herself in the months leading up to her death," Ona told him. "I won't try to be subtle. Her mind was going, and she'd lost a great deal of reasoning power. Not only that, she'd became increasingly unaware of what was going on around her."

As Sutherland told me this, I could only think of Marjorie that weekend and how sharp she'd been, aside from her occasional lapses. Was this the beginning of a setup for Ona and her husband to contest the will?

Ona continued what she had to say in Sutherland's office, telling him, "It was during one of my extended stays that I became aware of not only the presence, but the influence of the young writer Jason Harris, whom Marjorie had taken into her confidence. Frankly, I never liked him from the day I met him, and had strong feelings that he was up to no good where my sister was concerned. I raised that with her once, and she dismissed me, as she was prone to do, so I kept my mouth shut but continued to observe."

Sutherland asked Ona whether she was aware that Jason Harris had been murdered, and she said she was. She went on to say, "I was there during a time when a major portion of *Gin and Daggers* was being written. I'd seen my sister work on previous novels and was quite familiar with her work habits and approach to writing a book. This time, those things were conducted in a vastly different manner."

"How so?" Sutherland asked her.

"She was incapable of sustaining focus and attention at her typewriter, so she dictated the book in fits and spurts, and gave the tapes to Jane for transcription."

Sutherland asked what significance that might have.

"None in and of itself," she replied, "but Mr. Harris seemed intimately involved in the process. I saw him on a number of occasions take Jane's transcription and work it over with pencil. Once he'd done that, Jane would retype that portion to include his additions and changes."

"What percentage of the work would you say was changed by Jason Harris?" Sutherland asked her.

"That would be impossible for me to determine," Ona said, "although, based upon those portions of the book that I had an opportunity to observe, I would say it was substantial."

Sutherland placed his notes on our table at Bubbs and poured us each another glass of wine. He said to me, "When Jason Harris was found in the Thames, I tried to assign some meaning to his death, as it might apply to Miss Ainsworth's murder. I wasn't very successful, until Mrs. Ainsworth-Zara came to me." He picked up his notes again and continued telling me what had transpired in his office that morning.

Ona had told him, "It was obvious to me that Jane and Mr. Harris were concerned about keeping their activities secret from Marjorie. There was always consternation about having me in the house, and I had a constant feeling of being spied upon."

"By them?" Sutherland asked her.

"Yes, and by the new butler, Marshall. Be that as it may, it was the relationship between Jane and Jason Harris that was of most interest to me. They were lovers."

"How did you know they were lovers?" Sutherland asked her.

"Because I observed them. Once, when Marjorie was out of the house, I saw them embracing in the garden. It was dusk, and they probably thought their actions were covered by darkness, but there was quite a bit more light than they realized."

"A serious embrace?" Sutherland asked.

She replied curtly, "I know the difference, Inspector Sutherland, between a friendly hug and kiss on the cheek, and a passionate embrace."

"I must assume you do," Sutherland said. "Was that the only time you observed them displaying affection?"

"No. I saw them holding hands once. Jane was transcribing my sister's dictation, and Jason sat next to her. They touched hands a number of times, and they had an expression on their faces that was unmistakably carnal."

Sutherland waited for her to say more. When she didn't, he said, "Let's assume your observations are correct and that there was some level of romantic interest between them. What significance does that have?"

"I am convinced that Jason Harris murdered my sister in order to benefit, in some tangible way, from his involvement with *Gin and Daggers*."

One of Bubbs's waiters interrupted us and asked if we wished to order. Sutherland removed his glasses and said, "Time for a break, I think." We perused the short menu, and I decided on poached turbot in a sauce into which strips of vegetables were woven. Sutherland opted for partridge. We agreed to share a salad garnished with venison as a first course.

"Can't shake my Scottish love of game," he said.

"One of my friends from Maine had hare with a chocolate and raspberry sauce the other night at La Tante Claire," I said.

"That might be a bit much for this Scotsman," Sutherland said with a gentle laugh. "It's the chocolate that would do me in."

We talked of things other than his meeting with Ona Ainsworth-Zara until after we'd consumed our salad. I asked what else had been discussed.

"I told her that since Harris is dead, I would hardly consider him to have benefited from anything. Her response was that his death might have been nothing more than an unfortunate coincidence that robbed him of the opportunity to gain whatever benefit he was seeking."

I frowned; I didn't buy that, and judging from the expression on Sutherland's face, he didn't, either. "She told you she'd seen them in the garden when Marjorie was out of the house. I wasn't aware she ever left, at least not in recent months. She needed a wheelchair. Where did she go? Was this an isolated instance of her leaving the manor, perhaps to see a doctor?"

Sutherland said, "I asked the same question. Mrs. Ainsworth-Zara told me that her sister left Ainsworth Manor more than people realized. Evidently her chauffeur, Wilfred, took her out on a regular basis."

"How regular?" I asked.

"Once every two weeks, she told me."

"Had she ever asked Wilfred where he took Marjorie on these regular outings?"

"As a matter of fact, I did ask that, Jessica. We think very much alike, it seems. She said she'd tried to talk to him once, but failed to learn anything. As she told me, this Wilfred is much the archetypal chauffeur, deathly loyal to his employer.

She told me, 'It would take a severe form of Oriental torture to make him even admit he'd taken her anywhere.' "

Our main courses were served. As we enjoyed them, Sutherland leaned across the table and said in a whisper, "Those people at that table in the corner obviously know who you are, Jessica. They've been looking in your direction and commenting all evening."

"How unfortunate," I said, bringing a smile to his face.

When those dishes had been cleared, Sutherland said to me, "Well, Jessica, what do you make of all this?"

I'd forgotten for the moment about his meeting with Ona Ainsworth-Zara. Instead, I'd been grappling with how much to tell this handsome Scotland Yard inspector whom I found so attractive, yet was compelled to be on my guard with. Did he know about Jimmy Biggers, about the manuscript Biggers had delivered to me that afternoon, about Maria Giacona, David Simpson, the whole Jason Harris connection? I decided that if he did, he would have to be the one to bring them up.

I forced myself to return my attention to his question. "What do I make of it?" I repeated. "I don't know. I was thinking of how angry Tony Zara was when he left the reading of Marjorie's will."

"Are you suggesting he might have murdered his wife's sister?"

"No, but his suddenly leaving the country must raise some question with you."

"That occurred to me, of course. Here we go again, Jessica, thinking alike. I raised that with Mrs. Ainsworth-Zara, and she did not offer the expected defense of her husband. Quite the opposite, I would say. She actually seemed pleased that I was thinking along those lines. She told me that her husband was *awfu'* upset because Marjorie often made a fuss over him, enjoyed calling him her . . . what did she say?—her 'little Mediterranean darling' . . . her 'Italian duckie' . . . something like that. He assumed he would be included in her estate, according to his wife, and was furious when he wasn't."

"*Awfu'?*" I said.

"Did I say that? You can take the Scot out of Scotland, but you can't take the language out of him. *Awfu'*. It loosely means *very* . . . very upset . . . *awfu'* upset."

"This meal is *awfu'* good," I said.

"Not quite the proper usage, I'm afraid," he said pleasantly. "Getting back to my meeting this morning, I asked whether she was angry at being left out of her sister's estate. She said that she wasn't even surprised because, according to her, her sister had never forgiven her for marrying an Italian. He's a count?"

"He bills himself as such," I said.

"Dessert?" he asked, eyeing a dessert menu that had been placed in front of us.

"No, not for me, thank you," I said. "This has been lovely, and I'm very pleased to see you again, but I can't help but question the purpose of it. Clearly, you've gained nothing of substance from me."

"Well, Jessica, perhaps now is the time for you to provide such substance."

He stared at me. I shrugged. "Please explain."

"You've been doing as much investigation as I have, according to my sources. You've engaged the services of the inquiry agent Mr. Biggers, have made contact with Jason Harris's stepbrother, are the only person who had a look at Harris's body other than his stepbrother, and, in general, seem to have been devoting considerable time to this effort, at least according to Mr. Darling."

"According to *Lucas?*"

"I was chatting with him about this panel discussion tomorrow, and happened to ask how much participation you've given the convention. He said you've barely taken part."

"Which means I've decided to enjoy London. I've done some wonderful walking and sightseeing."

"Undoubtedly you have, Jessica, but I also have the feeling . . . no, to be more accurate, I have had information given me to support my feelings that you've possibly been learning things that would be of interest, and of use to me and the Yard in this investigation. Would you share what you've learned with me now?"

I made a decision at that moment that I would totally divorce the two large questions—who killed Marjorie Ainsworth, and whether she had written *Gin and Daggers* without undue help from Jason Harris. Whatever I knew that had direct bearing on the former, I would share with any and all authorities, beginning with Chief Inspector George Sutherland. Anything having to do with the authorship of the novel was not, it seemed to me, police business, not with the reputation of a dear and deceased friend on the line. I thought of the manuscript sitting in my hotel suite; that certainly would not be mentioned, at least for now.

There was, however, the conversation I'd had with Renée Perry regarding the alleged novel *Brandy and Blood*, and her assertion that Bruce Herbert had possession of it, and had murdered Marjorie Ainsworth in order to resolve the pending difficulties presented by it.

"George," I said, "I have run across some information that might possibly be of interest to you where Marjorie's murder is concerned, but it must be kept . . ." I smiled. "It must be kept *awfu'* private."

"Of course. Let me drive you back to the hotel, and you can tell me on the way."

He drove a relatively old racing-green Jaguar that he kept in pristine condition. He drove slowly, and I explained what Renée Perry had told me about the missing manuscript, and her accusation that Bruce Herbert had killed Marjorie.

"Does Mrs. Perry hold any particular credibility with you?" he asked.

"Frankly, no, and when I asked her directly, she admitted she had no proof."

"What about her husband? We've done a considerable background check on him. It seems he heads a publishing company that bears his name and is in precarious financial condition."

"Yes, I've heard that."

"And Miss Ainsworth charges in her will that he'd stolen money from her, and that she had loaned him a considerable amount to keep the company going."

"I was at the will reading and heard those things. As far as stealing money from her, Marjorie wouldn't be the first author to make such claims against publishers and agents without evidence to support it. Writers are . . . writers, and by the very nature of what they do and how they earn a living, tend to become distrustful and paranoid. I remember touring Dickens's house on a previous trip to London. I jotted down the contents of some of his letters that are on display, letters to his agent and to his publisher humbly requesting money with which to live and, without actually stating it, implying that there might be some hanky-panky going on with their accounting of royalties." I laughed. "I even committed one of those letters to memory. He'd written it to his publisher, Chapman and Hall, in 1836.

"When you have quite done counting the sovereigns received for *Pickwick*, I should be much obliged to you to send me up a few. . . ."

I delivered the lines in my best British accent.

"The same with all writers, I take it," Sutherland said.

"Yes, but I'm not sure I would put much credence in Marjorie's claim of having been cheated either by Perry House or by her British publisher, Archibald Semple. The loan is another question. I wondered whether there had been papers drawn when the money had been given to him."

"I questioned Mr. Perry yesterday," Sutherland said, "and asked him about that. He said there never had been papers, and he characterized the loan as being of a very small amount, nothing of the magnitude Miss Ainsworth indicated in her will."

"When Mrs. Perry was telling me her story about the agent Bruce Herbert, I actually wondered—" I stopped myself. It's so easy to comment about other people without having a solid reason for doing so. I once heard a song titled "Your Mind Is on Vacation, Your Mouth is Working Overtime." I didn't want that to be the case with me.

I needn't have worried. Sutherland said, "It occurred to me as you were telling me of Mrs. Perry's accusation that she might be attempting to divert attention from her husband as a suspect in Miss Ainsworth's murder."

I didn't acknowledge that I had thought the same thing, although I suspect he knew I had.

He drove me to the front of the Savoy and offered to buy me a nightcap. I declined, but asked him why he had seemed so cold toward me at Marjorie's burial.

"Can I be brutally honest with you without offending, Jessica?"

"Yes, by all means."

"Any good law enforcement officer knows that the biggest mistake he can make is to become emotionally involved with someone in a case, and I must admit I developed feelings for you from the first moment we met that could easily violate that principle."

I had expected to hear any one of a dozen explanations for his behavior at the burial, but not this one.

"I've been tempted to call you every day to invite you for lunch or dinner, perhaps a stroll through the park, a ride in the country, but I've managed to hold myself in check. As long as I am confessing such things to you, Jessica, I might also say that it is my wish that when this whole nasty matter is resolved, you allow us the opportunity to explore the potentials of a relationship."

"I . . . you're a very kind and attractive man, George, and I am flattered by what you've said. In the meantime, although I am not a police officer, I suspect I, too, would be better served keeping my natural and very human instincts in check while we seek the murderer of Marjorie Ainsworth. After that . . . well, after that we can discuss it further."

"Of course, Jessica. It was good to see you again tonight. I must, however, pick up on something you've just said."

"Which is?"

"You talk of *us* trying to solve the murder. Might I make a suggestion to you?"

"Of course."

"I know you are a skilled author, and because of the nature of the books you write, you have an insight into crime and the criminal's mind. However, we're talking here about a very dangerous situation, and I urge you to confine your interests to the conference and leave this investigation to me."

"I thought you welcomed my observations."

"I do, but observations are one thing, active involvement is another."

"I know that you mean well with that suggestion, George, and I will give it serious consideration. Good night, and thank you for a lovely evening."

He came around and opened the door for me. We looked at each other. I kissed him lightly on the cheek and went into the hotel with deliberate haste.

If I'd wanted to ignore the personal exchange that had just taken place with George Sutherland, it was impossible—Lucas, who'd been sitting in the lobby sipping a gin and tonic, sprang to his feet at the sight of me. "Come, sit with me, Jess, and tell me what happened."

I forced a laugh. "Nothing happened, Lucas. The inspector and I discussed the case, and he drove me back."

Lucas gave me one of his mischievous, knowing smiles. "Jessica Fletcher, I think it's wonderful."

"What do you think is wonderful?"

"That you and the inspector have a personal interest in each other." I started to say something, but he cut me off. "I've been observing it ever since you met him—the sparks flying, the furtive glances, the romantic electricity in the air. I can see it now." He created a globe in the air with his hands. "Jessica Fletcher, world-famous mystery writer, falls in love and marries Scotland Yard's chief inspector, moves to London, where she takes an active part in the Marjorie Ainsworth International Study Center for Mystery Writers, and lives happily ever after."

His eyes were wide as he awaited my reaction.

"Lucas, I think you should try writing another book, only this time put it in the historical romance genre. I'm pooped. See you tomorrow."

Chapter

19

 I didn't get much sleep after returning from my evening with George Sutherland. The manuscript saw to that.

Of course, I'd already read the book, and there were few differences between published book and manuscript—not surprising for a writer of Marjorie's status.

What interested me about the manuscript were the numerous margin notes in red, purportedly made by Jason Harris. He identified, by my count, fourteen names that he claimed came out of his own background, including that of a dog which, his notes indicated, had been his pet as a young boy.

There were other references he took credit for, things like a London clothing store, a couple of favorite restaurants, a telephone number that had been his in a previous flat, the gin enjoyed by the story's hero that was Harris's own favorite, and myriad other items meant to convince anyone reading this version of the manuscript that Harris had, in fact, written it.

I made a long series of notes of my own, and after I showered and dressed, I went to the London telephone directory, found the number I wanted, and dialed it.

"Semple Publishing," the operator said.

"Mr. Archibald Semple," I said.

"Might I enquire who is calling?"

"Jessica Fletcher."

Semple came on the line. "Mrs. Fletcher, what a surprise, good to hear from you, trust all is well, what can I do for you?"

I asked if I could see him that day.

"I don't see why not, although the day is a bit crushed, sales conference coming up, too many books in the hopper, not enough editorial hands to deal with them."

"Would an hour from now be all right?" I asked. "I can be there by ten."

"Jolly good, sounds fine to me, I'll clear the decks for you."

Every publisher's office I'd ever visited was messy, but they were all bastions of order compared to his. Manuscripts were piled everywhere, including on the carpet in front of his desk, creating a maze for visitors to navigate. He was sweating profusely as he got up to greet me. "What a pleasure, what a pleasure," he said, leading me to a chair and removing a pile of recently published books from it. "Sit, sit. Tea? Oh no, you probably prefer coffee. I'll see to it that you have coffee."

"Actually, Mr. Semple, I would prefer tea. One sugar and lemon."

"Of course, of course." He buzzed his secretary and put in an order for two cups of tea.

Once he was settled behind his desk again, he said, "Now, Mrs. Fletcher, what brings you here? This is such an honor."

"Well, Mr. Semple, I appreciate your kind words, but I'm afraid I'm not here on a social visit."

"Oh?"

"I was wondering whether you would have available Marjorie Ainsworth's manuscript of *Gin and Daggers.*"

He frowned and went through a series of "hrummmphs"

before saying, "Unusual request, highly irregular even for a writing colleague. Why, may I ask, do you wish to see it?"

"Mr. Semple, I won't beat around the bush with you. I'm certain you're aware of rumors that Marjorie did not write *Gin and Daggers*."

"Yes, preposterous, no basis to them at all."

"I feel the same way, but I think it's very important that those rumors be put to rest. I thought . . . I thought that if I could see her manuscript, it might help me become more secure in my own mind that no other hand was involved."

"Can't see what the manuscript would tell you, Mrs. Fletcher. Just like any other manuscript from her, a few additions by pen in her hand, and our editorial notes and corrections."

"Yes, I realize that, Mr. Semple, but there is a young man . . . *was* a young man named Jason Harris who, the rumor says, actually wrote the book. We met Mr. Harris at that fateful dinner at Ainsworth Manor."

"Yes, I remember him. I'd met him before."

"Really? Under what circumstances?"

"Haven't the slightest idea, some literary party, cocktail bash, whatever. I've heard his name mentioned in connection with *Gin and Daggers*, too, and I dismiss him along with the rumor itself."

"Be that as it may, Mr. Semple, there is a growing and serious question about the authorship of *Gin and Daggers*. May I see the manuscript?"

He had a great deal of trouble flatly refusing me, but that's what he ended up doing. "Mrs. Fletcher, I would consider that a violation of a publisher's privilege. After all, the relationship between a publisher and an author is akin, somewhat, to that of solicitor and client. Agree?"

"No, not when murder has injected itself into the relationship. I really can't see why you won't allow me to at least look at the manuscript here in your office, Mr. Semple. I don't intend to do anything with it, to carry it away, or to make a statement to the press about it. All I wish to do is see the pages."

"Quite impossible, Mrs. Fletcher. Damned sorry, but that's the way it has to be. That's the way I run my publishing company, always have. Please don't consider me discourteous or uncooperative."

"I don't think either of those things of you, Mr. Semple. I just wish you were amenable to my request." I stood and extended my hand across the desk. "At any rate, it was good to see you again, and thank you for allowing me to intrude upon a busy day."

"No trouble at all, Mrs. Fletcher. Anytime." He personally escorted me to the elevator. It arrived, and he held the door open with his foot as he asked in hushed tones, "You don't think there's any truth to the rumor, do you?"

I laughed. "Absolutely none, Mr. Semple. By the way, are you aware of the other rumor that Marjorie had written a novel before *Gin and Daggers*, and that it has never been submitted to publishers?"

He seemed sincerely surprised.

"According to the source of the rumor, it's called *Brandy and Blood*."

It took him a few seconds to go from serious pondering to raucous laughter, and he managed to say, "Funniest thing I've ever heard. You don't think the old lady, I mean, Marjorie, was contemplating a series, do you?"

"That was exactly what I thought when I heard the rumor. Well, again, thank you for your time."

"One final thing, Mrs. Fletcher."

"Yes?"

"Any word on who her unnamed lover is?"

"Not that I'm aware of."

"Seems to me that if I were investigating her murder, I'd look in that direction."

He was right; I would bring that up with George Sutherland the next time we spoke.

My next stop was the address I'd taken from the phone book for Cadence House, the publishing company that, according to William Strayhorn's column, was about to publish four novels by Jason Harris. It was located on Old Compton Street, the main avenue through Soho that I'd walked the other day, and that bustled with restaurants and cosmopolitan food shops, more international news stalls than I could ever imagine in one area, and, of course, a wide variety of sex shops and striptease clubs. Judging from the description of Cadence House in Strayhorn's column, I would have expected it to be located above a sexually oriented establishment, like David Simpson's agency. Instead, it occupied its own three-story building, very well maintained, and with the sort of heavy polished wooden doors and brass lettering one expects of a Harley Street physician, a Belgravia investment banker, or Newgate Street lawyer.

I stepped inside and found myself in an airy downstairs reception area. Large potted plants were everywhere. The decor was distinctly European-modern, as was the ravishing blond girl who sat behind an uncluttered teak desk. She looked Scandinavian; I thought of Morton Metzger's comment after his night at the gentlemen's club, and wondered whether she would address me in French.

"Good morning. Is Mr. Cole in?"

"Do you have an appointment?" Her accent was distinctly German.

"No, I don't. My name is Jessica Fletcher. I'm a writer from the United States, and am here attending the International Society of Mystery Writers convention. I was also a friend of Jason Harris, whose work, I understand, you are about to publish."

The look on her face indicated that while she might be an efficient receptionist, she had little interest in, or knowledge of, what went on in the company for which she provided such an attractive front.

"I think if I had just a few minutes to explain to Mr. Cole the purpose of my visit, he would want to see me. Would you try him for me?"

While she talked to a person I assumed was Walter Cole's secretary, I looked through a glass case in which Cadence House's most recent releases were displayed. Strayhorn had been right in his column; the titles and covers were obviously designed to appeal to prurient interests, although I did take note of a couple of esoteric Scandinavian novels that were a cut above the others, though sex was at their core, too.

"Mrs. Fletcher," the receptionist said.

I returned to her desk.

"If you would not mind waiting a few minutes, Mr. Cole will see you."

"Thank you very much."

I sat in a leather chair slung on a chrome frame, and watched the flow of sidewalk traffic outside the window. It was a lovely day in London, and just as I was beginning to feel disappointed at not being able to simply enjoy it, a young woman came down a circular staircase and approached me. She was every bit as beautiful and shapely as the receptionist; evidently, the hiring code for Cadence House contained requirements beyond typing and stenography.

I followed her up the stairs to the first floor, and then up another winding staircase to the top. Unlike the first floor, where a corridor led to a succession of office doors, a visitor to the top level came off the stairs and stood in the middle of a huge office that spanned the entire floor. At one end, behind a chrome and leather desk so large I assumed it had to have been dropped into the building by crane, sat Walter Cole.

My escort immediately descended the staircase, leaving me

to make my own introductions. I approached the desk and stopped a few feet in front of it. Cole had not looked up. He was hunched over a manuscript, a red pencil flying over the text. I decided not to interrupt, and simply waited. Eventually he glanced at me and said, "Jessica Fletcher. Famous American mystery writer. Sit down."

Walter Cole was a painfully thin man, his chest concave, his eyes sunken. He had thin, brown-gray hair that hung to his shoulders in shapeless strands. He wore a blue shirt and red paisley tie.

He continued working on the manuscript, oblivious to the fact that I had taken a chair and was staring at him. I cleared my throat; he didn't respond, just kept working.

"Mr. Cole, I . . ."

He abruptly dropped the pencil on the page and stood. "I've read all your books, Mrs. Fletcher. You're very good."

"Thank you."

"You ought to dump that stodgy British publisher of yours and let me publish you. I'll make you a better financial deal and see to it that distribution is a hell of a lot wider than what you currently have here."

"That's very generous, Mr. Cole, but I—"

"Can we make a deal? I can have a contract drawn up in ten minutes."

I shook my head and laughed. "No, I'm afraid I'm quite content with my present situation. I didn't come here looking for a publisher. I wanted to talk to you about Jason Harris."

His face, bearing a visible network of tiny red spider veins, broke into a smile. He came around the desk and perched on its edge. "Glad to see you keep up with the business, Mrs. Fletcher. Yes, we're very excited about publishing Jason's works. Shame he's about to achieve international recognition and won't be around to enjoy it, but that places him in pretty good company, wouldn't you say?"

"Yes, it has happened before. Mr. Cole, I met Jason at

Marjorie Ainsworth's house. I had only brief conversations with him but, based upon those conversations, I came away with the feeling that he had never really completed any work. Yet I read that you claim to have four novels he'd written."

"That's right."

"Are any of them murder mysteries?"

Now his crooked smile turned into a laugh. "What are you getting at, Mrs. Fletcher, that he turned out the sort of stuff Ainsworth did? If he had, I wouldn't be wasting my time publishing his output. Why he hung around her I'll never know. She was beneath him. Jason Harris was a brilliant writer, someone who will take his place with the world's literary greats once I get through publishing him."

"He was *that* good?"

"Even better than that, Mrs. Fletcher. A hundred years from now, he'll be required reading for school kids in their Great Books classes."

I had the feeling I was on the receiving end of terrible overstatement, and really didn't know what else to say.

"Don't believe me, Mrs. Fletcher? You'll have a different attitude once you read his work."

"I'm certainly eager to do that. Would it be inappropriate for me to ask to see one of the manuscripts?"

"Very."

"Well, if I share your view of it, I might be willing to lend a blurb for the dust jacket."

Cole shook his head and returned to his chair. He put his feet up on the desk, revealing dirty tan chukka boots with holes in their crepe soles. "Look, Mrs. Fletcher, I don't want to offend you, but having a blurb from a murder mystery writer is not the kind of endorsement I want for Jason. No offense, but murder mysteries are nothing but genre fiction, like Westerns and romantic novels. We're talking about a major literary talent here. I'm looking for other major literary figures to acclaim him."

I ignored the comment and said, "I'm fascinated that you would devote such effort and, I assume, money to promoting works of literary merit. No offense, Mr. Cole, but your publishing company obviously has made its mark with sexually oriented materials. This seems to be quite a departure."

"So what?"

"So I wondered why. As good as you say Jason Harris was, I can't conceive of his books generating the kind of income that your usual list does. Why change focus?"

He stood again and leaned against the wall behind his desk, his arms and ankles crossed, a scornful expression on his face. "Mrs. Fletcher, I took two hundred pounds and parlayed it into a very successful publishing company. I did it by giving the public what it wants—sex—and I've made bloody millions from it. Now I've decided that since I don't need money anymore, it's time I put my efforts into developing truly deserving artists of merit. You might say I've become altruistic in my middle age. You've made a lot of money writing silly murder mysteries. What are you giving back to literature?"

I stood and said, "I don't see anything to be gained by continuing this conversation, Mr. Cole. It was good of you to allow me to barge in on you, and I wish you the best of luck with Jason's books."

"Thanks," he said, "but I don't need good luck."

I went halfway to the circular staircase, turned, and asked, "Do you know Jason's stepbrother, David Simpson?"

Stuart laughed. "I know of him. He provides real girls the way I publish stories about them."

"Yes, I know that. Is he involved in any way in this project to publish his stepbrother's works?"

"Doesn't have a thing to do with it, Mrs. Fletcher."

"What about Jason's girlfriend, Maria Giacona? Have you spoken with her?"

"Never heard of her."

"I see. Well, thank you again for your time."

I was happy to leave the building and be out on the streets of SoHo. The sunshine felt clean and good after my encounter with Walter Cole. He certainly sounded convinced of the wisdom of publishing Jason Harris posthumously, but, at the same time, I had a feeling that most of what he'd said to me had been written by a public relations expert on the floor below, a company line, the sort of hype that would be used to create an audience for Jason Harris.

I walked to Dean Street, went up the stairs, and asked Carmela, David Simpson's receptionist, whether he was in.

"Haven't seen him all morning," she said without looking up.

"Well, I would like to speak with him. Would you have him call me as soon as he has a moment?" I took a piece of paper from her desk and wrote my name and phone and room numbers on it. She looked at it, casually tossed it to the other side of the desk, and continued reading the tabloid in front of her. There was only one other person in the reception area, a woman whom I judged to be my age, although she had applied her makeup the way a young girl does the first time she gets into Mommy's dressing table. She looked very tired, beaten down. I considered suggesting to her that we leave together and have a bite to eat, but knew that she would probably find that offensive, so I left by myself, returned to the Savoy, and called the room shared by Seth and Morton. Morton answered.

"What are you two up to today?" I asked.

"We were just about to head for the Tower of London."

"Mind if I tag along?"

"Gee, Jess, that would be terrific."

"Good, lunch is on me, and so's admission. I need a couple of hours of normalcy in the Bloody Tower."

Chapter
20

". . . and so ninhydrin spray has proved to be extremely valuable in raising fingerprints that might not have been identifiable before its invention. Ninhydrin is quite different from fingerprint powder. It reacts to the amino acids in the skin rather than to salt in perspiration, and works quite well on paper, cardboard, and certain wood surfaces. It is, by the way, toxic and must be used very carefully. We prefer that our officers in the field not apply it at the site of a crime, but we are using it extensively in our laboratories."

Members of ISMW who attended the panel discussion with Chief Inspector George Sutherland were treated to a fascinating morning in which new scientific investigative techniques were expounded upon. I'd always found that ISMW members fell into two categories, those who dwelt extensively in their books on technical matters, and those who included just enough detail to establish credibility, but who preferred to focus more on character and plot development. Judging from the questions that came from the crowd, most in attendance were from the former school.

Members of the panel lingered for a half hour after the

session for informal conversation with attendees. I had a few minutes alone with Sutherland and asked him whether Marjorie's mysterious lover could be considered a suspect. He told me he'd personally called Chester Gould-Brayton on that subject and had received the response he'd expected—that the solicitor-client privilege precluded him from divulging the lover's identity. "Frankly, Jessica," Sutherland said, "I really would be quite surprised if this unnamed romantic interest of hers had anything to do with her murder, although we intend to keep the option open."

Lucas Darling invited Sutherland to join a select group for lunch, but he begged off because of his busy schedule that afternoon. He wished me a pleasant day and said he hoped I had not taken offense at his personal comments the night before.

"Quite the contrary, George, I was flattered."

"May I call you again?"

"I thought we decided to postpone any personal considerations until Marjorie's murder was solved."

"Yes, and I consider myself a man of my word, but there have been times—rare, I admit—when I have been an outright liar, and this might be one of them." We both laughed, and he left the hotel.

Lucas took us to Dirty Dick's pub on Bishopsgate for lunch, and we enjoyed a pleasant meal in the atmosphere of synthetic dirt, grime, cobwebs, and dead cats used to carry through the pub's theme. According to legend, Dirty Dick's fiancée died on their wedding eve, and he was so stricken with grief that he shut the room that was to have been the site of their wedding breakfast and left everything, including the food, to decay. He never washed or changed his clothes again for the rest of his life, so deep was his sense of loss. An abandoned meal in a locked room—straight out of *Great Expectations*.

"What are you up to for the rest of the day?" Lucas asked me.

"I have some errands to run. I'll be back in time for the awards dinner tonight."

"I have a relatively free afternoon, Jessica. Why don't we spend it together?"

I told him that might work, but I had to check with my friends from Cabot Cove, Seth Hazlitt and Mort Metzger.

"We can all enjoy what's left of the day together," he said.

"I'll call you in a half hour, Lucas."

I went to my suite and did what I'd planned to do since getting up that morning. I called Ainsworth Manor. What I hoped was that Jane Portelaine would follow through on her offer to allow me to spend some time at the manor. I was somewhat optimistic based upon her pleasant greeting of me at the reading of her aunt's will.

Marshall, the butler, answered the telephone.

"Marshall, this is Jessica Fletcher. How are you?"

"Quite fine, ma'am."

"Is Miss Portelaine there?"

"No, ma'am, she's not. She's taken a brief holiday, she has."

"How wonderful. Where has she gone?"

"The Costa del Sol."

"Delightful," I said. "When is she expected back?"

"No way of knowing, Mrs. Fletcher."

"Well, I'm coming close to the end of my stay in London, and she had invited me to spend some time at the manor before I returned to the United States. I have some free time this afternoon, and really don't see another opportunity."

"That will be fine, Mrs. Fletcher, Miss Portelaine told me of your request before she left, and instructed me to accommodate you at your convenience. What time will you be arriving?"

"I'll leave right now. I might bring some friends with me."

"Oh, Mrs. Fletcher, I don't know whether Miss Portelaine would approve of that."

"Well then, I won't. Expect me, alone, in a little over an hour."

I quickly called Lucas and told him that something had come up unexpectedly, and that I wouldn't be able to see him until dinner that evening.

"Another secretive foray by Jessica Fletcher. Damn, Jess, when are you going to include me in these things?"

I laughed away his comment and said, "As soon as I embark on one that would be of interest to you. Have to run, Lucas. See you this evening."

My next call was to the concierge. "How quickly could I have a rented car delivered to the hotel?"

"You wish to hire a car, Mrs. Fletcher? Ten minutes, at the outside."

"Fine, thank you, I'll be right down."

As I waited for the elevator, I realized I was not only filled with anticipation at going to Ainsworth Manor; I'd made a decision that I never thought I would. I was about to drive on the "wrong" side of the road for the first time. I tried to boost my lagging confidence by telling myself it was about time I learned how to drive in a city and country I loved so much, and would undoubtedly visit again. It can't be that difficult, I reasoned; it simply demanded more attention than usual. I thought of Frank and how easily he'd adapted to it. I glanced up at the elevator's ceiling: if you're looking down on me today, Frank, give me a hand.

I was relieved that the automobile had automatic transmission. The thought of trying to manually shift gears with my left hand while sitting on the right-hand side of the vehicle might have presented too daunting a challenge.

The young man who delivered the car had me fill out a form. I showed him my American driver's license, and he asked if I'd ever driven in England before.

"No, but . . . well, when my husband and I were here years ago I did have a little bit of exposure to it."

He graciously offered to accompany me for a spin around the block, and I accepted. To my surprise and absolute delight, I made it back in one piece, my nerves a little frazzled, perhaps, but my ego inflating at a rapid rate.

"Cheerio, ma'am," he said as he got out of the car and looked at me through the open passenger window. "Where will you be going?"

"I thought I'd take a ride to the country, out toward Crumpsworth."

"Do you know your way?" he asked.

"Not really."

"It's quite simple," he said. "The major problem will be getting clear of town." He gave me explicit directions, which I noted on a pad of paper. "Safe journey," he said, stepping back and tossing me a little salute as airline workers do to the pilot after they've pushed an aircraft out from the gate. I drew a deep breath and pulled away from the curb.

As I drove across London in search of the road that would lead me in the direction of Crumpsworth, I kept reminding myself that this was all mind over matter, and that any fool could learn to drive on the opposite side of the road from which they were accustomed. Crossing the street as a pedestrian was more dangerous than driving in London. I'd almost been hit a couple of times myself because I looked in the wrong direction before crossing. Millions of British tourists came to the United States, rented cars, and drove on our side of the road. More people die at railroad crossings than in airplanes. The death rate from falls in bathtubs exceeds . . .

I silently cursed the British for continuing to use the left side of the road, after almost being wiped out by a double-decker bus and its aggressive driver.

There were a few times I considered pulling over and abandoning the idea of driving to Crumpsworth, but I persevered and, eventually, was out of the city vehicular chaos and on the relatively peaceful highway leading to Ainsworth Manor.

By the time I reached Crumpsworth and had turned off on the access road to the manor, I considered myself a veteran British driver. I was actually relaxed and smiling as I guided the rented car to my destination. "Thanks, Frank," I said aloud, casting a quick glance up at the sky. "Piece o' cake."

I hadn't had much time to think about anything but driving for most of the trip but, now that I was comfortable with it, I allowed my mind to wander to other subjects, particularly Jane Portelaine's having gone to Spain on vacation. How unlike her. Then again, people do change. Perhaps Jane's life had been smothered by her service to her aunt, a classic scenario—spinster caring for an ailing or tyrannical family member until that person dies, freeing the spinster to taste life not previously available to her. I thought of Peter Lovesey's female lead in his superb Victorian murder mystery, *Waxwork*. Jane had always reminded me of that character, staunchly loyal to the family but then, as in the novel, having everything and everyone change because of murder.

I opened the gate at the entrance to Ainsworth Manor, drove through, closed it, and proceeded to the front door. How thoughtful it had been of Jane to inform Marshall that I might be coming, and to welcome me at any time. He'd sounded much more pleasant than when I'd first met him. Perhaps Marjorie's demise had freed everyone in the household. I didn't like thinking that way, but the reality was that Marjorie Ainsworth's sheer presence was dominating. Poor Marjorie, I thought as I got out of the car and approached the door, thinking of Jimmy Biggers's comment about the residents of Crumpsworth disliking her. With all her success, that was a difficult legacy to leave. Would I be thought of that way by certain people when I died? I hoped not.

I'd just begun to knock when the door suddenly opened and Marshall stood there. He smiled and said, "I was beginning to worry, Mrs. Fletcher."

"I know I'm running late, but I decided to drive myself, something I'd never done in Great Britain before."

He looked past me at the rented car and his smile broadened. "Pleased to see you're here in one piece. It sometimes takes Americans days to get over their initial fling on our roads."

"Challenging, but not that bad. It's good of you to allow me to visit."

We stepped into the foyer, and I immediately noticed the heavy scent of Victorian posy that hung in the air. Amazing, I thought, the lasting power of some fragrances, although I didn't know how long Jane had been gone. She might have left that very morning for her vacation, for all I knew.

Marshall led me to the library and offered me tea, which I accepted, along with a tray of butter cookies. "Are these fresh from Mrs. Horton's oven?" I asked.

"No, ma'am. She's gone home to visit family in Manchester."

"Sounds like everyone's on holiday."

"I'm here, Mrs. Fletcher."

"I suppose someone must keep things going." I looked around the room and sighed. "Strange, standing in this room without Marjorie poised to enter it," I said.

"Yes, ma'am, it has affected us all quite deeply."

"Will you be staying on once the manor is turned into a study center?" I asked.

"Probably not. Such a center needs curators, not butlers."

He was right, of course, and I felt a twinge of sadness for him. Not only had Marjorie pointedly left him out of her will—his short tenure at Ainsworth Manor was certainly reasonable cause for that—but he would have to find another job. With household help in short supply, according to what I'd read, he probably wouldn't have much trouble.

"Well, Mrs. Fletcher, I am at your disposal, on Miss Portelaine's instructions. Please feel free to roam the house. A simple pull on any of the call cords will have me at your side right away."

"Thank you, Marshall, you're very kind. I did want to spend a few minutes in Miss Ainsworth's upstairs writing room." I laughed. "I once visited Stratford-on-Avon and spent an hour in the house in which Shakespeare was born. It was on Henley Street, I think. No matter. I really felt as though I were absorbing some of his intellectual powers and literary skills. I had the same feeling in Dicken's house in London. Silly, I know, but I suppose writers, especially those with romantic notions, tend to embrace such ideas. Maybe by sitting in Miss Ainsworth's chair, I'll soak up a little of her talent."

"Yes, I can understand that," he said. "Excuse me. I'll leave you to yourself."

As much as I wanted to get to Marjorie's upstairs study, I didn't want to appear too eager. I remained in the main floor library, sipped my tea, and browsed through books that went floor-to-ceiling on the west wall. She had a remarkable collection of other writers in the mystery genre; the study center she established was already off to a good start. She had an autographed copy of Agatha Christie's first book, *The Mysterious Affair at Styles*. Marjorie owned every book ever written by Margaret Millar, and they occupied a special shelf. All the greats were represented—Wilkie Collins, a complete collection of Poe, Sayers, James, Carroll John Daly, MacInnes, and right up through Hammett, Stanley Ellin, and McBain. The temptation to pour another cup of tea, pull down any one of the volumes, and curl up for a good afternoon's read was strong.

Marshall appeared in the doorway once or twice. He didn't seem to want anything, simply looked in, nodded, and moved on. As I left the library and went up the stairs, he was on the landing. When he saw me, he began polishing a silver goblet with his handkerchief.

"Do you need anything?" he asked.

"No, thank you, I'm enjoying exactly what I'd hoped to, a chance to revel in what this magnificent house, and the lady of it, means to me."

I took a few moments to examine prints on the wall before going to the door that led to Marjorie's writing study. I glanced back; Marshall continued to absently wipe the goblet as he observed me. I smiled, opened the door, entered, and closed it behind me.

Books, too, dominated this room, but because it was considerably smaller than downstairs, they created more clutter. I slowly circled the room, stopping to admire artifacts, pictures, and a row of leather-bound editions of each of Marjorie's works. I paused at the window and looked out over the gardens. How tranquil; what years of pleasure she must have gotten from this view.

I continued my stroll until reaching the door again. I placed my ear against it and heard nothing. I thought of the night Marjorie was murdered, and how I'd been awakened by a sound and had gone out onto the landing and . . . and saw that horrible sight in her bedroom. I shuddered and looked at my watch; it was later than I thought. I had to be back in London for the ISMW reception and dinner.

I went to Marjorie's desk and sat behind it. Although many things were on top, there was a certain order. A pile of unopened mail that would never be seen by Marjorie was to the left of a green desk blotter edged in scrolled leather. An ancient fountain pen in its holder was at the top of the blotter. I remembered Marjorie once steadfastly refusing to use anything but a fountain pen, just as she had resisted attempts to replace her old Underwood typewriter with something more modern. The blotter was covered with ink stains from letters addressed with the fountain pen, and fixed upon its porous surface.

I cocked my head in the direction of the door. Again I heard nothing. I slowly and quietly opened the middle drawer of the desk. It contained an assortment of pencils and pens, paper clips, and other practical items found in any office. I wasn't looking for anything in particular, which made it unlikely that I would recognize something of importance if I came across it. Still, I continued opening and closing the drawers, going down the three on the left side, then opening the top right-hand one. In it were four Greater London telephone directories. Sitting on top of that was a personal address and telephone book covered in green leather and etched with gold leaf. I removed it from the drawer and opened it to the *A* section. I expected to see dozens of entries. Instead, it contained only five or six. I scanned them, then turned the page to where names beginning with *B* started. I skimmed the list of people there, and turned to the *C* section. "Wait a minute," I muttered, quickly returning to the preceding page. My eyes focused upon one name beginning with *B*—Beers, Glenville, M.D. There was no address, just a phone number.

I sat back in the chair and tried to identify why the name meant something to me. I certainly didn't know anyone by the name of Beers, but it was familiar. Then it hit me. It was the name of an incidental character in *Gin and Daggers* who was casually mentioned toward the end of the book. Yes, Dr. Glenville Beers was the name of a character in Marjorie's latest novel, which represented a distinct violation of her principle that no real person's name ever be used. Why would she have included this person? Who was he?

I jotted down his name and number, thumbed through the rest of the book, replaced it in the drawer, and stared at a black telephone on the edge of the desk. Dare I make a call from the house? Would there be someone listening on an extension? I reached for the phone, having resolved that issue by telling myself that it didn't matter whether someone listened or not.

There was no reason for me to apply any significance to this person, this Dr. Glenville Beers I was about to call. Maybe, like many people, Marjorie did not always live up to her principles and allowed them to slip on occasion. He might simply be her personal physician, whom she wished to honor by including his name in one of her books before she died.

I dialed the number and listened to it ring a very long time before it was picked up. The slow, shaky voice of an old man said, "Dr. Beers."

"Dr. Beers, my name is Jessica Fletcher. I'm calling from Ainsworth Manor. I'm not sure how to explain this, but—"

"Mrs. Fletcher, I was beginning to wonder whether you would ever call."

"Pardon?"

"Would you care to join me for tea, or a glass of port? My home is no more than a fifteen-minute drive from where you are, and I would be sincerely pleased if you would come to see me."

He was expecting my call, this man I knew nothing about? I wasn't going to explore the matter on the telephone. "Yes, I would like very much to visit you. Would you give me directions? I have my own car." How fortuitous that I had chosen this date to rent an automobile and to drive myself.

He gave me directions from Ainsworth Manor, which involved heading back toward Crumpsworth and veering off onto a small road before reaching town. Dr. Beers lived in a village called Heather-on-Floyd, obviously situated on the Floyd River, which ran through the region. I told him I would be there as quickly as possible, gently hung up, and left the study. Marshall was standing a few feet from the door and was straightening a picture that, as far as I remembered, had been perfectly straight when I looked at it fifteen minutes ago.

"Did it work, Mrs. Fletcher?"

"Did what work?"

"Sitting in Ms. Ainsworth's chair. Were there vibrations you felt?"

I didn't know whether he was trying to be cute or was legitimately asking whether I had experienced the same sensation as when I'd been in Shakespeare's and Dickens's homes. "Yes," I said, "it worked quite well. My creative energies have been refueled. Thank you so much for allowing me this lovely time. It meant a great deal to me."

He escorted me down the stairs and to the front door, which he opened for me.

"When is Miss Portelaine expected to return?" I asked.

"I have no idea, Mrs. Fletcher. The strain of what has happened here took its predictable toll on her. It's good she's got away for some sun and rest."

"She's taken quite a chance in doing that," I said.

"How so?"

"Everyone who was here the night of the murder has been instructed to stay in the country until further notice."

"She cleared her trip with Inspector Coots."

"That's good," I said. "Has he been here recently?"

"I don't think so. If you'll excuse me now, I have chores to attend to. Please drive carefully, Mrs. Fletcher. It's beginning to get dark, and for someone unfamiliar with the roads, that poses an additional hazard."

"Thank you for your concern, Marshall, and for your hospitality."

I missed the turnoff to Heather-on-Floyd and almost reached Crumpsworth before realizing it. I turned around, found it, and five minutes later was in the tiny village of Heather-on-Floyd, which consisted of only a row of low buildings on either side of the road—no more than eight or ten—and the village ended abruptly the minute the last building was passed. I wasn't sure how to park on the narrow road; there were only two other cars, and they'd pulled up onto the sidewalk to take up less of the narrow roadway. I did the same in front of the number Dr. Beers had given me. A small sign was just above the buzzer: GLENVILLE BEERS, M.D., G.P.

I pushed the button and heard the buzzer sound inside. Moments later, the door was opened by a stooped old man with a full head of white hair and cheeks as pink as cherry blossoms, and wearing a red velvet smoking jacket over shirt and tie. His feet were clad in leather slippers. A pair of glasses hung from a black ribbon about his neck.

"Mrs. Fletcher."

"Dr. Beers."

"Yes. Come in, please."

He walked with the slow shuffle of an old person. I followed him into a small parlor dominated by large pieces of stuffed furniture. A pleasant fire crackled in the fireplace. He'd been reading; a book lay open on a table next to his favorite chair. A lamp of the type seen in doctors' examining offices cast a harsh white light over it.

Once I was settled in a chair next to the fireplace, he sat, leaned forward, and seemed to study me.

"I'm afraid I really don't understand why I'm here," I said, "but I have a feeling it's good that I am."

He nodded. "Yes, I think it is very good. Tea, or port?"

I started to say tea, but changed my mind. Somehow, I felt a glass of port in my hand would be more appropriate for what I was about to hear.

One hour later, I left Dr. Glenville Beers, got in my car, and headed for London. I'd already missed the cocktail reception, and the awards dinner would have started by now. I hoped Lucas wasn't too worried about me, although I didn't dwell upon that as I found my way into Crumpsworth, took the road back toward London, and, eventually, after a few near misses, pulled up with a great sigh of relief in front of the Savoy.

"Jessica, I have been frantic," Lucas said as I walked into

the dining room. "I was about to call the police. I heard you rented a car and drove yourself. How stupid. Why didn't you let me drive you? I told you I had the afternoon free and . . ."

I touched his arm and smiled. "Lucas, please, I've had an interesting but tiring day. I'm sorry to have given you cause for worry, but here I am, safe and sound, and awfully hungry. Where am I sitting?"

Chapter
21

"I can't believe you did this without consulting me, Jessica," Lucas Darling said as he paced the floor of my suite. Seth Hazlitt and Morton Metzger were there, too. It was nine o'clock the following morning. Sunshine blazed through the windows of the suite, but the weather forecaster on the BBC predicted that a storm of some magnitude would be hitting the city by late afternoon.

"Lucas, you are simply going to have to trust me," I said from where I sat at a rolling table on which my breakfast had been served.

"The lobby is swarming with press people again," Lucas said.

"Think of the publicity."

"I have been, but that's not the point. You simply cannot spring these bombshells without talking to me first. I am, after all, the secretary."

"I know, I know, Lucas, and please stop pacing. Sit down, and let's discuss this quietly. When you get this upset, your voice goes up an octave and you sound like a countertenor in an bad opera."

He sat.

"Let me see if I have this straight, Jessica," Seth said. "You got up to the microphone at the end of dinner last night and said you would be making a major announcement soon concerning the authorship of *Gin and Daggers*?"

"That's right."

"What Mr. Darling here is gettin' at, Jess, is that you shouldn't be comin' up with such surprisin' announcements," said Morton.

"No, I suppose I shouldn't, but I did, and that's that. In the meantime, I suggest we enjoy the day. We won't be here much longer."

"Just because the conference is coming to a close doesn't mean you can leave," Lucas said. "No one can until Marjorie's murder is solved."

I ate the final bite of my English muffin.

"When do you intend to make this announcement, Jess?" Seth asked.

"Tomorrow," I said, dabbing at my mouth with my napkin. I crossed the room to where I'd tossed my raincoat on a chair.

"Where are you going?" Lucas asked.

"Out for a good, brisk walk before the bad weather sets in. Anyone care to join me?"

Lucas jumped to his feet, ran to the door, and splayed himself across it. "You're not going anywhere until you tell me more about this announcement."

Seth and Morton came to my side; together, we formed a defiant trio. "Coming with us, Lucas?" I asked.

"Yes," he said glumly. We went downstairs and got into a waiting taxi. "Kensington Gardens," I told the driver. "The Albert Memorial."

"Why are we going there?" Morton asked.

"No special reason," I said. "It's a pleasant place to walk, and I haven't been there in a long time."

We left the cab and stood at the foot of four wide flights

of granite steps leading up to the neo-Gothic spire that juts 175 feet into the air and is ornamented with mosaics, pinnacles, and a cross.

"Who was this Albert fella?" Morton asked.

"Prince Consort to Queen Victoria," I said. "Come on, let's head for the palace and pond."

As we walked, Lucas asked, "Where did you go after the dinner last night?"

"To my room."

"I tried you there a number of times and you never answered."

"I heard the phone, but I didn't want to talk to anyone. I let it ring. The hotel operator took your messages."

Lucas looked at me skeptically. I smiled in return and picked up my pace. There was no need for him, or anyone, to know just then that after making my announcement at dinner, I'd gone to my room and called George Sutherland at his home. I felt a little guilty inviting him out for a drink because he must have assumed I wanted to pursue the idea of a personal relationship. He suggested a pub in Covent Garden called the Punch and Judy. We met in its quiet upstairs bar overlooking the piazza and I had an old tawny port, while he had a Courage best bitter. I tasted his; it had a wonderful nutty flavor, but I stuck with my port. We talked for an hour, and he drove me back to the hotel, which I entered with trepidation, but was relieved to find that no one I knew was in the lobby.

Lucas, Seth, Morton, and I strolled the parklike gardens of the palace where Victoria, and Queen Mary, wife of George V and grandmother of Queen Elizabeth II, were born, the only inhabited royal palace in London whose state apartments are open to the public.

"Beautiful, isn't it?" I said as we left the palace grounds and walked to the Bayswater Road in search of a cab. We approached a small stand from which a young boy sold newspapers. He shouted out the most provocative headline of the day:

"AINSWORTH MURDERER NABBED. READ ALL ABOUT IT, AINSWORTH MURDERER NABBED."

Lucas literally jerked the paper from the boy's hand and stared at the front page. "Look, Jessica."

We gathered around him and looked down at the headline. Sure enough, that's what it said.

"You look, you pay," the boy said. Seth handed him money and we moved a few feet away. Lucas read the short front-page article aloud to us. The gist of it was that Scotland Yard's Chief Inspector George Sutherland had announced that evidence had been gathered to support a murder charge against Count Antonio Zara, Marjorie Ainsworth's Italian brother-in-law. Italian authorities had been notified, and once an arrest was made, extradition proceedings would begin immediately.

"I never did trust him," Lucas said.

"Nor did I," I said.

A line at the end of the story indicated that other material concerning the Ainsworth murder could be found on an inside page. Lucas turned to it. The lead item was my announcement at the ISMW dinner that I would be revealing startling information about the true authorship of *Gin and Daggers*. My picture accompanied the story. Lucas looked at me and said, "You knew about this, didn't you?"

"About what, Count Zara being accused of Marjorie's murder? Of course I didn't. If I had, you would have been the first to hear."

His expression was a mixture of skepticism and confusion.

"Let's get back to the hotel," I said. "There's an empty taxi." We ran to it and got in.

"This was a lovely stroll, Jessica, but I don't see the purpose of it."

"Lucas, must there always be a purpose to everything? I just felt like a walk, wanted to soak up a little bit of London before we left. Now that the murder has been solved, I suppose we'll be able to leave on schedule."

"Fine with me," said Mort Metzger. "I can't stay here forever. I don't have many vacation days left."

I patted his knee. "Morton, it was so good of you to use your vacation to come here to give me support." I said to both Mort and Seth, "You are dear friends, and I am very fortunate to have you."

We pushed our way through a large crowd of press people at the Savoy who shouted questions at me, most pertaining to the announcement I promised to make, some dealing with the news that Ona Ainsworth-Zara's husband, Count Antonio Zara, had been charged with Marjorie's murder. I stopped and said, "The announcement I promised will be made tomorrow. As for the charges against Count Zara, I can only assume that the painstaking investigation undertaken by Chief Inspector Sutherland of Scotland Yard has successfully pointed to Count Zara, which comes as a relief to every other suspect . . . including this one. Please, I have nothing else to say until tomorrow."

Lucas, Seth, and Morton wanted to come up to my suite, but I dissuaded them. I went there by myself, locked the door, and sat down at the desk. *The Times* had been delivered to the room, and I carefully reread the front-page story and the inside items pertaining to Marjorie Ainsworth.

I went downstairs and used the rear entrance shown to me early in my stay by the assistant manager, grabbed a cab, and said, "Pindar Street, please."

Jason Harris's landlady was sitting on the front steps smoking a cigarette with a neighbor. She screwed up her face when I approached as though trying to remember where she'd seen me.

"Good morning," I said. "Has Mr. Maroney returned?"

She cackled. "No, and not likely he ever will."

"I want to leave another note under Mr. Harris's door."

"No need to do that," the landlady said. "She's up there."

"She?"

"The little dark one, Harris's bird. She paid up his rent, she did. Can't take that from her."

"Excuse me," I said, stepping between the two older ladies and going up the stairs. Jason's door was partially opened. I pushed it open the rest of the way and said, "Maria."

Maria Giacona stood by the window holding a handkerchief stained with blood to her nose.

"Maria, what happened?" I asked, going to her. Now I saw a purplish yellow lump above her left eye. "Who hit you?" I could think only of Jason Harris, of course.

She looked at me with those large, brown, pleading eyes and sat on a crate used as an end table. She continued to cry and to attempt to stem the flow of blood from her nostrils. I crouched down and placed my hand on her knee. I was about to ask her again who'd struck her, but the question was suddenly rendered unnecessary. I raised my face and sniffed the unmistakable scent of Victorian posy in the small room, certainly not the sort of fragrance Maria—or Jason Harris—would use.

"Maria, was Jane Portelaine here? Was she the one who hit you?"

She shook her head. I didn't believe her.

"We should get some ice for your nose and eye," I said. "Why don't you come with me and we'll find a pharmacy. That nasty-looking bruise is getting bigger every second."

She slowly moved the handkerchief away from her nose. The bleeding seemed to have stopped. "Lie down with your head back for a few minutes," I said.

"No, I have to go."

She started to get up, but I pushed down on her knees. "Maria, you must tell me if Jane Portelaine did this to you, and why."

She gently touched her nose with her index finger, and examined it for fresh blood. She said, "I heard what you plan to do, Mrs. Fletcher. You *are* going to announce that Jason wrote *Gin and Daggers*?"

"You read the paper."

"Yes, and saw it on the television. Are you really going to say that?"

"Yes, because I believe it to be true. I would do anything to avoid injuring the memory of my friend Marjorie Ainsworth, but I think there is a greater truth at stake here. Although Jason is no longer alive to receive the accolades he deserves, his talent should be recognized."

A small smile came to her face.

"I knew you'd be pleased, Maria. Where have you been? You disappeared so suddenly."

"I had to get away, Mrs. Fletcher. Jason's murder was too much for me to bear."

"I understand. I just wish you'd kept in touch, that's all. Why did you come to the flat today? The landlady said you paid Jason's back rent."

"Yes. I thought I would live here for a while. I couldn't bear to be near this place after he was killed, but now I have a need to touch everything that was his."

"I understand that, too." I did, of course. I'd gone through similar shifts in emotion after Frank died.

I suggested again that we find a pharmacy, and this time she was agreeable. We went downstairs and I asked the landlady for the location of the nearest one. She looked at Maria's face and shook her head.

I repeated my question, and she told me there was one

two streets away. Maria had started to walk in the direction the landlady pointed. I quickly asked, "The tall, thin lady who was here. How long ago did she leave?"

"The scarecrow? No more than fifteen minutes."

"Thank you."

The pharmacist invited us into the back room of his shop, where he prepared an icepack for Maria to hold against her face. He said there wasn't anything else to be done, except report the attack to the police.

"No one attacked me," Maria said. "I fell."

"And I'm the Duke of Windsor," he said. I offered to pay him, but he wouldn't accept anything.

We left the pharmacy and walked slowly down the street until we reached a small pizza parlor. "Feel like a slice?" I asked. "I haven't had pizza in a long time. Is the London version as good as we have back in the States?"

"I don't know. I have never had pizza in the United States."

"Come, let's enjoy some pizza and a cold drink and talk a bit."

She was more relaxed as we sat at a Formica table in the pizza parlor. I said, "Jane Portelaine is supposed to be on vacation in Spain. Why did she come to see you? Why did she hit you?"

"Mrs. Fletcher, I really don't want to talk about it."

"I suppose I can't make you, but I have tried to be helpful. Maybe I'm wrong. Maybe it wasn't Ms. Portelaine. Was it someone else?"

"Why do you think it was her?"

"Because I could smell her perfume. She uses a great deal of a fragrance known as Victorian posy. I smelled it in the room."

"I might as well tell you what happened, Mrs. Fletcher. There's nothing mysterious about it. I'd only met her once, through Jason, although I knew a lot about her. He would tell me what an ugly, nasty person she was, how much he hated her. He'd used her to get close to Marjorie Ainsworth, and said he wanted to stay close. Then she learned that Jason and I were lovers."

"Why would it bother her that you and Jason were lovers?"

"Because . . ."

"Because she'd been Jason's lover, too?"

Tears formed in Maria's eyes. I said, "I'd heard about them having a relationship of some sort, although I can't imagine she was nearly as meaningful to him as you were. Did you know about any romantic or sexual involvement between them?"

"No, I did not. I always assumed Jason was faithful to me."

"Had the relationship between them been going on right up until the time he died?"

The tears came freely now and she shook her head, not as a denial but as a signal that she wanted to stop the conversation. I said, "Yes, I understand. This must be very painful for you. Frankly, I'm not only surprised that Ms. Portelaine is here in London, but that she would actually strike you. She's never impressed me as the type of person who would resort to physical violence." I'd no sooner spoken the words than I realized they weren't exactly true—there had always been an edge to Jane's personality.

I finished my soda. "Now that Jason is dead, Maria, what would cause Ms. Portelaine to attack you? I could better understand it if a relationship between them were going on at this moment, but Jason is dead."

She wiped her eyes with a napkin, careful not to press on her nose or left eye, and said, "Thank you, Mrs. Fletcher, you're a very kind person. I think what you are doing tomorrow, letting the world know that Jason wrote *Gin and*

Daggers, is a wonderful thing." She stood, turned on her heel, walked from the pizza parlor, took a right, and, by the time I reached the sidewalk, was lost in a crowd of people.

The press was still at the hotel when I arrived. So was Lucas. He bounded toward me, grabbed my arm, and said, "Trouble, Jess."

I assumed he meant the press, and laughed it off.

"Not down here, Jess, up in your suite."

I didn't have a chance to ask questions because Lucas literally propelled me through the crowd and to the elevator, where a Savoy security guard kept others from getting on. We said nothing on the ride up, but the minute we were in the hallway, Lucas said in a stage whisper, "Everybody who's ever been involved with Marjorie is waiting for you. They are furious."

"Furious about what?"

"At your plans to announce tomorrow that Marjorie did not write *Gin and Daggers*."

"Why should they be furious? What if it's true?"

"Jess, we're—no, I take that back. *They're* dealing with stakes much bigger than your sense of honor and fair play."

"Who let them in?" I asked.

"I okayed it. I didn't know what else to do."

As we entered the suite, everyone started talking at once.

"Wait a minute," I said. "I take it there is a message you wish to get across to me, but I will get it only if I hear one voice at a time."

They sat on a long couch—Clayton Perry, Marjorie's American publisher; Bruce Herbert, her American agent; Archibald Semple, her British publisher; and the London book critic, William Strayhorn.

"Is it true that you are going to announce that Marjorie did not write *Gin and Daggers*?" Strayhorn asked.

"I really don't intend to reveal what I have to say until tomorrow, but yes, it does concern that."

"Are you crazy, Jessica? Do you know what this will do to Marjorie's reputation?" Perry asked.

"No, Mr. Perry, I am not crazy. Yes, I do know what this will do to Marjorie Ainsworth's reputation, and, in my judgment, it will do very little. Her preeminence in the field of mystery writing—all writing for that matter—has been established over the course of many, many years and involves countless books. If she did not write this latest book, her fans will still think of her as the writer of all the others that gave them so much pleasure."

"Don't do it, Mrs. Fletcher," Archibald Semple said weakly from the corner of the couch. "She was a British institution, and we do not make it a habit of attacking our institutions."

I pulled a chair from the desk and placed it in front of them. "Gentlemen, can we please separate concern over Marjorie's reputation and concern over the loss of profits if people are told that she didn't write *Gin and Daggers*?" I looked at Bruce Herbert, who had said nothing. He raised his eyebrows, closed his eyes, and turned in the general direction of the window.

I continued. "No one thought more highly of Marjorie Ainsworth than I did, and no one in this world is more concerned about honoring her memory. However, there is the matter of a young man named Jason Harris, whose throat was slit, whose face was battered, and who was tossed in the Thames. He is the one who should receive literary credit for writing *Gin and Daggers*. I'm sorry, but I intend to see to it that he receives his just due."

Strayhorn, the critic, stood and assumed a statesmanlike posture across the room, his elbow casually resting upon the mantel of the suite's small fireplace. "Mrs. Fletcher," he said, "I think it is safe to say that you believe in books."

I turned so that I was facing him. "Of course I do."

"We are very much in the midst of a society whose cynicism is unparalled. Nothing is trusted any longer—government, educators, physicians, solicitors, and publishers of books. The sales of hardcover books, particularly fiction, have been eroding at a steady rate for years."

He stopped talking. I waited. When he said nothing else, I asked, "What does this have to do with the issue we're discussing here today?"

"Can you imagine the sense of betrayal millions of people who loved Marjorie Ainsworth will suffer if you make this announcement?"

I had to give him credit; at least he was basing his objections on a larger, loftier principle than the others, who obviously had their pocketbooks uppermost in mind. At the same time, I found his thesis to be absurd. Pointing out to the public that a great writer had lost her faculties toward the end of her long life and had engaged the services of a younger, more energetic writer to complete her latest work, would hardly mark the end of civilization as we know it. I didn't put it to him quite that way, but I came close.

"What proof do you have?" Strayhorn asked, looking intently at me, the prosecuting attorney grilling a shaky witness.

"That will be revealed tomorrow, Mr. Strayhorn."

"I insist, Mrs. Fletcher, that you present your evidence here and now."

I returned the chair to its place beneath the desk. "No, I will not do that. Sorry, but you will all have to wait until tomorrow to hear the details."

I must have presented a firm façade because they stopped talking to me and started chattering among themselves. Eventually they drifted from the room muttering objections, interspersed with mild obscenities, and were gone—with the exception of Bruce Herbert.

"Bruce, is there something else you'd like to say?" I asked.

He looked at Lucas. "I'd prefer to speak to you in private, Jessica."

"Don't worry about me," Lucas said, "I'm like family."

"Not *my* family," Herbert said. "Please, give us five minutes."

I nodded to Lucas that he should accede to the agent's request. "I'll run downstairs and check on the convention's progress," he said, "but I'll be back."

When Lucas had left, Bruce Herbert said, "Jessica, I'm no fool. I know the subject you raised over cocktails yesterday about a series of novels, using the name of a liquor and a weapon in each title, was not an idea that came to you because of Marjorie and *Gin and Daggers*. You've heard about *Brandy and Blood*."

I suggested we sit down. "Yes," I said, "I know about *Brandy and Blood*. It's a novel Marjorie wrote before *Gin and Daggers*. She gave it to you, only you haven't submitted it anywhere, as I understand it."

Herbert looked at the floor, and then up at me. "Jessica, I have the distinct feeling that you are finding out more than anyone would really like to know—not only about Marjorie Ainsworth's murder, but about the young man she took into her confidence, Jason Harris."

I said nothing; my eyes and expression indicated I wanted to hear more.

"*Brandy and Blood* was not written by Marjorie," he said.

"No? Who wrote it, Jason Harris?"

"Yes. Because of Marjorie's advanced age, he sensed that she would not live much longer, so he batted out a novel in what he hoped was her style, and that could be sold under her name after she died. He tried to create the illusion that Marjorie had written the novel before she went to work on *Gin and Daggers*, but that isn't the truth. He'd sat at Marjorie's side—to be more precise, at Jane Portelaine's side—throughout the writing of *Gin and Daggers* and thought he'd gotten her style down."

"You're not suggesting, Bruce, that he was concerned about perpetuating Marjorie's financial estate?"

Herbert smiled. "It wasn't to perpetuate anybody's estate. When Jane Portelaine gave the manuscript to me and asked me to handle it, she said that Jason wanted a lot of money for it. Publishing it probably would have doomed Marjorie to an eternity of scorn."

"How so?"

"Well, it isn't very good. No, that's a gross understatement. It stinks."

I shook my head. "I can't imagine Jane committing such a traitorous act against her aunt."

"I don't know what her motivation was, Jessica. She told me she thought that as Marjorie's American agent, I would want anything that would be marketable under her aunt's name. At the time I thought she was sincere, misguided perhaps, but sincere. I suppose I also have to be honest enough to say that if it had been any good, I might have considered going with it."

"But you sat on it."

"Yes."

"What else did Jane say when she gave the manuscript to you?"

"Not much, really. I do remember that she seemed uncomfortable giving it to me. I actually had the feeling that Jason had some sort of hold over her. I wonder if that wasn't the case."

"You say the manuscript is terrible. I've had conversations recently with people who are praising Jason Harris's writing."

Herbert shrugged. "Based upon *Brandy and Blood*, they're wrong. Would you like to see the manuscript?"

"Yes, very much."

"I'm doing this with a purpose in mind, Jessica."

"Which is?"

"To convince you that Jason Harris did not write *Gin and Daggers*, was incapable of it. Once you see that, there'll be no need for you to go through with your announcement tomorrow."

"I'll have to make up my own mind about that."

"Of course." He went to the door. "I'll bring the manuscript back in a few minutes. It's in my room."

My phone rang. It was Jimmy Biggers. "I've been trying to reach you," I said.

"Been busy, love. What's this codswallop I hear about the Italian murdering Marjorie Ainsworth? Don't add up to me. Make sense to you?"

"Yes, perfect sense. I've thought all along he was the one who killed Marjorie."

"You did?"

"Yes."

"That's a bummer for us. I was hopin' you and me would solve this one and share the glory."

"Looks as though that won't happen, Jimmy. Sorry."

"Well, nothing ventured, nothing gained, as me mother used to say. By the way, did you enjoy your afternoon in Crumpsworth?"

"How did . . . Jimmy, I don't think it's standard procedure for a private investigator to follow his own client."

"Got to bend the rules sometimes, Jessica, especially with a born snoop like you. You never saw me, did you?"

"I don't know how I could have missed you in that ridiculous car of yours."

"Didn't use that one. Borrowed me a friend's little one."

"Where are you now?" I asked.

"Back at the Red Feather. I just come in from Crumpsworth."

"Why did you go back there?"

"You told me to keep an eye on Harris's stepbrother, David Simpson, so I been followin' 'im."

"David Simpson went to Crumpsworth today?"

"That he did, drove straight out to Ainsworth Manor."

"Was anyone with him?"

"I don't know who the bloke was, but he was skinny and had long hair."

"Walter Cole," I said, more to myself than to him.

"Say, Jessica, what's this announcement you're supposed to make tomorrow about Ainsworth's book?"

I laughed lightly. "Nothing you'd be interested in, Jimmy. Purely a literary matter."

"I'm not much for books, Jessica. I suppose I might as well pack up here and get on to somethin' else."

"Yes, I guess you should. Looks like the Yard did its job, which means we don't have a job to do. Thank you again. It's been an interesting collaboration."

"My pleasure. Maybe you and me could get together for a pint before you head back."

"I'll be busy right up until I leave, but if there is a break in my schedule, I'll certainly give you a call." As I hung up, I jabbed at an imaginary Jimmy Biggers with my index finger.

Bruce Herbert returned with the manuscript of *Brandy and Blood*. I thanked him and promised I'd read it as soon as possible.

"Do with it what you will, Jessica. It has no value to me." He placed it on the desk.

"Bruce, this manuscript aside, what is your evaluation of Jason Harris's future potential?"

"Future? He's dead."

"Yes, I know that, but it seems that certain people in the London publishing business think they can turn him into a posthumous literary hero."

"You mean Walter Cole. I read Strayhorn's column. Cole's

obviously banking on one thing, that the world will be told, with your help, that Harris wrote *Gin and Daggers*. If that happens, Harris will suddenly take on international importance. Of course, people will read what he's written, find out how bad it is, and that will be the end of it, but a big, fast profit could be turned. Think about that before deciding whether to go through with your announcement tomorrow."

I walked him to the door. "Bruce, I have to do what I feel is just and fair where *Gin and Daggers* is concerned. If I don't, I won't be able to live with myself."

"Even though it smears the reputation of a good friend?"

"Yes, and even if it diminishes the royalties her books will earn in the future. I'm sorry. I know it directly affects you and others who were professionally involved with Marjorie."

"Well, I suppose you have to do what you think is right, but give it some serious thought."

"I've been giving it nothing but. Thank you for the manuscript and for your candor."

Lucas had arranged that evening for a group of ISMW members to have dinner at the Mayfair Hotel, and to attend a performance of *The Business of Murder*, which had been playing in the theater situated in the hotel for more than eight years. I'd seen it twice—good enough reason to beg off—but Lucas was adamant that I join them.

I was thinking of ways of getting out of going to the play when the phone rang. I picked it up and heard Dr. Beers say, "Mrs. Fletcher?"

"Yes, Dr. Beers. How are you?"

"Quite fine.

"I didn't expect to hear from you so soon."

"I hadn't intended to call you today. Actually, I am not calling for myself. There is someone here who wishes to speak with you."

"Who?"

"I'll put him on."

"Mrs. Fletcher."

This was a voice I did not recognize. "Yes, this is Jessica Fletcher. Who is this?"

"It's Wilfred, ma'am, Miss Ainsworth's chauffeur."

"Yes, Wilfred. I'm . . . well, I'm surprised to be hearing from you."

"Mrs. Fletcher, would it be impudent for me to ask for some of your time today?"

"Absolutely not."

"It's my afternoon off and I thought I would drive into the city. Would it be proper for me to stop by at the Savoy?"

"Perfectly proper, and I'll look forward to it. When do you think you'll be here, Wilfred?"

He paused before saying, "As soon as I possibly can, Mrs. Fletcher."

Chapter
22

"Lucas, I am terribly sorry, but I couldn't possibly leave my friend in the condition he's in. He's come all the way from Maine to be with me and I can't abandon him."

"What about your doctor friend, Hazlitt? Let him take care of him."

"Please try to understand, Lucas. Have dinner and go to the theater with the others and enjoy it."

"How can I enjoy it? I've seen it fourteen times."

"Then see it for the fifteenth time and analyze how it has changed over the course of the years. I'd enjoy hearing your comments about that."

"Jessica, you are extremely exasperating."

"I know, and I have a great deal to make up to you. I'll try to do that at first opportunity. Thank you for understanding, Lucas. You are aptly named Darling."

I hated to lie to Lucas and was uncomfortable making my excuses based upon a fabrication that Morton Metzger had taken ill, but it seemed the most expedient way to get out of the evening. I hung up and looked across the suite to where Wilfred, Marjorie's chauffeur, sat stoically by the window, very straight and proper, one leg neatly crossed over the other, his uniform cap resting precisely in the middle of his lap.

I put on my raincoat and stood in the middle of the room. I drew a deep breath and said, "Well, Wilfred, I think I'm ready. My friends should be downstairs by now." I'd instructed Seth and Morton to meet us behind the hotel, just outside the entrance my assistant manager friend had shown me. Wilfred had parked the Morgan there a half hour ago.

He stood. I said, "You've done a wonderful thing, Wilfred, for Miss Ainsworth."

"It's Dr. Beers deserves any pats on the back, Mrs. Fletcher. The lady was fortunate to have him as a friend."

"And fortunate to have you, too, Wilfred. We'd better go."

We started for the door, but I stopped. Should I call George Sutherland one more time? No. He was too efficient for me to worry about his following through.

Seth was dressed in a black turtleneck, tweed sport jacket, and new Burberry raincoat he'd bought that afternoon. Morton was in his Cabot Cove sheriff's uniform. "Ready?" I asked them.

"I hope you know what you're doing, Jess," Seth said.

"I think I do. Besides, if I don't, I have the two of you for support."

Wilfred drove at a leisurely pace through London and towards Crumpsworth. Morton, Seth, and I said little to each other during the trip. It wasn't until we'd turned onto the road leading to Ainsworth Manor that my heart began to trip. "Remember," I said, "we're not here to take any physical action. The important thing is that our arrival be a surprise."

"I'll take only what action is necessary," Morton said, his jaw jutting out.

"I'm sure there won't be any action necessary, Morton, but it is comforting to know an officer of the law is with us."

Wilfred went through the process of opening and closing the gate and headed for the manor. Instead of veering to his left, however—which would have placed us at the front door—he turned right and followed a narrow gravel road to the back of the house and to the garage, which had been added to the main structure. He clicked an electronic door opener that was clipped to the sun visor, and the garage door slid open. Inside was one other vehicle, a blue Ford Escort belonging to Jane Portelaine. Wilfred guided the Morgan into the garage, turned, and clicked the electronic device again. This time it closed the doors. He turned off the Morgan's lights, leaving us in virtual darkness, except for a small, low-wattage lamp at the far end, beyond the Escort.

"Careful as you walk," Wilfred said as we got out of the Morgan and quietly pressed the two back doors shut. Wilfred closed his door with normal force, and we fell in line behind him until reaching the door leading into the house.

"What's beyond this door?" I asked.

"The pantry, ma'am, which leads directly into the kitchen."

"Is Mrs. Horton still away?"

"Yes."

I looked at Seth and Mort. "Ready?"

They nodded.

Wilfred used a key to open the door and led us into the house. The pantry was very large, and its shelves were stocked with enough provisions to ride out a replay of World War II. Our path was illuminated by light from the kitchen. A large butcher block took up the middle of the room; copper pots and pans hung from a circular rack above it. The four of us stood around the block and listened. The sound of voices could be heard coming from the adjoining dining room. There was laughter; it sounded like a party.

I turned to Wilfred and whispered, "I think you have gone far enough with us. What I would like you to do now is to go upstairs and let us take over from here."

He was about to protest, then simply nodded and left

through another door connecting the kitchen with a narrow flight of stairs leading to the upper floors.

I went to the dining room door and pressed my ear against it. Now I could hear the voices with more clarity. A man said, "It actually worked, it bloody well worked." He laughed raucously.

"I propose a toast," another male voice said, "to literary excellence and to the world of books." Everyone laughed now. As I heard glasses clink together, I opened the door and stepped into the room. It took those at the table a few seconds to realize that someone had joined their dinner party. Jane Portelaine was the first to see me. She half rose, and her face reflected her shock. The others realized something had happened and turned. I took a few more steps into the room, and Seth and Mort joined me.

"What in hell . . . ?"

"Good evening, Mr. Harris," I said. "I see you're sitting in Marjorie Ainsworth's chair at the head of the table. How appropriate."

"Who are these people?" the publisher Walter Cole asked.

"These people are my friends. Officer Metzger is a law enforcement officer. I see you and Mr. Simpson have joined this celebratory party."

Harris, who'd displayed some initial bravado, turned and looked at Jane Portelaine with eyes that sought help.

She stood, came around the table, and faced me. She looked the way she had at the reading of her aunt's will— rose-colored lipstick outlined the contours of her mouth, and her hair was in that loose, becoming style. And, of course, there was the heavy scent of Victorian posy. "How dare you enter my home without my permission," she said.

"I didn't think you'd mind, Jane. After all, you'd instructed Marshall to accommodate me at my convenience." I looked at Marshall, who'd abandoned his butler's uniform for a more appropriate jacket and open shirt. He looked panicked.

Harris stood. "What in bloody hell is she talking about?" he snarled at Jane. "Invite her?"

I said, "Mr. Harris, Jane did not invite me this evening. She invited me yesterday while she was soaking up sun on the Costa del Sol."

"It was a good time to let her do her snooping around," Jane angrily answered Jason, "when no one was here." She turned to me and said, "Please leave this house immediately. You are not welcome here."

"I don't think your aunt would feel that way, Jane."

"My aunt is dead!"

"Yes, we all know that. The question is whether it was necessary to brutally do away with her in order for Mr. Harris to gain some measure of financial success that his own literary talents aren't capable of generating."

Harris sat down again and assumed a posture of nonchalance. He smiled at me, which offended me deeply, and said, "I don't see why you should be upset, Mrs. Fletcher." He lighted a cigarette and drew casually on it. "After all, I think you've had enough evidence presented to you to make the point that I did, in fact, write *Gin and Daggers*. You've had a chance to go over the manuscript."

"I assume it was you who gave it to your stepbrother, Mr. Simpson here."

"Yes . . . well, not exactly, but what does it matter?"

"It doesn't. I had an opportunity yesterday to see Marjorie's original manuscript. It contained none of the names and events you marked on the copy given to Mr. Simpson. Obviously, you, with Jane's help, inserted those things after Marjorie had finished dictating it to embellish your claim of authorship. Unfortunately for you, there was one name you should have changed."

"What's that?" Harris asked, trying to sound incurious but failing.

"The name of your mentor's friend and lover."

"She had no such person," Jane said.

"Oh yes she did, Jane."

David Simpson displayed no emotion at all. He sat and stared at a large silver candelalbrum in the center of the table.

"You are not his stepbrother, Mr. Simpson. That relationship was created so that you could identify the body dragged from the Thames as Jason. How big a slice of the pie were you to receive for that criminal act?"

He said nothing, but continued to stare at the ornate centerpiece.

I looked around the room before asking, "Where is Ms. Giacona?"

If Jane Portelaine had appeared to be angry before, her face now flooded with rage. "How dare you mention her in my house."

"You didn't have to hit her so hard, Jane. She didn't deserve that."

"She's nothing but a slut."

I looked at Jason. "But a useful one, obviously. She *is* a very good actress, Jason. She had me thoroughly convinced at first that she was deeply in love with you and was anxious to right the wrong of having your work attributed to someone else."

Harris got up once again, came around the table, and stood next to Jane. "Why don't you get out of here, Mrs. Fletcher?"

"To do what, make my announcement that you wrote *Gin and Daggers*? You didn't really think I intended to do that tomorrow, did you?"

The first words out of Walter Cole's mouth were "*I* thought you were going to. You damn well announced you were going to. That's why we're celebrating tonight."

"A wasted celebration, I'm afraid. I think the only announcement to be made will be that Jason Harris murdered Marjorie Ainsworth."

I said it directly to Harris, and my words had their intended effect. His mask of defiance cracked a little, and he took a step toward me, as though to strike. Seth and Morton took their own instinctive steps forward, which caused Harris to think better of it.

"You can't prove anything," Harris said, leaning back against the edge of the table.

"I don't think it will be difficult for the police to establish the fact that the body found in the Thames, and falsely identified as being you by your bogus stepbrother, was part of an elaborate, ill-conceived scheme."

Harris started to say something but stopped himself.

I shook my head and smiled. "What a wonderful play this would have made. Why didn't you write it, instead of acting it out? It might have had a long run in the West End."

Walter Cole stood. "I don't know what any of this is about, but I'm leaving. I've done nothing but agree to publish Jason's works. No crime in that for a publisher."

"Unless you were part of the conspiracy to enhance Jason's worth in the marketplace. I have a feeling, Mr. Cole, that you were in on this from the very beginning—that the four of you sat down one night, probably with a few bottles of wine, and decided to pull a grand hoax on the world."

I looked at Jane Portelaine. "How could you have betrayed your aunt this way?"

Until I asked that, she'd been glaring at me with a face of stone. There was a discernible tremor in her long, lean body, and her fists were clenched at her sides.

"Marjorie Ainsworth was a difficult person, Jane, but she did not deserve to have her life end that way."

"She was old, about to die anyway," Harris said from where he sat in Marjorie's usual chair, a freshly lit cigarette dangling from his fingers.

Now *I* was angry. I said, "I suppose the person floating in the Thames was old and about to die, too."

Suddenly the room was bathed in harsh white light that

poured through every window. Automobiles could be heard outside, along with the voices of many men. Marshall bolted from the table and ran into the adjacent drawing room. He looked through windows to the front, turned, and shouted, "There's bloody police everywhere."

"We can continue this discussion at Scotland Yard," I said.

"There'll be no discussion with me," Jason said. "I didn't kill the old lady, although I wouldn't have minded doing it. I hated her, but I didn't have to be the one to kill her." He looked up at Jane. "Tell her how you did it, Jane, how you drove the stake into the witch's heart."

I stared at Jane, said nothing.

"It wasn't hard, was it?" Harris said to Marjorie's niece. "Over as quick as that."

I continued to look at Jane and noticed that the nature of her trembling had changed. Now it was less born of anger and more rooted in other emotions. I asked softly, "Why, Jane?"

She slowly shook her head and lowered her eyes.

"Was it so important to you that Jason have a career he didn't deserve that you would kill your own aunt?"

Jane's voice matched the softening of her face. She slowly shook her head and said, "No."

"Why did you kill her, Jane?"

"Because . . ." She slowly turned and looked at Jason Harris, who was smiling at her. She looked at me again and said, "Because I would lose him if I didn't."

The smug expression on Jason's face caused me to want to rake it with my nails, throw lye in it, disfigure it the way the body dragged from the Thames had been disfigured.

The heavy metal knocker sounded against the front door. Marshall returned to the dining room, his face plastered with fright. "What do we do?" he asked Jason.

"Invite them in," Harris said, stubbing out his cigarette

and standing. He came around the table and said to me, "I have news for you, Jessica Fletcher."

"And what might that be, Jason?"

"That I win no matter what. When this is over, my name is going to be very big and valuable in the publishing community." He looked at Walter Cole. "Am I right, Walter?"

"I had nothing to do with any of this," the publisher said again.

The police, led by George Sutherland, came through the front door and surrounded the dining room table.

I started to say something to Jason Harris, but was interrupted by a voice from the group. "I knew it all along, I did."

Jimmy Biggers pushed past two uniformed police officers and winked at me. "We did it, Jessica."

"Yes, Jimmy, we did. When you told me that Mr. Simpson was on his way to Ainsworth Manor, and that he had someone with him whose description matched that of Mr. Cole, I knew my instincts were right, and that there would be a gathering of sorts here tonight."

"We'll do us a press conference together, Jessica, as soon as we get back to London."

"I'm not sure I'm up to press conferences, Jimmy, but we certainly will stand together." I winked at him. "Good for business."

He returned my wink and grinned.

I looked at Jason Harris and repeated what I'd started to say before Biggers interrupted. "You know, Jason, you're absolutely right. The public loves a name embroiled in scandal. The problem is you don't have the talent to give the public what it will expect from you. Then again, you'll have plenty of quiet time in the penitentiary to sharpen your literary skills. Some pretty good books have been written by lifers."

Chapter
23

Seth Hazlitt, Morton Metzger, Lucas Darling, and I sat with George Sutherland in his office at Scotland Yard. It was the following morning: the weather in London was what tourists always claim it is, chilly and damp. Tea in Styrofoam cups had been purchased from a vendor who serviced the Yard. It wasn't an elegant tea service, but the tea tasted good.

"I can't believe that dreadful man Montgomery Coots," I said, "bouncing up and down on TV this morning, claiming he knew all along it wasn't Count Zara who'd killed Marjorie; that it was Jane. The nerve of him to talk about how Scotland Yard almost derailed the investigation by accusing Zara."

Sutherland, who'd removed his jacket and sat behind his desk in shirt, tie, and dark brown sleeveless sweater, laughed gently. "I think we can withstand the attack on our reputation by the Crumpsworth inspector." He leaned forward and said to me, "I must admit, Jess, that when you asked me to announce that we'd identified Zara as the murderer, I came this close to denying you." He held his thumb and index finger an eighth of an inch apart. "But I must admit it was effective.

Obviously Harris, Ms. Portelaine, and the others felt confident they were off the hook."

"Well, George, all I can say is that I appreciate your going along with me for twenty-four hours."

"What an evil woman," Lucas said.

"Jane?" I said. "I don't think she's evil, Lucas. I'm not excusing her for having killed Marjorie, but there is a mitigating factor, I think."

"Which is?" Sutherland asked.

"A lack of premeditation. The others were involved in a classic conspiracy. For Jane, ramming the dagger into her aunt represented extreme frustration and fear. I suspect she'd never had a relationship with a man before, let alone with such a handsome, dashing, and supposedly talented one as Jason Harris. She would have done anything to keep him."

"Ms. Giacona has been very cooperative," Sutherland said. "According to her, Harris had Marshall, the butler, plant the pendant your husband gave you in Miss Ainsworth's bedroom to cast suspicion on you, Jessica."

I touched the pendant and said, "If Inspector Coots had his way, I'd be defending myself in the Old Bailey right now."

I looked at Lucas. "I don't wonder that Maria is being cooperative, after taking Jane's blows. When I saw that girl's face—and I am not excusing her, either, from having been part of the scheme—I knew deep inside that Jane had killed Marjorie. Until I saw how capable she was of physically venting her anger, I would have dismissed that notion."

"Any word on the Maroney fella?" Morton asked.

Sutherland shook his head. "We'll find him."

I said, "I certainly was wrong there. I assumed it was Maroney who'd been killed and dumped in the Thames, but then I thought back to when I'd seen the body. It was such a fleeting glance, but the head was too small."

"Harris was certainly effective at getting others to do his dirty deeds, wasn't he?" Seth said. "He got Jane to kill Marjorie, and then convinced—or paid off—Maroney to find a drifter down by the docks, kill him, and disfigure him so that he was unidentifiable, then dump him in the river."

"Yes," I said, "and that would never have been established had Maria not been there when that deal was made with Maroney."

"I'm intrigued with this Dr. Glenville Beers," Sutherland said. "Miss Ainsworth and he had this intimate relationship all these years, and no one ever knew about it?"

"Wilfred, Marjorie's chauffeur knew," I said. "She trusted him implicitly, and for good reason."

Sutherland stood. "Ready for your tour?" he asked, putting on his jacket.

"Sure am," Morton said. He'd had the Savoy do a fast cleaning and pressing of his Cabot Cove uniform in anticipation of spending the morning with one of Scotland Yard's chief inspectors. His respect for Sutherland was manifest in the fact he'd removed his Stetson upon entering the office. Morton generally left it on no matter what the event or who the person.

Sutherland talked as he led us to what's commonly known as Scotland Yard's "Black Museum." "We moved into this glass and concrete edifice in 1967," he said. "The previous headquarters on Whitehall was built on the scene of an unsolved crime."

"How'd that happen?" Lucas asked.

"They were digging the foundation and discovered a woman's body. Her head and arms had been severed. They tried their best to find the murderer but never did. Somewhat unpleasant having police headquarters constructed there."

"Sounds like headquarters back in Cabot Cove," Morton said.

"It does?" Seth and I said in unison.

"Don't you remember when the new jail and sheriff's office was put up five years ago? The construction workers found those tires Tommy Detienne had reported stolen from his Buick a year earlier?"

"I'd forgotten about that," Seth said.

"Never solved that crime, either."

"Shall we continue?" said Sutherland, tossing me an amused smile.

The "Black Museum" was the name given the Yard's archives by a reporter who considered it to be dark and evil. It's not open to the general public, and a visit takes a special invitation from a high-ranking member of the Yard. We couldn't go much higher than George Sutherland.

After we'd all entered the museum, he carefully locked the door behind us and conducted a tour that lasted almost two hours. It represented a remarkable monument to crime, to the criminal mind, and to detection. Death masks taken from prisoners hanged at Newgate Prison in the 1800s were displayed. There were sections on forgery, rigged gaming devices, burglary, drugs, kidnapping, and, most startling, sexual perversion. It was man, and woman, at their worst.

Many of the displays were chilling, but one in particular has stayed with me to this day. Sutherland said as we stood before it, "A young Southampton girl celebrated a birthday in 1945. One of her gifts arrived by post and contained a card telling her that the gift would bring things closer to her. It was a pair of binoculars. There they are." He pointed to them in the glass case.

"Before the girl had a chance to look through the binocs, her father put them to his eyes, and adjusted the focusing screw. Sharp spikes sprang out from each eyepiece, blinding him for life. Whoever had intended to injure the young girl was not only a madman, but a remarkably skilled craftsman. He'd carved the binoculars from wood, fitted the spikes inside them on a rachet of sorts, used a coiled spring to activate them, and done a beautiful paint job with black rexine and enamel. To this day no one knows who is responsible for this grotesque crime."

"A nut, like Jason Harris," Morton said.

"Yes, or, as we Scots say, *deleerit*."

"That was quite a tour, Inspector," Mort Metzger said after we'd left the museum and were standing in the Yard's main lobby.

"Yes, we're quite proud of it," Sutherland said. "We use it in our training of senior detectives. Do you have a crime museum back in Cabot Cove, Sheriff?"

"No, not enough happens there for a museum, 'less we display tires that got stole off Detienne's truck, or the picture window that got broke in Miss Boonton's house."

Sutherland said, "I'd say your sheriff is a modest man, Jessica. I've heard about murder cases you've had a hand in solving back home."

"Just a few, George, just a few."

"Well, shall we go to lunch?" Sutherland asked. He'd insisted upon taking us to a farewell lunch at Joe Allen, on Exeter Street, which has been serving up American food since 1977 with great success. It was sweet of him to suggest that particular restaurant as a gesture to our American heritage. I would have preferred something more traditionally British, as I'm sure Lucas would, but Morton and Seth seemed delighted with the opportunity to be able to order what London insiders say is the best hamburger in town, and to garnish it with french fries and salads.

One of Sutherland's uniformed staff drove us in an unmarked black police vehicle. As we were getting out in front of Joe Allen, and the uniformed officer held open the door for me, we all became aware of a commotion at the corner. "Grab him, somebody grab him. He stole my purse," a lady's voice cried.

We watched as a young man burst through a sizable crowd and ran in our direction.

"Oh my God, it's him," I said.

"Who?" Seth asked.

"Him, the one who mugged me."

The young man with pink hair, black jacket, and silver earrings headed straight for us.

"I'll get 'im," Mort Metzger said. As the young man was about to race by us, Mort threw a body block, sending the thief sprawling to the concrete. Within seconds, Mort was on top of him, twisting his arms behind his back.

"What in hell do you think you're doing?" the young punk rocker screamed.

"Sheriff Metzger, Cabot Cove, Maine, United States of America. You're under arrest for the mugging of one Jessica Fletcher. You have the right to remain silent . . . ."

"I never even bin in the bloody States."

By now we'd all formed a circle around Mort and his prey.

"Are you sure this is the one who mugged you?" Sutherland asked me.

"Yes, positive. How could I miss anyone who looks like that?"

"What's the old bag yappin' about?" the mugger asked as Mort, now aided by the bobby who'd driven us, jerked him to his feet and flattened him against the wall.

"You mind your manners and mouth, son," Mort said. The bobby put the cuffs on him.

Sutherland looked at me and grinned. "If you press charges, Jessica, you'll have to return to testify at his trial."

"I will?"

"Afraid so."

"It would be a great inconvenience, George, and I know my schedule won't allow it, but there is my civic duty to consider, isn't there?"

"Yes, most definitely," he said.

I looked at the young man, looked up into George Sutherland's green eyes, and said, "Well then, book the bloody bloke!"

Dedicated to the memory of Richard Levinson
1934–1987